Nacht und Nebel
Night and Fog

NACHT UND NEBEL

NIGHT AND FOG

FROM THE DIARY OF
FLORIS B. BAKELS

Prisoner no. 4381 Natzweiler Concentration Camp
Prisoner no. 99718 Dachau Concentration Camp

Translated and adapted by
Herman Friedhoff

THE LUTTERWORTH PRESS
CAMBRIDGE

The Lutterworth Press
P.O. Box 60
Cambridge
CB1 2NT

First published in the UK by the Lutterworth Press, 1993
ISBN 0-7188-2881-X

British Library Cataloguing-in-Publication Data:
A catalogue record is available for this book from the British Library.

Printed in Great Britain by
St Edmundsbury Press
Bury St Edmunds, Suffolk

CONTENTS

Foreword by Professor L. de Jong   vi

Preface to the English Edition   vii

Notes on the Translation   xi

Introduction   1

1 Prologue (1877-April 1942)   4

2 German police prison (April-July 1942)   18

3 Police transit camp (July-November 1942)   37

4 German Army Remand prison (November 1942-July 1943)   66

5 Concentration camp, Natzweiler (July 1943-September 1944)   110

6 Ottobrunn Annex (September 1944)   161

7 Dautmergen Annex (September-November 1944)   163

8 Vaihingen-Enz Annex (November 1944-April 1945)   172

9 Concentration camp, Dachau (April 1945)   201

10 Liberated (April-May 1945)   213

11 The journey home (May 1945)   218

Epilogue to the English edition   232

FOREWORD

German concentration camps caused such immense suffering that it is understandable that those who survived months and even years of this ordeal should prefer to forget. Such amnesia can help to heal the wounds superficially, but at a deeper level of consciousness the memories remain to haunt the victims and break out involuntarily at unguarded moments, as tears or in dreams.

Many have suffered irreparable psychological damage and I fear that almost all of them endured experiences to which they can never be reconciled. Nevertheless some relief may be obtained by bringing their memories to the surface and describing them in words or pictures. For those capable of such self-expression some ghosts may be laid by recording what actually happened - which would otherwise disappear without trace - and this in turn may kindle sympathy for the survivors and reinforce the world's determination that concentration camps and the organized torture of human beings should never again become possible.

As for the German concentration camps, I do not know of any publication which records reminiscences so truthful and so striking as in this book which Floris Bakels has written after thirty years of mature reflection.

I hope and believe it will not be read without stirring deep emotions, including a high regard for the personality of the author.

Professor Louis de Jong
former Director of the State Institute for War Documentation
Amsterdam

PREFACE
TO THE ENGLISH EDITION

The original Dutch edition of *Nacht und Nebel* appeared in 1977; 1992 saw a fourteenth reprinting. A hardback German editon followed in 1979 with the same title, the paperback in 1982. In 1981 it came out for the first time in a world language, Spanish, as *Noche y Niebla*. Why then has it not been available until now in the premier world language, English?

Having been a publisher in Holland for most of my working life I have always deferred to the arguments of my colleagues in the Anglo-Saxon market as their knowledge of this field is greater than mine: too many books on World War II, they told me, author entirely unknown. As a keen observer of the wider world of publishing - and for some years President of the Royal Dutch Publishers Association - these arguments have never entirely convinced me. Books on subjects related to World War II and the Holocaust continue to be published in great numbers, often by authors entirely unknown to the general public, though they may be familiar to a few experts. The real reason turns out to be much simpler: the only unbridgeable gap between our two countries, which are in many ways so similar and hold each other in high regard, is not the Channel nor the North Sea but the Dutch language. We Dutch strengthen this barrier by insisting on speaking English with the English.

The gap has now been filled by my old friend and erstwhile colleague Herman Friedhoff, with the critical help of John Swanzy and Herman's wife Polly. Herman is himself the author of a recent book in English on a World War II subject. I too am familiar with the complex problems of the undervalued art of translation. Between 1948 and 1954 I used the evening hours to render the 1.7 million words of Churchill's *The Second World War* into Dutch.

The English language, the English, England, the United Kingdom of Great Britain and Northern Ireland .... England had become a place of legend for us Dutch during that period. Early in August 1948, some three years after the liberation of my country, I left Amsterdam harbour as one of a six-member crew in a 22-metre yacht for a voyage to Torquay to watch the first Olympic sailing competition after World War II. At that time all mines had not yet been swept from the North Sea. After passing through the big locks at the end of the canal linking Amsterdam with the sea at dusk, we set full sail to catch the weak northerly wind. It fell to me to take the midnight watch. The sea was wonderfully phosphorescent. At last, after five years of Nazi occupation, three in two prisons and six concentration camps, I was on my way to England!

Approximately eleven hours later, at dawn, we sighted the British coast near Lowestoft. I was deeply moved. There finally was England. England, where our Queen Wilhelmina had resided. England, whence Churchill had directed the war. England, with its BBC and Radio Orange - banned to us in Holland. England, continuing to fight alone between June 1940 and June 1941. England, to which 1,600 Dutchmen escaped and which many more tried to reach, where the RAF bombers took off on their journeys across our country to Germany, where secret agents were trained to be dropped into our country - including those caught in the horrible England Spiel. England, its entire south having been one immense army camp, one large airfield, one large naval port on the eve of the invasion in June 1944. That mighty, heroic country overseas whence our liberation had to, and did, come. England that morning in August 1948 was a faint strip shrouded in morning haze.

However, in the evening of the same day this great ally did not quite live up to our expectations. We planned to sail triumphantly into Dover harbour. In prison I had often softly sung *The White Cliffs of Dover*. But at dusk thick fog suddenly descended. All our crew posted on deck to keep watch, front, aft, port and starboard. One of us sounded the foghorn with a sort of bicycle pump. Far away but also fearfully close we heard the smothered roar of ocean vessels. In my imagination I saw mountainous funnels towering above us. In those days yachts did not yet have radar. Our skipper, experienced in navigation at night, ordered the sails to be lowered; we proceeded very slowly on our diesel engine. According to his repeated calculations we should be bang slap in the middle of the Dover channel, and we could occasionally vaguely discern and identify a beacon. But no lights were visible anywhere. We moved forward at a snail's pace. New calculations were made. Even the normally imperturbable skipper now became slightly nervous. He insisted we had arrived at the entrance to Dover harbour. Suddenly, high above us, a blurred green and a blurred red light appeared on each side, followed by a blinding searchlight scanning our ship, and a voice boomed out over a megaphone, 'Who are you?'

The next morning we protested to the harbour master: this was not really the way to welcome the President of the Royal Dutch Yacht Club and his crew. He apologized. He thought no ship would be mad enough to sail into Dover harbour in such thick fog, so he had turned off all harbour lights for reasons of economy. He had not reckoned with the enthusiasm of the Dutch!

NOTES ON THE TRANSLATION

Others, more qualified, have proclaimed that translating is an art. It certainly presents problems, aptly phrased in a French dictum: "Les traductions sont commes les femmes; quand elles sont belles elles ne sont pas fidèles et quand elles sont fidèles elles ne sont pas belles."

Floris Bakels writes a stylish Dutch which does not easily transfer into stylish English. My aim was above all to be fidèle, but I hope that some of the beauté has survived. The main problem, however, resided in the diary entries, one third of the book. Occasionally written on a half full stomach, as in Utrecht prison, most were scribbled on an empty one under tremendous duress. Sometimes full sentences flowed from his pencil stubs, more often only phrases without much structure. It is difficult to imagine such circumstances. Again I have been faithful to the original rather than transcribe it into more fluent English. The credibility and flavour of this visceral document would otherwise have been lost.

At the request of the publisher all Bible quotations come from the Revised Standard Version (RSV). The author rarely had a Bible, although he tried hard to replace the ones lost. Once he had a French Bible, at another time even a Norwegian one, usually he had none and quoted from fickle memory. Consequently there is no consistency in the original. But it would have been needlessly confusing not to be consistent in this version.

The text has been firmly cut. The original is riddled with names of Dutchmen who have no meaning elsewhere, and there are repetitions which can easily be dispensed with fifty years later. So also can references to peculiar Dutch conditions that would have required lengthy and distracting explanations.

The use of 'kraut' for 'German' may not please everyone. It is nevertheless the only correct rendering in English of the Dutch 'mof', in common usage in Holland for at least a century. In German, 'kraut' stands for cabbage, often associated with sauerkraut. Of course, no one likes to be called cabbage, but then it is not meant to be complimentary. It is fairly innocuous compared to pig or bastard and in no way racist, for we are all of the same race (Caucasian). After five years of struggle against the daily satanic presence of Germans it would have been dishonest to weaken the Dutch author's fury by replacing 'kraut' with 'German' for his 'mof'.

The author frequently changes from past to present tense and back again. Some of these changes can be attributed to style. Most, however, originate in the way the book was written in 1976/7. The diary texts on their own do not constitute a readable narrative. There were gaps, there were also scraps that make no sense to anyone but the author. Yet, Floris Bakels had all of them in front of him when writing. Here the present tense heightens the immediacy of the events, as in the diary entries quoted.

Text between [square brackets] contains further information relevant to the English edition, from the notes printed at the end of the original Dutch edition.

I have had help from several native Britons, sometimes from specialists, such as Colonel Mike Davidson for military terms, and a renowned lexicographer, Edmund Weiner, for some of those delightful ambiguities in the English language. Much thanks to them. Only one has read the entire manuscript and saved me from many pitfalls: John Swanzy, who read history and English at Cambridge and like me served in World War II. I am most grateful to him, and to my wife Polly whose typing skills match her critical aptitude. Finally, gratitude is also due to those who stimulated an English version of this truly unique war document: Professor M. R. D. Foot, historian of (among other subjects) the Special Operations Executive (SOE); and the biographer of Churchill and historian of the Holocaust, Martin Gilbert CBE.

INTRODUCTION

National Socialism came to power in Germany at the end of January 1933. The Führer, Adolf Hitler, almost immediately started preparing for World War II. This was to claim the lives of some 50 million people, half of them civilians, including an estimated six million Jews.

On 10 May 1940 the Führer invaded the Kingdom of The Netherlands. He crowned a five-day war with the terror- bombardment of Rotterdam, its second largest city. The occupation that followed was to last five years. Unlike Belgium and France where military governors took control, a civil overlord was installed in Holland, probably with a view to future annexation of what the Germans called their 'sister nation'. The occupying forces, led by former Austrian Chancellor Seyss-Inquart, controlled all civilian government activities and this made resistance extremely difficult.

The occupying power introduced an extensive army and police apparatus to track down those involved with resistance and turn them over to German courts. Whenever this did not produce the required result - the death sentence - those caught disappeared in prisons, hard labour and concentration camps, often without trace.

The *Sicherheitspolizei* or Sipo (secret police) caught me on 9 April 1942 as a result of betrayal by an *agent provocateur*. Three years in two prisons and six concentration camps followed.

Nacht und Nebel (NN) Häftlinge (prisoners) were political prisoners from Germany and German-occupied countries who for one reason or another - whether sentenced to death or not - disappeared without trace in 'night and fog' on instructions from the Gestapo, SD (*Sicherheitsdienst*) or Sipo (*Sicherheitspolizei*). They were sent to particular concentration camps in Germany or France and treated abominably. Natzweiler in the French Vosges mountains was one such camp, where I spent fourteen of my thirty-six months of imprisonment.

The concept derived from a decree by Field-Marshall Wilhelm Keitel, Hitler's Chief of Staff, dated 12 December 1941. It dealt with

1

civilian resisters whose treatment was intended to deter others by a) letting the accused vanish without trace and b) refusing any information about their whereabouts or fate. The decree provided for the deportation of those not executed within a week in secret to a prison in Germany where they would be tried, again secretly, by a German court. Whenever this caused problems those arrested would be sent to a concentration camp. Seyss-Inquart enforced this decree rather erratically, ironically shielded by Himmler. In Holland the Germans tacitly admired the Resistance. Convinced of victory - this was the end of 1941 - they wanted to cooperate with their 'Germanic sister people'. Dutch Nazis were considered unfit. The right people would be found among resisters, 'the most valuable Dutchmen whom one couldn't do without' (Rauter, Himmler's SS chief in Holland). One of my fellow prisoners had been interrogated by Himmler himself. He was told that a number of Dutchmen would be saved for later, after some others had been executed. 'Useful' resisters were sent to NN camps. That a large number succumbed nevertheless, not by bullet, rope or cudgel but through hardship, illness, starvation and ill-treatment, is another matter. The Germans, meanwhile, came to realize that they would lose the war.

I was able to keep going because God gave me the power to do so; because - except for one moment of total despair - I was absolutely determined to go on living; because I loved my wife and family too much to give up; because I inherited a strong constitution; because I had many excellent friends who helped pull me through; and because from mid-July 1942 I unburdened my soul in a diary, kept at great risk and despite almost impossible conditions.

My diary *ex carcere* has been preserved pretty much intact, owing partly to the courageous efforts of several fellow inmates. After the liberation it was placed in the care of the Dutch State Institute for War Documentation where a typed copy was made of the 3,000 barely legible scraps of paper. In 1947 a small selection from the diary was published under the title *Imagination as Weapon*. This little book contained fifty sketches, memories of happier times, which alternated with pieces that revealed the contrasting reality of prison and concentration camp. They were fragments of the vase, not the vase itself.

During the years after 1945 I felt unable to distance myself sufficiently from those wartime experiences to commit them to paper comprehensively in a book. Moreover, hundreds of books appeared with the wartime experiences of others. In addition, I had to use all my strength to build a new life and a new career as a publisher. Now, however, encouraged by my family and friends as well as by Professor de Jong, then Director of the State Institute for War Documentation, Amsterdam, I have come to say what must be said, convinced that this is one of the reasons why God spared me while calling to Himself so many of my excellent friends, in whose memory and honour this has been written. We should be chary of the word 'hero', yet many of them were heroes, during their lives, during their resistance activities, during their suffering and during their slow or quick death, for freedom, humanity and justice.

I have still another purpose. For 12 years, 1933-1945, the demoniac spirit of German National Socialism raged over mankind leaving unimaginable horrors in its wake. German power was broken in 1945, as was Japanese power soon after, yet since then nothing has really been solved. For example, little has been done to ensure that a recurrence of the massacre of six million Jews cannot happen again. There is no repentance. On the contrary, man has continued to renounce God on the road to materialism and unbelief, even anti-belief. The alarming symptoms can be seen all around us. There is no limit to our greed and conceit. Those crying in the wilderness who warn of future catastrophes are right. As the author of this book I add my voice to theirs. The dead compel me to do so.

When you read what those possessed by the devil perpetrated, do not simply heave a sigh and say, 'let's not think about it, those days are past, we live in peace'. These days are not past, we do not live in peace.

It may help people today and in the future to acquaint themselves with the experiences of World War II survivors, particularly their experiences of occupation and of the concentration camp; they may learn how a reign of terror operates and how to resist it. Future generations may appreciate that, while Satan appears to rule, God is almighty and always present. This might one day come in useful.

Floris Bakels
Bussum, 1977

1. PROLOGUE
1877-April 1942

GRANDPARENTS

A century ago Father's father was a Mennonite minister on Texel, one of a string of islands in the northwestern corner of Holland. The 'Admonition', where he preached, was a simple barn. He visited his parishioners on horseback; with a wide-brimmed black hat and cape he galloped across the fabulous island, where northwestern storms alternated with southwestern gales. Sometimes his interest in natural science seemed greater than in theology.

Father's mother, the daughter of a modest shipowner, was something of a comedian, full of tricks, and keenly interested in royal dynasties and the great of this world. Mennonites who were ill or otherwise indisposed she would treat with saucepans full of hot soup and jokes. Father's father died at the age of 76, of pleurisy contracted while perched up a tree in a high wind, carrying out some obscure experiment. His wife died in our home in The Hague at the age of 93. The day before her death she was still full of jokes, but the next morning she felt too tired to get up and quietly breathed her last.

Mother's father was a member of an old patrician family from Twente, an area of east Holland. For centuries they had been burgomasters, vicars, notary publics or judges in and around Oldenzaal near the German border. Mother's father spoiled the professional record by attending a textile school and subsequently setting up the Palthe textile factory with two of his brothers. They prospered greatly and several considerable fortunes were made. With his wife and many children Mother's father lived in a very large house in Hengelo, while during the summer the family moved to his country seat near Denekamp. As Mother's mother, also from Twente, played the piano extremely well - particularly Beethoven sonatas - the grand piano always moved with

4

them. Mother's mother died at the age of 68. Her husband remarried and moved to a vast villa in The Hague. He lived to 94. In view of what follows it is significant to note the longevity of these forebears, a tradition which was carried on by my parents.

PARENTS

My father had a very happy childhood on Texel. He played with the local sheep-farmers' sons and took violin lessons from the tailor, while his father prepared him for entry to the gymnasium, the most academic and testing of secondary schools. During the holidays the minister sailed the Zuiderzee with both his sons. In each port they would go ashore to sketch the landscape.

At fourteen father moved in with two aunts in Haarlem where he attended the municipal gymnasium. He was then thin and melancholy. I've never understood how they managed it financially, but his parents sent both their sons to Amsterdam University at a time when grants were unknown. My father studied law without conviction, though with great diligence, suffering incessantly from homesickness, longing for the beauty of his native island, and yearning to be a painter. During his last years as an undergraduate he lived in a room of a house that stood in the grounds of the zoo; so it was to the accompaniment of the mighty roar of lions and tigers that he mastered the civil code. Towards the end he felt overworked and unhappy. However, this did not prevent him from being awarded two doctorates on the same day, one in law, the other in political science, the latter *cum laude* (with distinction). Armed with recommendations from his professors he was able to secure an unusually high post for his age at Amsterdam town hall. He sustained this function, which gradually filled him with horror, for three years.

My mother was the eldest of four sisters and two brothers. In old, yellowed, family photographs she looks a serious, handsome young lady with black hair and a determined chin, very conscious of herself, her family, the glory of Twente and the invulnerability of the beautiful and the good.

In those days, around 1895, the culture of Twente families was orientated towards nearby Germany. One read - and recited extensively - Goethe and Schiller. One played Beethoven, Mozart and Brahms. One took singing lessons in Leipzig and Dresden. One went on holiday to Wiesbaden and Heidelberg. One bought clothes in Hannover and danced in Bentheim.

It was a famous actor who introduced my father to the van Wulfften Palthe family and to my mother. Two more contrasting characters would be difficult to imagine. Father: highly intelligent, although socially unsophisticated, emotional, without a prestigious name, and without money. Mother: five years his junior, a plump beauty, self-confident, socially accomplished, unflinchingly convinced of the rightness of her opinions, and provided with both a well-known name and money.

It was clear that these two were attracted to each other and why: both shared a strong character and absolute integrity. They were married in 1903. The couple settled in Hilversum, looked after by the single servant they could afford. Father commuted by train to Amsterdam town hall, where he continued to suffer from the farrago of bureaucracy, the stickling for regulations of ambitious officials and the unreliability of his alderman (full-time elected councillor). After three years he left the town hall, bought painting material and started to paint.

This was a bold venture. He had never been taught how to paint and did not know anyone in the art world. A competent lawyer and the husband of an accomplished wife, he had seemed well placed for a successful career. Instead he threw all this overboard and, with the unwavering support of his noble wife, started work as an unknown painter, trying like every serious artist to achieve the unattainable. That he succeeded so soon as an artist was due to his boundless respect and admiration for the process of creation, as well as his talent, his unremitting application, his wife's faith in his abilities and the financial independence provided by her family.

It took five years of marriage before a child arrived: my brother came first, followed by two sisters and finally me (on 19 July 1915). From 1920 the parental home was in a quiet stately street in The Hague, where most of my childhood was passed.

CHILDHOOD

My childhood was extremely happy, both at the time and in retrospect. Undoubtedly I took most after my father. As a child I was not strong and rarely to be found at school. I suffered from asthmatic bronchitis and, being the youngest, grew up under the fond protection of parents, brother and sisters. I loved home; our house consisted of twelve rooms, some mysterious. Girlfriends from school supplied me with homework. In red ink that glittered a goldy green I did sums, wrote exercises and made little maps of the Dutch provinces. I also had appendicitis and frequent other ailments.

At eleven my parents felt my asthma and bronchitis had to be stopped. They sent me to a lady who taught Swedish remedial gymnastics. She was worth her weight in gold. After three months of these gymnastics, my bronchial asthma had disappeared never to return. In addition, my parents bought a houseboat and a 12 foot dinghy on the Kager Lake. Sailing was in my blood and I mastered it at once. From then on I became healthy, even strong, in the end as strong as a lion. This turned out to be very useful later on.

Secondary school was a happy time too. Until then my friends were exclusively female. The girls with their long hair and ribbons, their short skirts, their bare arms and legs, their high-pitched voices and enigmatic behaviour, enchanted me exceedingly from the age of six. The enchantment remained, but at the gymnasium at last I also acquired male friends.

Father, both artist and lawyer, sat on many government committees while working hard in his large studio, where he continued to paint until his death on 9 July 1956. He was well-known as a painter during his life. Mother ran the household with the help of servants, usually from Germany or Austria, and administered the finances. Father had no idea about money and made the most of it. Once, having painted a portrait, he complained months after delivery about the absence of payment. Mother explained that it had been transferred by giro. Father could not believe this, so Mother got the money out of the account, showed him the bank notes, and put them back into the account. Father chuckled timidly.

We hardly ever went to church. Although his father was a clergyman, Father was no more than a liberal-Christian, perhaps even a non-Christian. However, he deeply admired the Creator whose presence in nature he felt strongly. Jesus Christ did not mean much to him and I have never seen him read the Bible. Yet Father was convinced that an independent anti-God existed, an Evil Power, and that Good and Bad were locked in a continuous battle, whose outcome was always uncertain. He had to support Good. While painting Father felt allied to God. Mother did not do anything about church either. My parents could not be classified, either religiously or politically, though they usually voted Conservative. Politics were felt to be beneath our dignity.

Meanwhile, around 1930, the world economic crisis became tangible. Soon my parents' fortune produced hardly any income. They confronted this potential disaster admirably. Father, though not commercially minded, proved to be an excellent portrait painter and accepted many commissions, which were handsomely remunerated. Mother contributed by taking in 'girls of good breeding' as paying guests.

After my gymnasium finals I turned 17, but I did not know what I wanted and applied for the army. A curious step, for no Bakels had ever been in the army. I was rejected on 'medical grounds' because they did not need me. Like many friends I then opted for Leiden University and read law. Father thought that with a law degree I would make an excellent burgomaster. My degree course started in the summer of 1933, some months after Hitler's rise to power.

I cannot remember any of my family or friends getting excited about politics in those days. We read a serious newspaper. Radio had hardly penetrated. England was far away across the sea; France was a large country, whose frivolous capital was particularly good for honeymoons. Otherwise people went to Switzerland in giant grey D-trains, luggage in large trunks, and stayed a night at the Schweizerhof Bale on their way to a family hotel in the mountains. We knew that in neighbouring Germany strange things were happening. Some terrible loud-mouth had sprung to prominence whose speeches we could now listen to on a gigantic radio full of lamps and coils concocted by my brother. Occasionally we also saw him on the newsreel in the cinema, an odd-looking type with a cow-lick of hair across his forehead and a Chaplin moustache. Some people we knew, respectable ones among them, considered this movement in Germany not all that bad and there were even some who joined the NSB (Dutch Nazi Party) in 1934, 1935, even in 1936, when it had stopped growing as many left. As far as the Jews were concerned ....

From the age of eight to seventeen, I attended numerous concerts of the Residence Orchestra, usually with Mother. Initially I regarded the tympanist high on his pedestal behind the orchestra as some demi-god. The leader was Sam Swaab. One day at dinner Father mentioned that Swaab had been refused membership of the prestigious club *De Witte Societeit* in The Hague, purely because he was a Jew. I must have been thirteen (in 1928) when confronted for the first time with the concept of Jewishness. Later several classmates turned out to be Jewish. And now this shrieking upstart with the strange runic sign on his sleeve suddenly turned on Jews. We dismissed this as quite ridiculous and carried on with everyday life.

This was unforgivable.

THE FAMILY

Our family was a strong community, a fortress out of which we could operate and in which we found safety. Father, intellectual and artist at the same time, did not educate us but guided us unwittingly with his emotional gentleness by words, deeds and example. His family loved and respected him. Mother acted in a more pedagogical way. She organised the household, the finances and the social contacts. She was much more of a socializer than father. She held strong, often rather Victorian, opinions which often made discussion difficult. Both parents gave us much love which we returned happily. The entire family was highly affectionate as well as reliable, not without self-assurance and fairly critical of our fellow human beings.

The reader will wonder whether such a protected and happy boyhood did not make me especially vulnerable to the hard suffering that would follow. Clearly not. Clearly to the contrary.

UNIVERSITY AND INTO SOCIETY

Towards the end of August 1933, I rented a room at 60 Rapenburg, a seventeenth-century jewel on the canal near the main University buildings, Leiden having no colleges like its 'twin' Oxford. I joined the Student Corps, a fairly exclusive union, formed a club with contemporaries, even more select, and undoubtedly became arrogant. I became addicted to driving cars, an expensive hobby, and, of course, girlfriends. The latter worried my parents more than the former, particularly my Victorian mother. Consequently I found myself back in the parental home during my last years, commuting when necessary. However, my mother had not anticipated that one of her precious paying guests would introduce a poor cousin from Switzerland, of Dutch parentage, whom she generously took in as well. I first saw this new addition as I was standing in our hall, and she came down the stairs. This had the effect of a *coup de foudre*. We fell deeply in love and soon got engaged.

In early May 1938 I duly graduated in full ceremonial dress, only one contemporary having beaten me to it.

It was extremely difficult to get a job at that time. I wrote many letters applying for many posts. I had a high opinion of myself and refusals were taken as a personal insult. Not until April 1939, when war seemed already inevitable, did I get one, as a junior civil servant: legal clerk at the Agricultural Crisis Bureau of the Ministry of Economics in The Hague. Never have I earned so little for so many useless activities. One major annoyance was that when at last I had written something it had to be signed by someone else. Shortly afterwards I was asked to join a solicitor's partnership as a junior, a job I had applied for a long time before, and been refused. Thus I entered this honourable profession on 1 July 1939 in Rotterdam, at the bottom. One month later two senior partners were called up for the army, which precipated a quick rise in the hierarchy.

My future wife had meanwhile offered her services as governess and nurse to a wealthy family. The son celebrated this by throwing dirty socks in her face. Now a vain and ambitious solicitor, I felt embarrassed to be collecting a nurse at the huge front door of the vast house on her evening off. Of more importance was the fact that Hitler had invaded Poland and precipitated World War II.

MARRIAGE

It may well have been the awful psychological shock of 10 May 1940 that caused a lapse of memory about those first eight months of the war. It was a time of high tension and weird incidents, but we could not imagine that good old neutral Holland would actually face a dangerous war. It nevertheless seemed advisable to my future wife and me to get married. We did so on 5 January 1940 in The Hague, an icy though sunny day. Because of the mobilization and our limited funds it was a simple wedding without festivities, parties or receptions. Our honeymoon consisted of three days in the country some thirty miles from Rotterdam.

THE WAR OF MAY 1940

On 10 May 1940 we were woken by the roar of engines in the dawn sky and the bark of anti-aircraft guns. Surely there must be some mistake: a misplaced Dutch exercise, stray German aircraft, British planes violating neutral airspace. We turned the radio on. It mentioned passing German Junkers and Heinkels, both names new to us. We went out into the street, evidently not the only ones. Everywhere on that early May morning people were talking excitedly. We walked to the river Meuse. At a transformer station we noticed three soldiers nervously busy with a machinegun. We thought they must belong to some elite group as their uniforms seemed unfamiliar. It was 5.30am. Far away on the river we saw seaplanes and rubber landing craft full of soldiers. Further along we saw a lot of smoke. Rumours among the crowd that there had been a German surprise attack were confirmed when we returned home and heard on the radio a proclamation of Her Majesty Queen Wilhelmina: Holland was now at war with the German Reich.

During those five days of war we were either glued to the radio or swapping news in the street or telephoning the office. Outside one was often stopped by military in various degrees of panic. There was a constant stream of rumours about traitors, German spies in nurses' uniforms, executions, bandits firing from windows, great victories over the Germans, the departure of Queen and cabinet. Sometimes we ventured out to the harbour where, on 11 May, we saw the flagship of the Holland-America Line, the *Statendam*, on fire. From the top floor of our office, in the caretaker's flat, a high-ranking officer, well-known to us, turned out to be sending messages by telephone about the German troop movements across the river.

The May war was a nightmare, the abominable crown of this Satan's work coming to Rotterdam on 14 May at 1.30pm. The Stukas came down out of the clouds, sounding like trumpets of death and bombed the city in waves. The apartment below ours stood empty. We fled there, dragging our dog Max along. All windows were open to reduce the shattering effects of bomb explosions. For the first time - it would happen often in the future - my senses witnessed an event that I could not rationally comprehend and therefore considered impossible: the murder of a city. You saw Stukas screaming down, you saw the black dots fall from the bomb hatches, you saw the towering pillars of smoke, you heard the explosions, you smelled the fires, you felt the dike vibrate, our house rocked and there was absolutely no way you could take it in: the krauts* were deliberately flattening the centre of Rotterdam.

Max lay trembling across our knees, we could barely restrain him. When the attack stopped we saw large columns of people, loaded with luggage, hurrying to the west. 'The entire inner city is aflame, the hospitals, the churches, thousands of houses, thousands upon thousands of dead ....' is what they shouted. The sky was full of monsters of whirling smoke, grey, slate, black, while flames from the burning city centre cast a lurid red light. The sun had first become yellow, changed to orange, then to deep red. The fire approached our building so we grabbed a suitcase filled with silverware and fled in panic. Max dragged us along. In the west of the city a Palthe cousin had a house. We fled there. A few hours later we learned that the Dutch army had capitulated.

My wife and I retreated to a bedroom, embraced and tried to put order into our thoughts. This failed. We were convinced that shortly wild armies of krauts would storm into the city, rape the women, shoot the men, loot our homes. People emptied their wine cellars and the bottles. I could not endure it any longer and went back to the street. Large crowds gathered, ambulances and private cars drove in the direction of large ships moored at quaysides. The sick from inner city hospitals were being evacuated to them. A robust man threw open the gates of a timber merchant's yard. Hefty chaps, me among them,

---

* For an explanation of the use of this term see Notes on the Translation.

emptied the entire timber store in a few minutes and started constructing scaffolding and walk-on bridges from the quayside up to the ships to enable ambulances to drive on board.

That evening, trembling, exhausted and, above all, consumed with hatred, my wife and I considered whether we should end our lives and, if so, how. I also contemplated walking up to the krauts and killing a few before it was my turn.

THE OCCUPATION STARTS

However, the next day we were still alive. Rotterdam burned like a torch of monstrous proportions. We worried about my parents in The Hague, who in turn would think we had been crushed beneath collapsing buildings. We borrowed bicycles and set off for The Hague, some fifteen miles away, with Max running beside us. And then, for the first time, we could laugh a little. To left and right beside the congested road, crowded with fugitives, lay wrecks of the kraut's aeroplanes, tens, perhaps hundreds, between the dead bodies of thousands of cattle, obscenely swollen, legs stiff in the air.

Once in The Hague, however, we were livid with rage to see masses of people on terraces lounging as if there were no war, no royal family evicted, no city murdered and no army capitulated. There and then the seed was sown that grew into compassion for suffering victims, contempt for submissive profiteers and, later, murderous hate for traitors.

Back in Rotterdam, still fiercely burning (even six months later, in October, I saw the contents of a warehouse still smouldering), my partners and I tried to bring order to the chaos. At first the office on the river Meuse could not be identified, but later, after climbing across smouldering ruins, I found our small safe, scorched. Propped on a bicycle, it was taken to a garage where it was opened with a blow torch. We recovered an amount of 1,080 guilders in half-burnt notes and crooked coins. A few days later we took these to a tiny branch of the Bank of The Netherlands where we received 1,084 guilders in return. Initially, we were given temporary office space with a shipping company but then after some months we moved into a reasonable semi-permanent office. Our senior partners had been demobilized. While thousands of Rotterdammers kept working for months on end in the rubble, our life under occupation gradually returned to normal.

RESISTANCE STARTS

In the early days the Germans, led by Seyss-Inquart, uttered reassuring, even conciliatory words. I won't deny feeling somewhat relieved. The Netherlands Union was founded and I joined at once, like hundreds of thousands of compatriots. I even helped out in one of its offices, like many other volunteers. But soon the kraut showed his true colours. In late summer 1940 he introduced anti-Jewish measures. In spring 1941 I appealed to all my learned colleagues in Rotterdam by circular letter not to sign the so-called Aryan declaration which was intended to reveal Jewish origins. I believe no solicitor signed it. I also started a primitive newsletter. This was done because I had noticed that many people were lulled into accepting the situation or were simply afraid. At home I typed letters in rather bombastic language and distributed copies in Rotterdam and The Hague, dropping them at random into private letterboxes. This gave me profound satisfaction.

After a few months I felt that the Netherlands Union had tied itself too much to the German apron-strings and resigned my membership in an extensive, fully documented letter to the triumvirate who were its leaders. I kept a copy. This came back to haunt me later.

During the autumn of 1940 I gradually became unmanageable and bad tempered. In retrospect I suppose I had turned slightly crazy. An emotion until then unknown took hold of me: hatred, hatred of Germany, the Germans, every German, their language, their culture, Goethe, Bach, the entire Teutonic caboodle. I could not accept the events as an official war between two countries, which the strongest had won. I viewed them as a criminal case, fortified by my experience of Rotterdam's bombardment. The presence in Holland of a *Reichskommissar* with all the farrago of German government offices and regulatory measures I judged to be a farce, a sinister comedy. We were really dealing with gangsters and nothing else. Later I was proved to be only too right. My indignation increased again when these gangsters introduced into our country a new type of jurisdiction, *Landesgerichte*, courts with German judges. That was the limit: German gangsters judging Dutchmen.

[Some people have since tried to convince me of an affinity between Dutch resisters of 1940-45 and groups like the PLO, IRA, Croats, Basques, even the Rote Armee Faktion, the German terrorists who call themselves Red Army Faction or RAF, etc. After all, these people argue, the German occupying power regarded the Dutch Resistance in the same way that you now look upon Palestinian, Irish, Basque, etc., resistance: as terrorism. Like you, they say, these resisters are freedom fighters. There is, however, no connection at all. Holland was indubitably our country, overwhelmed by a foreign military power run by a criminal government without any legal justification. No terror measure was too much for the occupier. In every respect, therefore, resistance in Holland was a duty. Rarely if ever did Dutch resistance activities willingly or knowingly endanger the lives of innocent citizens. In most cases the other groups fight against legally established governments and cause bloodbaths among innocents. This is not a judgement on their aims, simply a correction of a false analogy.]

My work suffered, of course. For my wife and others I must have become unbearable. The worst sin of the Germans is that they taught us to hate. Hate saps the spirit. Hate also corrodes the tubes of love. Anyone who hates that much cannot properly love again. Whatever resistance activities I engaged in were not primarily for love of my country but out of pure, undiluted hatred. Love for my country came much later.

I discussed with my wife whether to leave for England. Rumours suggested there were regular crossings in dinghies, even canoes, at night. Rightly or wrongly we decided against it, even after the offer of a trip aboard a small boat with an outboard motor.I felt more damage could be caused to the enemy in Holland than in England where military men, sailors and pilots would be needed. Military matters were a closed book to me. I preferred to resist with pen and word.

I had acquired a fear of bombers after my Rotterdam experience. British planes often visited our city, occasionally dropping a bomb. Our dog Max and I started to tremble the moment heavy rumbling started in the sky and the anti-aircraft batteries opened fire. We therefore moved to Pijnacker, a quiet garden-village. I commuted to Rotterdam on a romantic little electric train. We listened in secret to the English news with maps at hand. It required ingenuity to turn the knobs until finally you heard, 'This is the BBC Home Service. Here is the news and this is Frank Phillips reading it.' Max was put outside, as he would bark when someone approached the house.

One day a young client on legal aid joined our solicitor's office. He talked a different kind of language: espionage, secret transmitters, weapons and blowing up Nazi installations. A junior partner joined in and he boasted family connections with Philips, the electrical giant. We would make more transmitters. More people joined us. One of them turned out to be a Sipo *provocateur* who betrayed all of us, as I learned in prison.

ARREST

Almost nobody can predict the future. Usually one cannot perceive the logic of events even after they have happened. Still, some have an intuition about what will happen and when it does they think, 'How stupid of me! That is precisely how it had to happen.'

When on 9 April 1942 I heard the front doorbell ringing at 6.30am I knew at once. Immediately I think, 'That this should happen to me is excessive. A revolution has started.' The bell rings again. My brother is a guest and staying on the first floor. My wife and I remain in bed on the second, frozen stiff. We hear voices. People mount the first staircase. Someone, alone, mounts the second staircase. This is atrocious.

'Floris, are you awake?' calls my brother.

'Yes.'

'Floris, are you really awake?' 'Yes.'

'Floris,' - other feet mount the staircase too - 'there are two gentlemen here from the German police.'

I stay put. I have been ill for three days, a heavy cold and stomach upset. On the left and right of our bed stand krauts in grey rubbery raincoats.

'Sind sie Herr Backels?'

'Yes.'

'Sind sie Herr Doktor Floris Berchtold Backels?'

'Approximately, yes.'

'Also, stehen sie auf. Sind sie Frau Doktor Backels?'

No reply.

'Let's assume she is. Now get up. You, Hendrich, have a look round.' They turn their backs to our bed. We get up. I notice one kraut rummaging in our chests and suitcases. There, under a loose floorboard, my secret papers are hidden. I move to the bathroom, one rubbery raincoat following.

'Keep quiet and no nonsense.'

'May I have a bath?'

'No. Get dressed. We have no time.'

I get dressed, dizzy from my cold. The second fellow walks to the landing, to go downstairs.

'Careful,' my wife says,'there's a dog in the room downstairs.'

'Doesn't worry me, I've got a gun,' says Hendrich. Both men have kept their hats on. I get hot under the collar.

'In my home you take off your hat,' I tell them and repeat it in German.

'Funny lot, these two,' says Hendrich on the landing, his hat still on. I am ready. We are all now on the landing, my wife in her blue and white striped bathrobe. Hendrich clasps a batch of papers in one hand. I notice that they include the papers from beneath the floorboard. We go downstairs. My brother has chained Max in the front room. The dog does not bark, nor growl, just looks.

'You can eat something. Five minutes.'

My wife gives me two sandwiches. I ask for a cigarette. I get up and eat while smoking. I look at Max in the front room. Max returns the look, sparkling, motionless. Behind the dog is the wide window, beyond the window the street. However, in the street is a grey car with a chap who looks pointedly at our house.

My brother asks in German, 'What's wrong with my brother? Can we help?'

No reply.

I look at my wife. She looks at me with unnaturally clear eyes, in a friendly way, encouragingly. The kraut returns. In his hand he holds all my papers.

'Ready.'

'Well, Frau Doktor, your husband is coming with us. Perhaps he'll be back tonight.'

She asks whether I should take some toileteries. This alienates her from me, briefly. Does she not believe in 'tonight'?

'No. Please follow me.'

I take her hand. 'Put your coat on,' she says, 'you haven't recovered yet, it's cold outside.' She helps me into my dark winter coat, the front door is open, the buds of the plum tree are bursting, the sun shines.

'Perhaps I'll be back tonight,' I tell her. Both krauts are standing very close, looking on. 'Be brave,' I add. We leave. My wife stands in the door in her bathrobe. She looks at me continuously, in a friendly way, unnaturally friendly, her eyes sparkle unnaturally. 'Darling,' I hear her say. There is nobody in the street. Not a soul.

The Mercedes' numberplate reads POL-1A 9807. I get in at the back, one Sipo man next to me, the other in front beside the driver who does not turn round and keeps quiet. He starts the car, puts it in gear. I look at my home, no one to be seen. The car drives off quickly. In the streets of Pijnacker no one can be seen either. We turn one way, then a U-turn on the already crowded main road to Rotterdam and our office.

I'm sitting in my office with a kraut while others search it. Some time later: 'Also mitkommen'. Together with the seized goods I am delivered to the hall of the Sipo headquarters. I notice Dutch flags, radios, pamphlets. In a corner I fill my pipe with cigar stumps and smoke. The rubbery raincoat walks up to me and knocks my pipe out of my mouth. Again I get the feeling that something is happening to me which does not belong to me. A mistake of fate. A wrong position of the points. I will have to reverse a bit and can then travel normally in the right direction.

We go upstairs, into a large room. Under heavy guard there are some thirty men, standing more or less to attention. Suddenly I notice my junior partner. Later also the young client. What has happened? Nothing really, not yet. 'Perhaps he'll be back tonight.' I did not even need toileteries. You'll see, soon the performance will be finished. But those papers . . . .

'Alles raus!' but slowly, two at a time. Outside. In each car a driver is waiting. Because of my long legs - and amid laughter - I'm ordered to sit next to the driver. Two more in the back, a guard between them. We drive off, stop, drive a bit, stop again, a convoy is being formed. Shouting krauts with lists call out names. Then, eighteen cars behind each other - I'm in the fifth - we drive through Rotterdam on the road to The Hague.

THE ROAD TO SCHEVENINGEN PRISON

Suddenly I feel sick. The cars have moved away from each other. We drive at a correct 95 kph, often overtaking. The guard in the back offers us a cigarette. My hand trembles ridiculously. I shiver, spasms following one another. Under my armpits it feels cold even though I am almost suffocating in my winter coat. The speedometer now points to 90, I look at the door next to me,its handle. We overtake a huge lorry emblazoned with the name Verkade (the biscuit manufacturer). I'm related to them. I have to swallow hard, swallow repeatedly. I have to throw up, the driver will have to stop. What is 'to throw' in German? Erbrechen, sich erbrechen, ich muss mich erbrechen, and then at 50, 40, 30 perhaps the doorhandle, a ditch, the meadow, but thirteen more cars are behind us, isn't there a village, a hamlet, with streets? I clear my throat. 'Ich muss . . .' no sound follows. We are southeast of Delft, to the east lies Pijnacker, with my home, with my wife, my love, my darling. 'Ich muss . . . .'

Some light appears, there above Pijnacker, above the distant church tower, a wide silvery ray of light, the tower lights up. There is also a grail, a wide swathe of light, I am in it, a hand lifts me above this life to where there is only silence and light.

And I hear, 'Fear not. It is Me.'

2. DEUTSCHES POLIZEIGEFÄNGNIS SCHEVENINGEN
(German Police Prison Scheveningen)
9 April-17 July 1942

CELL 712

The cars move right up to the prison wall at the point where two heavy doors are now wide open. From the doors to the cars and all around them some sixty, seventy Sipo men stand guard, their ugly scowls straight out of a third-rate gangster film. We walk through the gateway, past heavy sliding doors, across a courtyard, into a low building with brick walls and barred gates. My junior colleague manoeuvres deftly to stand beside me when we are all placed along the wall, facing it, hands behind our backs. He whispers. At first I do not hear him. He now whispers more clearly and at length, about our young client, files, transmitter lamps, weapons. I do not quite understand. I listen to the monotonous music, the music of the prison: sustained rattling of keys. My leg is being kicked. A guard instructs me to lift this leg, the right leg, up and keep it up. One by one we are now led to a room for searching. We can keep our clothes, all other possessions are taken away and itemized on cards. I sign my card. I am allowed to keep a small leather wallet with pictures. Thank God. Also my winter coat, and my smart black hat. I am taken through a long corridor carpeted with coconut matting to Floor F, Cell 712.

At the back of the cell a little man stands to attention. He does not greet me. A mattress, a blanket, a pillow, a saucepan and a mug are thrown inside.

The cell measures some 2 x 3 meters (6½ x 10 ft). On the floor are dark tiles, the walls are plastered and painted yellow. At the back stretching the full width of the cell is a wooden bunk with a strawbag and horse-blankets, no sheets or pillow-case. Above it, in a corner, a wooden shelf. Against one wall stand a fold-back table and a stool; in a corner near the door the 'tun': a grey container with a number on it and a bucket inside with carbolic acid. There is also a tiny galvanized iron washtub, lavatory paper, an iron mug, and a spoon. Near the ceiling at the back run the central heating pipes. Above the door are two small barred windows with two cardboard black-out shutters.

In the centre of the door is a small hatch, 20 x 20cm, which can be lowered outwards after having been opened with a picklock; above it a spy-hole. The door is locked with a heavy lock and two bolts, one above, one below. On the wall next to the door is the cell card with my name and other details. On the other side is a bell which triggers a sign outside.

THE CELL BARRACKS OF SCHEVENINGEN

The *Deutsches Polizeigefängnis* Scheveningen (German Police Prison) was managed by the SS and Sipo, wearing their familiar peaked caps and deathheads. The warders were addressed as *Herr Wachtmeister* (Sergeant, Sir). For some jobs they chose prisoners as assistants: *Kalfaktoren or Flurwärter* (odd-job men or floor attendants).

The day starts with the bolts. Far away, at the beginning of the corridor, the regular clicking of the two bolts on each door starts as the floor attendants slide them back: click-click, click-click, getting nearer, and accompanied by a croaky 'morning' at each cell. Next the *Wachtmeister* arrives with his bunch of keys. He opens the hatches with a picklock. Faces appear at the hatches of cells opposite, pale, laughing, gesticulating, gullible. I notice a friend. One is not allowed to put one's mug on the hatch; it has to be held out when the floor attendant arrives who fills it with 'tea' or carrot-water. The bolts remain drawn back until evening.

The morning is reserved for airing, one side of each corridor at a time, some fifty men. The *Wachmeister* opens the doors, but one can only step outside when ordered, one behind the other, the 'tun' in hand. One then marches to the rubbish heap, puts the 'tun' down for cleaning by a group of prisoners, and continues to the airing yard, a sandy enclosure perhaps 15 x 50 metres (50 x 165 ft) west of the barracks, encircled by a high wall. High above the wall one can distinguish clouds and gulls, far away. In the centre of the yard the PT coach, a fellow prisoner, instructs us in light exercises. Those not wishing to join in are stood on one side, in a particular place. Smoking is prohibited. Warders with pistols mount guard. Above the airing yard is the wide, open sky, so important for prisoners. After airing we march through other corridors back to the rubbish heap to retrieve our buckets, now cleaned and supplied with fresh evil-smelling carbolic acid. Some cells carry an inscription on a piece of cardboard:

Ich bin Jude (I'm a Jew)
Einzelhaft (solitary confinement)
Strenge Einzelhaft (stringent solitary confinement)
Kalte Kost (cold food)
Keine Begünstigung (no favours)

Back in one's cell the issue at stake is how to pass the time until lunch. Quite soon one adopts a go-slow routine. Instinctively everything is done as slowly and ponderously as possible, to fill up time. The prison librarian - a quiet man, not a prisoner - provides a few books every week. I read them as slowly as possible, place a bet with myself about the number of letters in any one sentence. One book I have been given, a historical novel, contains a description of an execution. I warn the librarian to withdraw it from circulation. Often I read ten or twenty pages so deliberately that I have no idea of the contents.

Lunch arrives at noon. Hours in advance we know what it will be: in prison one acquires an astonishing heightening of the senses. That seems logical. Man's brain can accommodate a certain quantity of impressions. In prison nothing new is added. A vacuum develops. This cannot be filled with new stimuli so one's awareness of what already exists is heightened. At 9am you smell what is being prepared in the kitchen, 200 metres away. You hear the furtive *Wachtmeister* ten cells away before he arrives to peep through your spy hole. Every change in your cell, introduced during airing by policemen on the trail of iniquities, strikes the eye on your return; a photo stand has fallen, slippers moved, the plate on the shelf is not upright any more but lies flat: colossal changes because of our heightened sensitivity and undernourished visual faculty.

In Scheveningen the midday meal was always 3/4 litre (1½ pt) of quite reasonable stew. After ten minutes the empty saucepans were collected; you therefore have to do in ten minutes what you wanted to last for hours. I therefore transferred the stew to my plate immediately. I later struck an heroic deal with a cellmate: we would eat only half at midday, the other half we would keep until the sun entered the cell, around 3pm. That way you could enjoy three hours of anticipation. At 5.30pm you get a mug of tea and a piece of bread. With this bread I was so inventive in my efforts to prolong this small pleasure that I hardly dare write them down. For instance, I stored chewed pieces of bread outside the wall of my teeth and in hollow molars to retrieve them later with my tongue. This served as a sort of dessert. However, others went further. Sometimes we got a little sugar. I would put some of it in the tea, stir only lightly, and drink the tea quickly. The hot water allowed the squirming stomach a little grip, letting itself be tricked briefly. But the sugar sediment remained in the mug. This could then be spread on slices of bread. That way you derived double value from the same sugar. And usually I managed to postpone eating the bread until evening, just before turning in. This was announced, far away at the end of the corridor, by the approaching double click of bolts: click-click, sleep well, click-click, sleep well, CLICK-CLICK, SLEEP WELL-from the *Kalfaktors*.

My cell boasted a high window facing west. As mentioned, the sun found its way into my cell at about 3pm and shone steadily in until shortly before sunset, yellow, yellower, vivid yellow, lemon yellow, orange yellow due to the reflection on the yellow paint of the wall. In addition - and I shall hear it until I die, and I shall never be able to explain why to anyone - came the long drawn-out wail of a whistling buoy far out at sea. The yellow and the wail . . . .

The first day in Scheveningen I gave my cellmate half of the food from my saucepan. He gobbled it up disgustingly. His beige, previously white shirt smelled. I realised that soon I would be like him. Curiously, he was not a political prisoner but had been jailed for sex offences. I do not know why he was put in what we called the Orange Hotel, not because of the colour of the bricks but after our Royal House of Orange whose defenders we were. I do know that he was suspected of indecency with boys, about which he talked to me with great reluctance. More candidly - and in greater detail - he reported on his performances with women. He clearly practised a mixed trade. From time to time his lasciviousness was expressed in strings of obscenities, in a hoarse voice, about what kind of women he liked and in what ways and about who in the prison he most desired. He was no stranger to sadism either. He depicted his fantasies in such vivid detail that the copulations became almost visible, his words floating in a flood of saliva. Otherwise he grumbled all day long and treated me with malicious sarcasm. After a few days he was taken away, never to be seen again.

Fear

The first fortnight was one of slow suffocating agony through fear. The krauts deliberately kept us in the dark. We did not know or hear anything. What is going to happen? Am I going to be interrogated? How will I be interrogated? About what? Why am I here? What do they know? Is this because of the letter to the three leaders of the Netherlands Union which left little to the imagination? My pamphlets? The transmitter lamps? The non-existent weapons, often requested but never received? Have they discovered something? If so, what? What did they take away from my home? Did they discover that particular file in the office? What did I put in those letters? They contained codewords. Did they understand them? How do I extricate myself? Why did they also arrest my junior colleague? It must therefore be a case that concerns him as well as me. What could this be? What has he said? What about the young client? We had barely done anything together. Thank God, it must be a mistake, we will be released. We have not done very much, not yet. . . .

Prison. What did I know about it? As a lawyer I had often talked to detainees in the detention prison of Rotterdam: unfortunate wretches, pale, smelly, in their suits of brown baize with the round iron number on its chest, usually wearing clogs. They had appeared to me completely unreal: dried out, sterile, with eyes that twinkled mechanically.

Prison. One reads about dungeons, chains, rats. About languishing prisoners wasting away, bars, straw and rags, water and bread. About a spider, the companion of the incarcerated. Now, the first from the Bakels clan, I myself was in prison. That was . . . an honour. This was the Orange Hotel.

In this quod
Is no sod
Only Holland's glory,
a true story.

However, horror stories abounded about this prison. They tortured; I had heard that the krauts had taken the little son of a prisoner who refused to give anything away, and in front of his eyes twisted an arm out of its socket. Yet, a robust buoyant tone prevailed in talk about the Orange Hotel. Such as the production of OZO (*Oranje zal overwinnen* or Orange will be victorious), guilder coins with the queen's head sawn out, and similar childish pastimes in which I had happily participated until 9 April.

Those first days I try to cultivate the defiant mood of the Orange Hotel and Holland's glory. I march up and down, softly singing songs from the English radio: *The White Cliffs of Dover, Chattanooga Choo-Choo, Shoeshine Boy* and especially the English soldier's *It's a long way to Tipperary* . . . but, surprisingly, it does not help. It has the opposite effect, it increases fear. This heralds further revelations: first alarming, then liberating.

Slogans become empty. There are thousands of slogans, life is full of them. Almost all of them have proved to be untrue. It has become evident that we have strayed from reality in every sense and turned up in a labyrinth of fiction on the wings of slogans, fallacies and deceptions, where we can only hold out enmeshed in a maze of new misconceptions. All of it is untrue, I realised. Take war, battlefield, field of honour, God, Queen, country, and heroic death. The dishonest trumpeting of war as a dramatically edifying affair is centuries old and has often been exposed by learned authors. But clearly not effectively enough. Even in our midst we found people who had not understood anything, even though it was plain for them to see. War is a dirty pool of blood, on both sides. The 'field of honour' is the most loathsome concept of all. God - who dares use His name? Country - who fights for it? Most people fight to save their bacon. At best they fight for all the people in the world, for justice, for freedom - indeed, unequivocally and literally. In our time we do not fight simply for our country - something nobler is at stake.

The traditional catchwords show their falsehood when life is really at risk. This redoubled my fear. The first fear - of torture and possible death - was followed by a second fear springing from the unmasking of tradition, those powerless and obtuse slogans. Every certitude crumbled. Yet, curiously, when conditions deteriorated, slogan and tradition were found to contain at least some validity, something quite primitive that acted on one's instincts. But by then fury had taken over from fear. Our situation became so serious that even enmity diminished after a time. Now and again, I did not regard the Germans as an enemy to be destroyed, but as fellow human beings who were possessed, even as fellow sufferers. Writing this down shocked me, but it is true and therefore must stand. Eventually the situation grew too serious for enmity among people. Though later, when it became even worse, this attitude changed again.

During this first period in Scheveningen, isolated from society, I often got frightened by this new insight into the rhetoric of war. I thought, 'you are going soft.' Fear of death makes you a coward, gets such a grip on you that you become soppy, whining, mumbling about fellow men and such like. I am not certain but inclined to believe that fear of death gave rise both to clear insight and to softness.

SUFFERING AS THE MOTHER OF PRAYER

All proverbs, phrases and sayings - as distinct from slogans - are true. Like the Dutch saying: need begets prayer. Someone struck by grief and unable to digest the burden alone will turn to his Creator with an appeal for help. That appeal is nearly always a request to remove the suffering, or at least to alleviate it. This is not the intention of prayer. A devout prayer calls for strength and divine presence, with an added promise to acquiesce: Your will be done. One asks for strength to match the cross one bears. While it is true that need begets prayer it is also true that as the suffering diminishes so does the compulsion in matters of faith. When all goes well one tends to forget prayer. God is good for emergencies. He tends to be ignored when there are no complaints. This is an awful truth, evidence of shallowness and ingratitude, even stupidity. Apparently it also provides a decisive argument for those who deem themselves unbelievers to discard faith as an illusion and a lot of fuss about nothing. This argument is dangerous because nothing can be put against it. In the middle of repression and suffering people come to faith. Not on their own merit but by the grace of God and at the same time because of the cross they have to bear - whether they want it or not. However, people are themselves responsible for sustaining their own faith, by prayer. A man at prayer is invincible. Many hundreds, even thousands of those caught by the Germans came to faith. Innumerable diaries, letters, farewell letters and other testimonies confirm this.

FAITH

Several things under the German terror helped people to find faith: the feeling of guilt, the uncertainty, and the Gospel. Almost everyone has feelings of guilt, and rightly so. Almost no one will claim to be without guilt. The occupation contributed to it. We hated the Germans, our fellow human beings, with a deadly hatred which was sometimes translated into action. There was a war on and during a war crime abounds and the law is set aside. Anyone who kills in normal times with malice aforethought is a murderer and commits the most serious crime. Anyone who does it to one officially designated by the government as an enemy performs a duty. That's how it is and it is tragic. It creates a feeling of guilt, perhaps even guilt itself. Someone with a feeling of guilt will not be surprised when he is punished. I felt that the wrong meted out to me by the Germans was punishment, especially in the beginning. Of course I did not accept the punishment as a well-deserved penalty from the Germans. The punishment was determined by God, against

24

Whom I had sinned ceaselessly during my twenty-six years. The Nazis were only an instrument. They treated me unjustly, God treated me justly.

Next there is the uncertainty. People long for certainty. They try incessantly and in many ways to create certainties in their lives; the time and manner of death remain the great uncertainties and this is accepted only because it is inevitable. But the creation of absolute uncertainty, from A to Z, was an essential part of the German system of terror. Arrest took place unexpectedly. Until your interrogation you were not told why. You did not know where you were being taken until you arrived there. The duration of imprisonment remained unknown. Transport to prisons and camps took place unexpectedly, the destination was kept secret. Members of the family were either not informed, or told very late, and they never knew your whereabouts. German imprisonment meant that every second of every day anything could happen, including execution. That created the greatest uncertainty for the prisoners, and deliberately so. The Germans hoped it would break our spirit. But in reality that very uncertainty was a most forceful stimulus for inner strength through faith. When everything and everyone has been lost, you grasp instinctively for the one primary certainty: God's presence.

And finally, the Gospel. The Gospel, the good news, addresses itself particularly to the underdog. You only need to flip through the New Testament to learn that Christ devoted Himself especially to the poor, the disabled, the sick, the deprived, the humble, the sinners and the outcasts, to whom He promised salvation in the hereafter. On the other hand, the rich and mighty will have great difficulty in entering the Kingdom of Heaven. Obviously therefore the prisoners of the German occupying power were extremely susceptible to the Gospel of Christ. When you are burdened with a feeling of guilt, in the utmost uncertainty, beaten, kicked, humiliated, abused, tortured and starved; when you are threatened day and night with death for activities deemed criminal only by the aggressors and no one else, activities which you undertook as a duty, it is plain that you will be strongly attracted to words of comfort, and promises of salvation hereafter; then add to these feelings a certain disdain for earthly life which the Bible encourages. Facing death, surrounded by demons, tightly cut off from the outside world, wife and children, relatives and friends, you feel at first 'forsaken by God' - as Jesus himself exclaimed on the Cross - until the marvel occurs when God turns out to be unmistakably present, witness my 'vision' near Pijnacker on the way to three years of torture. It is ironic that it was in the kingdom of the devil that the prospect for divine revelation was especially great. All the conditions were fulfilled to perfection.

I am writing this down after some hesitation, and with a question mark. Are these conditions so perfectly fulfilled in the German prisons and camps in order to give divine revelation a new and indeed greater opportunity? Has our imprisonment perhaps not been a satanic but a divine enterprise? I am too inadequate to provide an answer. I would say that for me it was both at the same time. The reader must not ask me now how this is possible. Nor should the reader later ask anyone else, for no human being can understand it.

AIRING

Airing time could be full of surprises. In the first place I learned to appreciate the varied skies. The fresh air and open sky above were essential. There were birds too; they simply flew over the wall. A sparrow flew up and away. Oh, to have wings. . . . The airing yard boasted a small garden. One of my cell-neighbours had been appointed gardener. An excellent choice for he had lived in a mansion with vast gardens. He looked healthy and busied himself with spade, rake and watering can. In his care the little garden flourished. Another neighbour was obviously a naval officer. His expression, face, bearing: clearly a naval officer. Especially the way he walked: erect, stepping rhythmically, straight arms swinging generously, chest pushed forward, chin up. It was a proud, strong way of walking. At first, with my legs quickly becoming weak and rubbery, it gave me a lot of trouble to follow suit, but in the end I managed. Physically you move agreeably when mentally you feel well. I discovered that you could turn this round: you can start with the right movements and cheerfulness will often follow. The same applies to laughter. Usually laughter is the result of mirth. In particular circumstances it is to be recommended to start laughing, in the hope that mirth will follow.

One day in the airing yard a row of implausible new-comers stood against the wall. They had bald heads and looked tanned. At first you thought: these are really healthy fellows. But on closer inspection the reverse turned out to be true. The suntanned faces were more like draped skulls and the fairly decent suits hung in long folds on their bodies. The trousers hung curiously straight and when someone moved his leg it looked like a wooden leg, a pole. I realised they looked cadaverous. They smiled dimly at us. 'We've come from Amersfoort,' one of them whispered.

Zur Vernehmung (Interrogation)

Secrecy formed an important part of German terrorism. Terror required influencing us by means of fear. This fear was powerfully fostered by the menace of unknown but suspected cruelties to come. Impelled by pure fear, many gave away coveted information during their interrogation without having been touched at all. We should have an indescribable admiration for those who kept their mouths shut under torture and flatly refused to betray others.

To hold out against overwhelming might when all alone in the world, not to give an inch, not to forsake one's principles even once - or request favours, particularly a stay of execution! It is almost impossible to imagine such strength. But anything can happen and one should not be too quick to judge, nothing should be rejected as immoral. I have the greatest respect for those convicted to die who did not ask for a pardon out of pride. They did not want to plead with the enemy for their lives. They deemed this an intolerable humiliation. Which it was. Nevertheless, when life is at stake one becomes desperate to wriggle out of this dilemma, if only for the sake of wife and family. I too would have done so. This also applies to remaining silent, not mentioning names, under torture. The Germans used horrendously vile means to force people to talk. I know several who refused none the less. They are true heroes.

Some survivors told me that the threat of torture is worse than the torture itself, and that the beginning of the torture is worse than continued torture. You had to stand the threat and the first pains. Once beyond that you were usually saved. It became a matter of pride, a match, obstinacy. 'You bastards, do you really think you can break my spirit?' If you fight for yourself, you're lost. But I had fought for a noble cause, far more important than me, and therefore could hold out.

I have come to the conclusion that each must follow his own conscience. Consciences differ. I cannot condemn anyone whose reactions are extreme in situations that are extreme. After the sex offender I had several other cellmates, among them a mystic of limited education who sat and stared in front of him while loudly making calculations about the date of his release, conjuring up endless figures. As hunger increased, the interrogation failed to materialize and awful noises could be heard in other cells, I became more afraid. My *Zellenkarte* (cell card) mentioned sabotage, aiding and abetting the enemy, distribution of leaflets, (in German, of course). Day and night I racked my brain about what they might know. I too started to make calculations.

Gradually I felt myself split into two. The one half of me tried to become 'the new man'. Long-forgotten Bible texts floated back into my consciousness and after a few days I became fascinated by the words: whosoever has faith can move mountains. I believed and would therefore move mountains. If God were for me, who would be against me? I did not then have a Bible, nor spiritual guidance. I was all alone with God and an appalling struggle started that would lead to a crisis. I began to believe that if I had enough faith the cell door would be opened. That it remained shut was evidence of my unbelief.

Then, after two weeks, the day of my interrogation finally arrived. My interrogators were first SS Untersturmführer Walthes, later SS Hauptscharführer Heyduck. It revolved mainly around my relationship with our young clerk, his accomplice and their organization. Their attitude was initially rather good natured; no one touched me. They hardly asked any questions. The kraut opposite simply told me about the young client and others who belonged to an illegal organization. This was news to me, as was its name: *Leeuwengarde* (Lion Guard). My contacts with both were described accurately, including the gist of our discussions. They only asked whether all this was correct, which I confirmed. I could hardly do anything else. They asked for more names. I did not know any. Then it happened:

'You now have an opportunity to tell us more, Herr Doktor.'

This was a threat, accompanied by the offer of a cigarette, and it made me panic. Fortunately I could truthfully explain that I did not know any other names.

Next came the question: 'Where did you hide your gun?'

Again truthfully I could say I did not possess any weapons. Suddenly my interrogator, his ugly face bursting open like a melon with pips, threw a heavy revolver on the desk.

'That's yours, isn't it?'

I replied, never having owned a pistol, that I did not even know the difference between a revolver and a pistol and that I had also never tried shooting with any kind of gun. He looked at me with great satisfaction.

'Correct. It's not yours. It's mine.' The idiot: I now knew he could lie!

The discussion then focused on the papers they had found, several leaflets and particularly the copy of that long letter (translated by them into German) to the three leaders of the Netherlands Union, expressing estimably, extensively and eminently clearly my view of the occupying power, Queen and cabinet in London and other related subjects. Therefore the Nazis could be in no doubt about my feelings. I could only confirm them. Other affairs, apparently unknown to the *Hauptscharführer*, were not mentioned. A typist arrived and the minutes were dictated. The first words were 'I am Dutch-Royalist minded'.

COMMUNICATION

In the cell I had a packet of lavatory paper. I took a pin from a clean shirt that had been delivered and pricked out letters, words, in the lavatory paper. In dainty lettering, I wrote whole letters to fellow prisoners, which took a nice long time. During airing I handed the letters to whom they concerned.

In the evening a different sort of communication was possible. You always hear and read about prisoners communicating by knocking signals on walls. That was no use in Scheveningen. The next-door neighbours could be contacted by loud talking, while others could not be reached at all with knocks. The central heating pipes provided some conduction for sound; voices from far away sounded metallic, as if from a broken-down steel loudspeaker. They gave the impression of voices from another world.

Late at night there was a lot of sound-traffic between cells, distorted, bedded in concrete, sinister. I could make out snippets, glean some information. Was it true? I strained to understand, one ear against the wall, when some contact was made via others who passed it on. Yes, I had heard accurately. The president of our Leiden University Club was being held in a cell on my floor F. Chained up!

About a month after my arrest the entire prison was in subdued uproar. A lot was passed on, shouted on and signalled on. The Germans had shot dead seventy-two men. They turned out to be 'the 72' of the OD (Order Service, a semi-military resistance group), an act of terror which convulsed the whole country. They had been transported to Sachsenhausen concentration camp and were not shot from the front but in the back of the neck.

CALAMITY

The lavatory paper also served another purpose. The corners of pockets in trousers, jackets and coats always contain dust. And dust can be mixed with remnants of tobacco. Early on I had already searched all my pockets. Tobacco and dust were put on a piece of lavatory paper and rolled into a deformed cigarette. New cellmates were instructed to do the same. The difficulty was to find a light. Throughout my imprisonment cigarettes played a major role for everyone, without exception.

Occasionally - not often - calamity occurred on our corridor, especially late at night. One evening German shouts approached, accompanied by a curious sound, shuffling followed by panting. The uproar reached my cell, clearly some sort of cruelty: panting, groaning, indeterminate knocking and, of course, 'Los, los Mensch! Schneller, schneller!' (get on with it, man, faster, faster). The next day it turned out that a number of prisoners as punishment had been made to hop frog-like the entire length of the corridor, from start to finish.

A Miracle

In the evening around 5.30pm when bread and skimmed milk had been brought I would allow myself to work out the number of days I had been in prison. Only then, not before, as that would be unfair. Early on I had just calculated once, now I did it three times. Occasionally I would count carelessly, on purpose, for I then got different results, in which case I allowed myself to count four times, which took up more time and killed several more minutes. I counted: 44 days, and again: 44 days, whereupon I cheated by counting 30 days for May instead of 31, thus reaching only 43, so now I could count once again. Hey ho: 44 days. This amounted to a large gain: several minutes. During which the bread was left untouched. Another gain. A good day. And tomorrow would be for shaving, another good day.

The bread was sliced, though not cleanly, so the sides stuck together. Very gently I would tear them apart. There were always four, one of them a crust. I would put my handkerchief on the foldback table. Splendid! I could eat from a tablecloth. I would look at the picture of the woman on the wall and slowly count to one hundred. Then I would say a prayer. Now I could drink the skimmed milk slowly, sitting at the table, eyes closed. At the bottom of the mug would be a thin layer of wet sugar. I would lick the mug clean. I would then put the slices of bread on the shelf above the bunk to eat when the sun had set.

First I must walk. As in cheap crime novels: six steps diagonally one way, six back. Yesterday it was two hundred times back and forth, today therefore it will be two hundred and fifty. I start pacing, looking at my feet. My feet had become huge appendages on the end of thin poles, on top of these were rubbery knees, linked by more poles to a lifeless belly, a sunken chest cavity, a turkey's neck, and a bald pate. I walked. The 'tun' smelled worse as the spring air filtered in through the open window near the ceiling. The evening light grew yellower, ever yellower. All the time, morning, afternoon, evening, the boom of the whistling buoy at sea can be heard in the distance.

'Hello,' I heard. And knocking, from 714, which had been going on for some time already.

'Hello, what's the time?'

'About eight, perhaps ten past eight.'

'Almost another day gone then.'

'Yes.'

'I've been here one hundred and two.'

'Really?'

'There's supposed to be a deportation tomorrow.'

'You going?'

'Don't know.'

Knocking. Stony sounds in concrete. He fell silent, spotted trouble no doubt. The back wall was now more yellow than yellow. I pull the cardboard blackout shutter half-way across the window. The yellow softens, the sun disappears.

My God, the door is flung open, in the door a monster, Wachmeister SS Rottenführer August Fischer.

'You've been talking.'

'Not really, Herr Wachmeister.'

The swollen scarlet face, a lump of raw meat crushed between cap and collar, gazes at me with glazed eyes.

'What're you here for?' The fleshy mouth screeches. I can hear the other prisoners listening.

'I don't know. I'm suspected of . . . .'

He steps inside, with boots like heavy iron. The glazed eyes have a squint. The right arm points at me. I look. The hand at the end of the arm holds a piece of paper. The piece of paper in the hand on the arm is, I believe, being offered to me. The meaty face breathes, I smell dried sweat. The corners of his fleshy mouth curl. I take the piece of paper. I open it slightly. I see the handwriting.

When I looked up the door had closed. There was no one there any more. The blue tram to the sea whistled. It was getting dark. I opened the blackout shutter and stood under the window, beside the door in order not be observed through the spyhole. I opened the piece of paper a bit more. I read: 'My own darling'. I stretched and stood on tiptoes to reach the fading light. 'I'm hard at work for you'. I stretched further. 'You shouldn't really believe that they . . . .' I could not read any more. I could read the secret letter from my wife, which the enemy through God's mercy had brought me, no further.

WOHL NICHT (PROBABLY NOT)

A few days after this phenomenon I was taken from my cell to a waiting room. There I found myself face to face with my *Sachbearbeiter* (official in charge of my case) together with a senior partner from our solicitor's firm who told me in the best German he could muster that he needed information about a case I had been involved in. It was clear that this was just an excuse. Firstly, because the complete file was in the office, and secondly, because his questions were so silly that I feared that even the guard would see through the deception. My colleague interspersed his questions very cleverly with information about our young client, and his associates, incriminating documents relating to them, 'unpleasant material' present in the office etc. He was able to make it clear to me that all this had been found by him and our staff and destroyed without the Sipo knowing about it, so that I could take this into account when interrogated. For at interrogations the main question was always: what do they and what do they not know? But I had already been interrogated . . . .

Having dealt with the case, my colleague started asking the *Sachbearbeiter* about my situation. Why did they keep me? After all I could not have harmed the occupying forces. I was as gentle as could be, and so on. The German, with his hangdog face - like an afterbirth, as one of my cellmates described it - chuckled. But still, he said, 'der Herr' had yet acted in a way that was not *deutschfreundlich* (friendly to the Germans). But he added reassuringly, 'Aber erschossen wird der Herr wohl nicht' (but he will probably not be shot). My colleague and I looked at each other, first smiling, next in amazement, then blankly as his words sank in, finally alarmed. We also looked at the German, whose facial expression had lost its joviality and as if by magic changed to malice. I felt myself grow cold, my hairs stood on end. 'He is serious. He really means he will *probably* not be shot. *Probably* not. Therefore perhaps he will. My God, what have I done after all?'

That was how it happened. Each word, each gesture, each indication made an excessive impression on Sipo prisoners. We became sensitive to each word, each impression, to sounds, smells, even displaced objects as a result of fear and hunger, but also of the long confinement, the worries, the rigid prison regime, the absence of any contact with the outside world. *Erschossen wird er wohl nicht* - I sensed disaster, like a hunted animal.

A few weeks later there was a startling event: the distribution of the *Schutzhaftbefehl*. I knew quite a lot of German, but what could this onerous document mean? Literally, it meant a protective custody order. How? Who? What 'protection'? For days I worried constantly. What could it mean? Much later, in Amersfoort, I found out. It was an arrangement to detain a suspect in order to protect the state from him. The thousand-year Third Reich had to be protected from me. Towards the end of May I was woken by a distant but approaching all-embracing, strident rumbling. Aeroplanes. Bombers. The first airborne fleet. From west to east. The English, the RAF! Everywhere in the prison one heard knocking, signalling, vague words, exclamations. The invasion, they shouted, the invasion has started! It was spring 1942. . . .

It turned out to be the first of numerous air attacks by the RAF during the night of 30-31 May 1942 on Cologne with 1,130 bombers. English and American readers should appreciate that most Dutchmen, both outside and inside prisons, resisters as well as the non-committed, assumed that the war would finish in 1942. This affected the Resistance and the Jewish Council as much as the expectations of the silent majority. Wishful thinking? In retrospect, yes. But did not Stalin call for an invasion on the continent in 1942?

RELIGIOUS MANIA

In mid-June during airing my junior partner's laces came untied again. He stopped to retie them, thereby contriving to make contact with me. This had happened before. Last time it lost us a week's airing. Clearly an important message had to be passed on. Once again he managed to get behind me in the line of running prisoners. He hissed, 'I've had a visit from my wife - will probably be free shortly - the Sachbearbeiter told me that you too could perhaps be released if only you would at last tell the truth'.

Back in the cell it started. I began to reflect and reflect again, continually thinking, fretting, brooding, calculating and concocting webs of fantasy. Did the Germans possess some decency after all, and would they prefer you to tell them the truth? Was that going to be rewarded? Why had I lied during my cross examination, at least concealed all sorts of things, when I believed in God, in His power to save me? How could God be expected to stay with me when I had denied some activities out of fear of incriminating other people? Had this not been horrible unbelief? Was it not true that when acting apparently absurdly, indeed dangerously, one would be rewarded by God and saved? Was it not true that one could move mountains when one had faith? I too wanted to. go home, already my colleague had received a visit and would probably leave and I had not. My wife waited for me, needed me, did not have anyone else . . . .

I began to detect good omens. I calculated with dates, lucky numbers, particular terms. Small incidents, words overheard, suddenly looked like indications. Of course, that was the key: I simply had to tell the whole truth and God would help me.

Was this the onset of madness? The truth could lose me my life. Oh horror, unbelief crept in again. Do not be afraid, do not pursue human rational arguments, trust blindly, prove your belief, take the path of no return. This continued for days on end, nights on end. Until I too got a visit from my wife.

One afternoon they collected me and took me to one of the interrogation rooms. The door opened. God almighty! She is sitting at a table, next to the *Sachbearbeiter*. In honeyed tones he says: 'This is a surprise, eh?' I cannot say anything. I look at her. She smiles. She produces delicacies, also bread and butter. I start eating at once, gawping at her.

At last I say, stupidly, 'How d'you like my moustache?'

She answers in German, 'Hideous.' She also gives me a New Testament. I desperately want to escape to my cell. She chats with the *Sachbearbeiter*, asks when I will be released. It is a completely unreal meeting.

'Have you got any more bread?'

Sorry, I haven't,' in German. Oh, a visit in prison!

This visit prompted new indications, whispers, suggestions, numbers, combinations, a distinct guidance . . . . But I also heard that our beloved Alsation Max had died. That same evening I rang the bell in cell 712. My God, what have I started? After a long wait an unknown *Wachmeister* appears.

'What's wrong?'

'I'd like to see Herr Sachbearbeiter at once,' in German.

He studies my card: Heyduck. He disappears. There is no way back. I do not want to retract. Be brave, remain strong, believe at last. The Germans do not have any power. Only God has power.

An hour later Heyduck receives me. 'Well, Herr Doktor, what's the matter?' Smiling he offers me a cigarette which makes me dizzy. I tell him everything. I explain that as a Dutchman and a Christian I want to reveal the truth. I will not - thank God, cannot - betray anyone, but on my own have done more than admitted at first. I talk a long time, he listens attentively, affably, the atmosphere is spooky. I realize that I am playing with my life.

When I have finished the *Sachbearbeiter* says, 'Well now, we've assessed you correctly after all. The secretary isn't available at this moment. We must somehow document all this.' I am returned to cell 712.

Panic gripped me. Oh God, what have I done? I had relied on God and done my duty. I had endangered my life and the happiness of my wife and members of my family. *Erschossen wird er - wohl nicht?* Probably not shot. But then, faith moves mountains, be quiet, you will be released. Have I therefore done this only to be free? Not to obey God? But I am entitled to be free, am I not? Is that not reasonable? Am I not allowed to pray for release? No, that is not allowed, your release is not the issue, His will be done, even when it means your death penalty. Could it therefore be execution?

It continued like that, days and nights. I prayed and it got worse. The day arrived when my colleague did not turn up for airing. He had gone home. That was at the end of June. I then started making new calculations. They were keeping me a few days more to tease me. Releases were always on a Saturday. I added up dates and worked out dates. It would be 04-07-1942. I wait, I have to believe. God would now test my faith. He had sent my wife for some purpose, I was therefore allowed to ask for Christ's sake: let me go on Saturday 4 July.

That day arrives, the great day of the great marvel. God will do it. It depends on holding tight. I will move the mountain. I all but close the blackout shutters, to achieve subdued solemn light. I throw myself down on my knees on the tiled floor and start praying. I am praying hour after hour, more and more urgently. I go into a trance. I have vague visions and begin to be certain. We are aired, 'for the last time' in the airing yard, my poor fellow inmates will have to stay. Back in cell 712, I pray ever more fervently. Far away, in the corridor, a rattling of keys. Doors open, doors close. Dutch and German voices. Shouting, running up and down. They come my way. They are near. Almost opposite. A door opens, shuts. I kneel in front of my door. Close by I hear keys, voices. Boots thunder past, and return. Directly opposite a door slams shut. Now it is going to happen. The steps return, pass my cell, move on, further away. All noise dies. Deadly silence in the prison. A mistake, it is a mistake. I am holding on, they will come and collect me shortly. God has promised.

Far away saucepans rattle, the food trolley approaches. The hatches swing open. Food is served. My belief was insufficient, I had not asked in the right way, I did not know anything about prayer, God could not betray me. Hold tight! Especially now. My meal has arrived. I put it away. I would be released any moment, so I would give it to a neighbour. The empty saucepans are collected, but I kneel on the floor and pray. I prayed for hours on end, the silence of the weekend had already arrived.

Then I became mad. You know, when you become mad, that you are mad. You notice someone trying to climb up the wall, standing on top of the tun, on the stool, falling. You hear someone sob, roar, yell. Who is it? He should control himself. You cannot believe that this is you yourself, there are two of you. Nothing can be done. The regulatory mechanism has broken down. And God is nowhere to be found. Neighbours in their cells start to shout. The door swings open. My friend Fischer, his face scarlet, shouts, 'What's going on here? Calm down!' I grab onto him. He disappears quickly, returns with a *Kalfaktor*, a saucepan with food and a jigsaw puzzle of the painting *The Lost Inheritance*. One neighbour shouts, 'You've got to wash in cold water at once.' The door shuts. Sobbing, I undress. I wash myself with cold water. Shivering I start laying out the jigsaw puzzle, meanwhile emptying both saucepans ravenously. I hear my neighbour humming as he paces up and down his cell. I am exhausted, broken, desperate, senseless.

This was the first of three or four crises during my years of imprisonment, and probably the worst. Without any doubt it was a case of pure religious mania, as some wiser men than I explained much later. They pointed out that I had tried to force my will on to God. A few days later the *Kalfaktor* whispered, 'In two days you'll be deported.'

On 17 July at 1.30am lights are switched on. There is uproar all over the prison. 'Get ready for deportation. Quick, quick, man, get on with it.' My second statement had never been put in writing.

BEHIND THE NET CURTAINS

A romantic little train took us in the middle of the night to Amersfoort. We passed Pijnacker. Everything was blacked out, I could hardly see anything. A wild thought occurred to me: why not make a break for it, regardless? Reason won. In Amersfoort a column was formed of those condemned to suffer mightily. We walked to the camp, flanked by a heavily armed escort. The long column shuffled slowly forward. For a change, we were not pushed for speed. As the eastern sky paled we arrived through wide avenues in a fashionable district of Amersfoort.

I then saw a strange phenomenon. Behind the ground and first floor windows of most detached houses, shadowy figures became visible behind net curtains, especially children. When you looked carefully you could see they were wearing pyjamas or nightdresses. Mostly the shadowy figures stood motionless. Occasionally someone waved hesitatingly, secretly. Waving children were rapidly pulled away. We were parting with civilization, we were now in the realm of ghosts.

3. POLIZEILICHES DURCHGANGSLAGER AMERSFOORT (PDA) (Police transit camp Amersfoort) 17 July-13 November 1942

THE KZ OR KL (KONZENTRATIONSLAGER) GERMAN CONCENTRATION CAMP

Daunted by the almost impossible task of describing a KZ in such a way that the reader gets an accurate impression, I initially wrote many pages trying to present the details of a KZ objectively. These have been scrapped; others have done the job better. Nevertheless, I still have to make some introduction to its horrors. The reader will have to understand KZ terminology intuitively.

The SS management could not regulate everything in a KZ itself and therefore gave Häftlinge (prisoners) some self-government; in several camps we hardly saw the SS - except at roll calls - but its reign of terror was administered by more or less highly placed fellow prisoners: the *Lagerprominenz* (prominent camp figures). Among them were the *Lagerälteste* (camp seniors), the *Block-* and *Stubenältesten* (block and room seniors) and the *Blockschreiber* (block clerk); the men of the *Schreibstube* (administration) and the *Lagerpolizei* (camp police); the *Stubendienste* (room services) and many others, among them the *Kapos* who commanded the work parties supervised by *Oberkapos* (chief *Kapos*); and under the *Kapos* there were *Vorarbeiter* (foremen). There was, therefore, an extensive hierarchy of 'prominent prisoners'.

For the preservation of one's life - literally - it was important in every KZ whether the *Lagerprominenz* consisted of criminal prisoners or political ones (often German communists). The latter were, of course, infinitely preferable to the former. Where the day-to-day camp

37

management fell to the *Befauers* or *Befristete Vorbeugungshäftlinge* (prisoners with limited preventive custody) - we called them *Berufsverbrecher* (professional criminals) or *Grünen* (greens) from the green triangle on their clothing - the miseries could hardly be guessed at. In some camps a mortal power struggle was waged between *Grünen* and communists, while the SS stood by laughing.

The activities of fellow prisoners in their capacity as *Lagerprominenz*, particularly the *Block-* and *Stubenältesten* and the *Kapos*, had to match those of the SS of course. *Prominenz* who exhibited any form of softness, let alone the more or less humane ones, were rarely left in their function. But there were also quite a few exceptions to this rule. I have had experience of excellent *Lagerprominenz*, among them many Dutchmen (I too was a *Lagerprominenz* for a short while). Who can explain this strange, capricious, absurd system? Was it a reflection of the continuous struggle for power, political or otherwise, at the top of the KZ? Whatever the motivation, however, those who wished to please the SS had to show brutality. I myself have been maltreated more often by fellow prisoners than by the SS.

There were many sorts of *Führer* and *Prominenz* but also many sorts of prisoner. The *Grünen* have already been mentioned. Political prisoners wore a red triangle on their coats and trousers, 'bible-explorers' or Jehovah's witnesses a purple one, sexual offenders pink, anti-social people black, and Jews a yellow star. A letter stamped in the centre of the triangle indicated nationality. Dutch political prisoners wore the red triangle, the point downward, with an H for Holland.

In general the lay-out of concentration camps did not differ one from the other. Most important was, of course, the enclosure: as a rule concrete poles bent over at the top, connected by many rows of barbed wire, often electrified; sometimes a double enclosure with a path in between; occasionally a ditch as well. At set distances were wooden watchtowers, so-called miradors, garrisoned by SS with machineguns and searchlights. You entered the camp through a gateway, heavily guarded.

Immediately inside the camp there was the parade ground, sometimes a very large space. Prisoners lived in barracks, *Blocke*, divided into rooms, *Stuben*. Then there was the kitchen building, the hospital (called *Häftlingskrankenbau* or HKB, *Krankenrevier* or *Revier*), the *Schreibstube* (orderly room), *Effektenkammer* (inventory room, where the personal belongings of the prisoners were stored and meticulously detailed on cards!), sometimes a wash-room, a lavatory-block and a 'bunker' for extra punishment. Often there was also a crematorium with a high chimney, called *Kamin*, usually connected to the bathroom. Not all camps had gaschambers.

THE TENTH PLANET

This gives a brief summary of the factual details of a KZ. The reader must forgive me for the profusion of German terms: without them a KZ cannot be fathomed at all. Incidentally, all those in a position to judge - i.e. former inmates - agree that it is impossible to describe a KZ adequately because it belongs to a different world, another planet. Not unlike the essence of dreams, which are equally hard to describe. This is probably the reason why so few people have ever attempted to make a KZ film, while POW camp films abound. The only adequate means of expressing it may perhaps be with music. Convinced of my utter impotence, I shall nevertheless make a second attempt at capturing life in a KZ.

The *Häftling* is never sure of his life, truly not for one second of the day or night. Anything could happen at any time, and if one tried to imagine something really bad, something worse would really happen. We were deliberately and continuously terrorized on behalf of public authority. The terror was carried out by people who were usually common criminals, as in nightmares. They exercised a satanic power over us. Catholics with their vague ideas of hell could not conceive of a worse hell than the KZ. Fear of their satanic power dominated everything. We were *Häftlinge*, not people; they talked about 'hunderd Stück' (hundred pieces). We did not have names, only numbers. We did not have hair, not even armpit or pubic hair. We did not have any personal belongings, apart from dentures or spectacles; not even a toothbrush.

The class system and hierarchy of ordinary society did not exist in the KZ. The humblest slave labourer might be a general in normal life, the *Lagerälteste* in his exalted position, a road mender. There was hardly any contact with the outside world; in some camps not with one's family at home either. No letters, no parcels, nothing: *Nacht und Nebel*.

Second only to fear, hunger and cold ruled. Like fear, hunger dominated every second of the day and night. As a result of hunger the most unbelievable things occurred, including cannibalism. The cold was even worse. In winter, the cold from frost and snow could bring us, walking skeletons, to greater despair than fear, famine or even maltreatment.

In the camp and at labour-units there was not a moment without ill-treatment. All the time, even at night, some people were being ill-treated somewhere. The wailing, crying, screaming of men being abused . . . . Large-scale maltreatment occurred every day, including

39

murders. Unofficial murders, official murders, in front of the entire body of assembled inmates. The language was German, but Polish and Russian were also used.

Almost nobody bore up well, not even the most prominent Dutchmen. Everyone had physical complaints. In addition we were concerned about those we had left behind. Outside the KZ a world war raged. Our country was occupied; it became a war-zone again in September 1944 (the Battle of Arnhem Market Garden). I do not know how it was possible, but we were always apprised of allied war reports. We knew what was happening in Holland. We imagined the most terrible things happening to our people at home - if still alive - and we were powerless to do anything.

But this was not all. We were degenerating, in every respect, and we knew it. Some have said and written that once *Häftlinge* reached the state of *Muselmänner* - live skeletons, almost without consciousness - and even the less afflicted, they would be demoralized and without any veneer of civilization, bestial, intent only on preserving their own lives. This is a monstrous falsehood.

Yes, some did become bestial, but they were rarer than those - mostly political prisoners - who tried to remain themselves, to lift themselves above their weaknesses. There was a profusion of splendid acts of self-sacrifice, self- denial, altruism, heroism, charity and neighbourly love by *Häftlinge*. I will report on these in due course. But we did recognize that we were degenerating. And this produced a new fear. Anyone who retained his consciousness and his reason was inevitably aware of degeneration, and needed all, really every last ounce of his physical and mental reserves to sustain him.

However, there is another, entirely different, reason why a KZ cannot be described credibly. I have already mentioned the all-pervasive satanic power, the hell of the KZ. But precisely because of that there also was a heaven. Like the light from a lighthouse, which by day can only be seen as a pale spark out at sea, but which at night radiates dazzling rays for miles around. Similarly, the presence of the Almighty was firmly felt in the KZ, whereas in normal life it might only appear as a pale spark.

This is the real message I wish to convey.

THE BAPTISM OF FIRE

On 17 July 1942 our group from Scheveningen were treated in the PDA to its *Emfangszeremonie* (reception ceremony). This was an attempt to dehumanize us in a few hours, to deprive us of our identity.

You lost your luggage, all your personal belongings. You were shorn of all hair, armpit and pubic too, crudely, with a blunt pair of clippers. You received a number (mine was 918). You received a uniform of the Dutch army, often covered with bloodstains, sometimes riddled with bulletholes. You got clogs, socks, leggings. You also got rags for underwear: shorts with one leg, without crotch, half your size, double your size, like the uniforms. You received a fatigue cap. All this accompanied by shouting, beating, kicking. I managed to wangle in my pocket Bible and a photograph of my wife.

That first day in the Polizeiliches Durchgangslager Amersfoort we, unrecognisable scarecrows, were introduced to German drill, as well as camp rules, how to report, how to greet etc. The camp senior, the block seniors, the *Kapos* all ran around, kicking, shrieking, terrorizing the bewildered herd of slaves, supervised by the critical SS bosses. This over, we could attend the first evening roll-call exactly as prescribed. Immediately afterwards we made the acquaintance of the Geman beast in its undisguised demoniac shape.

A *Häftling*, returning from an outside party, was found during a search to have hidden stolen potatoes in his clothing. At roll-call he was led before the assembled inmates by those who were going to murder him. His face seemed a healthy red, on closer inspection unnaturally red. Indeed, as red as blood. Before long he lay on the ground, potatoes pouring out of his pockets. He curled up so his back received the full force of the kicks. Eventually he rolled over onto his back. That was fatal. One guard stripped off his trousers; even more potatoes poured out. The look on the guard's face changed. The cold indifference disappeared, it became attentive, eager, satisfied, almost happy. Later I would recognize this look as that of a sadist about to commit murder.

The booted *Unterscharführer* kicked him between the legs. Sensing death, his victim screamed like a pig, and tried to get up. The second kick hit him again between the legs, with a dull thud. Already the brute had drawn blood and he started smiling, baring his teeth so his lips almost disappeared. He kicked and kicked again. The sound changed suddenly. It turned into a smooth smacking. The boot had conquered resistance and penetrated further. Now the booted foot disappeared completely. The other boot had to retreat to avoid being stained red by the pool of blood. The screaming became a rattle. The rattle became silence. The boot continued.

This was our first day in the PDA. In utter despair, praying desperately, I tried to get some sleep on my board in block III. Could I survive this?

Very early next morning, after a wake-up call of booming blows on a bell, we were told the morning ritual. Washing, dressing, *Betten bauen* (making beds), collecting a mug of 'tea', drilling again, morning roll-call. Our group was drafted into the *Holzfällkommando* (tree-felling work party).

These were the phases a *Häftling* had to endure in order to survive. The mental digestion of suffering was, of course, much easier if you were incarcerated because you had been active in the Resistance - mostly non-Jews - rather than simply because you were a Jew.

THE MORNINGS

Whilst ex-prisoners often suffer today from nightmares of the KZ, at the time I enjoyed invariably blissful dreams. These were consistently and rudely interrupted by the loud clanging of the bell, which signified waking-up time. It was then still pitch dark. Instantly lights were switched on and the *Stubenälteste* rushed through the dormitory with his henchmen, with or without truncheons, shouting at us to get out of our 'beds' and, if necessary, beating us. The upper part of the body bare, you first had to wash, naturally without soap or towel, in an overcrowded washroom full of grumbling, coughing, spitting men. Getting dressed was horrible, especially when you had become soaked at work the previous day. It is extreme misery to wrestle into soaked, smelly uniform trousers and jacket and to wrap sodden muddy leggings round your spindly legs, and then those damned clogs rubbing the sores on your feet. At one stroke you lost all the body warmth of the night.

Among the many mental obsessions of the Germans was their preoccupation with *Betten bauen* (making beds). Straw bag and blankets had to be arranged with extreme precision. Literally accurate to the millimetre. A board or ruler was used for the hundreds of beds to determine whether they were really flat and level. This was checked regularly. The SS, drawn up on one side of the dormitory, looked across all beds, first the ones on the floor then those one up, then two up, to see whether all were flat. If not, hell broke out. The beds were furiously pulled apart, everything had to be done all over again, your number was registered, etc. etc.

After all this you went in darkness to the morning parade in your chilly wet rags, already dog tired, to face a day full of death and damnation.

I had been allowed to keep a tube of toothpaste - not a toothbrush! - and a large bottle of vitamin tablets, both presents from my wife in Scheveningen. In an attack of serious hunger I had sucked up all the toothpaste, delighting in the peppermint taste. And, after that - what shame! - also all vitamin tablets, one after another. This did not have any unusual repercussions. In the course of those three years, completely unacceptable, often dirty or contaminated substances entered my stomach without ever causing trouble. Once I ate 4½ litres (1 gallon) of brown bean soup without a pause. That too did not have any consquences. My stomach appears to be made of steel.

BERG

One of the deputies of commandant SS Obersturmführer Heinrich Stöver was SS Untersturmführer Berg. Rumour had it that Berg had lived in Holland for some time, employed by a timber merchant. Berg was one of the most dangerous SS men. He would look affable, peering at you from a distance, then suddenly he would loom up and turn unpredictably violent: a cold-blooded murderer. After a few days on the tree-felling party I was already an almost broken man, particularly because of those damned wooden clogs which rubbed painfully, causing boils, and every small wound became an abscess within an hour in a KZ. We lugged chunks of tree trunks across a stubble-covered field, two men to a trunk. Progressively slower, often stumbling, limping. I then saw Berg, in the distance, watching, a riding whip in his hand. Although more than a hundred yards away I knew he was observing me. He approached slowly.

'Stop, you!'

We stopped.

'You, tall misfit, what's your trade?'

'Lawyer, Herr Untersturmführer.'

'Ah, a solicitor. You are a solicitor, aren't you? I'll teach you how to work.' My workmate was kicked. 'Away with you.'

He dropped the tree trunk and moved away.

'You carry that on your own. Get going, man, lift it up.'

He hit me viciously with the riding whip. I lifted the trunk. I managed to get it on my shoulder. It did not quite balance. Berg watched as I moved it. The tree, now balanced, swung slowly left, then right, to and fro.

'You shall work, you swine. You're worse than the Russians.'

I tottered away, weighed down by my 60 kilo (132 pound) trunk, my knees buckling, the whip lash glowing, and my clogs filling with blood. I then imagined Jesus, stumbling and falling under His Cross on the way to Golgotha. After dropping my tree at its destination and returning to collect another one, I spotted Berg in the distance harrassing another

victim. I could now pick up a lighter tree. I went on. I had no energy left
for crying.

Schonung (Mercy)

The next day I reported to the surgery, my feet a mass of open wounds.
There was such good business for the 'doctor' that the queue of
Häftlinge stretched far outside the door, many Jews among them.
Although orderly behaviour and absolute silence were essential, many
Jews groaned, mumbled, moaned and even started quarrelling, which
endangered all of us. At any moment a medical *Kapo* could rush out
and kick us all away, the often seriously wounded Jews first. Though
pro-Jewish, I could not hold back my outrage.

'You wretches, I love you and we're doing our best to help you, at home
and here, but you make trouble for all of us. Shut your traps, you idiots!'

That is how it was, nothing could be done about it. In what was
called their Palestina work party they suffered more than we, but it did
not stop many from constantly causing problems, even during roll-call,
by their undisciplined behaviour, quarrelling, moaning. If you said
something about it, they looked surprised, mumbled excuses or curses,
tried to whisper explanations, then fell silent for a while before starting
all over again. It was, of course, the intention of the SS to turn us all into
antisemites. Ultimately they achieved the opposite. Oh, those poor,
dear Jews in the PDA!

At last my turn came to appear before doctor Klomp, a Dutch Nazi
wearing those hated boots. I took off my leggings and 'socks' - which
were stuck to me - and showed him my wounds. The doctor looked at
them.

'What's your name?'

'Bakels.'

'Did you study at Leiden, chemistry?'

'No, doctor, that's my brother. I read law.'

'In that case I've met your brother in Leiden. Put bandages on and
four weeks Schonung,' he called to the male nurses, and inspected the
next patient.

The Theologians Convention

The piece of paper ordering only light work is immensely valuable. It
ensures that during the period mentioned you do not have to attend the
tree-felling party and can stay inside, in the potato-peelers' shed; you
join the potato-peelers' party. Every morning after roll-call some
hundred feverish, wounded and crippled people, a sorry pack of bruised

men, join me in stumbling to the wooden hut to peel potatoes for ten to twelve hours a day. Almost all of them are elderly, and obviously intellectuals. Near the door there is a huge trough for the peeled potatoes which are constantly stirred with a pole and water. At the door watch is kept, in rotation. When a *Kapo* or SS man comes into view the look-out softly calls 'white mice'. The most diverse activities are immediately abandonned and everyone ardently returns to peeling potatoes. The guards see through this device and sometimes approach the shed from the back and unexpectedly fling the door open.

I am seated at the back of the shed among a surprisingly large number of clergymen, six Protestant pastors and one Catholic priest. After my solitary religious struggle in Scheveningen I am deeply grateful for this company. First we tell each other our life's history. One or other also gives an occasional lecture, while our hands turn sour from the potato juices. I myself give a small lecture on the profession of a lawyer while one by one the potatoes plop into the bucket between our miserable bandaged legs. Soon I start asking questions and get replies, sometimes from one of the Protestant pastors, often from the Catholic 'comrade'.

'Did Jesus say that there's one shepherd and one flock?'

'Yes.'

'Did He also say that where two or more are gathered together in His name He is among them?'

'Certainly.'

'May I deduce from this that Jesus meant that all who believe in Him form one community of faith, in fact one church?'

'You could put it like that, yes.'

'There should therefore be one Christian church.' 'Yes.'

My work-mates are speeding up their peeling.

'But some of you are Roman Catholic, some Dutch Reformed, some Calvinists, and other different sects.' 'Whether the serpent actually spoke . . . .'

'And that is not all. I understand that there are also Orthodox Greek Catholics. And Baptists, Methodists, Old Catholics, Seventh Day Adventists. Are there not Latter Day Saints or something like that? And the Jehovah's Witnesses here who get up at once when the bell sounds and start singing a hymn? And what other denominations are there?'

'Yes, there are many more, in Holland, England, America . . . .'

'But Jesus said there should be one Christian church.'

'Yes, true.'

'Then you are all in default.'

Silence. Then: 'We all indeed believe in the same God, there is only one God.'

'Right. And so do millions of Muslims, and Jews.'

'Yes, they all believe in the same God, but the roads to Him are different.'

'You and I believe in God through Christ?'

'Yes, indeed.'

'If there are so many roads that lead to God, is it necessary to add several Christian ways as well?'

'There are all sorts of differences.'

'Important ones?'

'Yes and no. Some are important, yes, such as the differences between Catholics and Protestants.'

'Really? Are they that important?'

'Yes. Catholics have a Pope, worship Holy Mary, have many saints, sacraments, confession, Holy Communion.' 'Does that make a lot of difference when you are in trouble, like us, facing death?'

'It makes a difference, yes, but not much when it comes to the point.'

'But it is to the point, now, and always.'

'Yes, that's true, we now see that.'

'Do you propose to remove these differences when you're released?'

'We have certainly learnt a lot here in the PDA. But there are many churches, many organizations, boards, legal structures, institutions, customs, traditions, agreements, peoples, countries . . . . It can't be done just like that.'

'I appreciate that, but it's wrong and has to be changed.'

The next day, a bit more hungry and more of a wreck, we continue. My theologians are a little less sympathetic.

'Here we go. As you know I had a "vision" when arrested. If I'm released and if I then want to join a church, which one would you recommend? Shall I opt for the Catholic Church? It's big, old, international, has beautiful churches full of images, candles and flowers. All rather attractive to me.'

'Your family is not Catholic.'

'If they're anything at all, they're Mennonites.'

'Then join the Mennonites.'

'Why?'

'Because you come from a Mennonite environment.'

'Why not something else, with or without the epithet Christian?'

'You're mocking us.'

'Not at all. You're fine chaps, really, and well versed in many things.

You're theologians. I've only got God, and Christ. But I have still more objections, if you want to know.'

Another day passes. Peeling is now fully automatic. There is a lot of coughing because of the dust from the potato bags. In addition to being sour, our hands begin to crack.

'You had more complaints. Like what?'

'Your behaviour here is not always impeccable. Shouldn't clergymen set an example? Some of you complain too much. Sometimes you're selfish, try to organize food, even dishonest . . . .'

'Yes, that's true. We're only human.'

'You preach the Gospel *ex officio*. Here too, but not enough.'

'You're right to mention it. We too are afraid.'

'Servants of God's Word, afraid?'

'Yes, afraid. And we too are rotting away from hunger.'

'Give us this day our daily bread. Do you get your daily bread?'

'Yes, too little as you know.'

'Enough.'

'No, not enough. We're all rotting away from . . . .'

'Yes, I know. But you get enough, that is if you have faith.'

Silence.

'Are you on familiar terms with God?'

'How do you mean?'

'You always speak so patronisingly. As if you talk to God regularly and know precisely what He wants, regrets, welcomes. How can you be so sure? And all that singing . . . .'

'What singing?'

'In your Protestant church they sing abominably. Wailing. Without any joy. The hymns often have maddeningly silly words. And then there are these wooden men with velvetty bags for marbles to hide your few coins in. And at the front are special seats for important people, sometimes with a name tag. I thought everyone was of equal importance to God. And Christ was particularly interested in publicans, i.e. Nazis, and sinners. He washed his disciples' feet . . . . And then the Pope!'

'What about the Pope?'

'The Pope, rigid with power, money and robes, on his throne in Rome, has the nerve to pretend to be God's vicar on earth.'

'Did you never hear about Peter, the first Pope, and his mandate?'

'Certainly, but I haven't read anywhere that Peter and his successors should sit rigidly with robes on a throne, that their pronouncements *ex cathedra* were infallible, that people should kneel in front of them. If I were Pope . . . .'

They laugh, at last. 'Well, if you were Pope, what then?'

'I should step down from my throne, put on ordinary clothes, put huge amounts of money into my pocket, take leave of everybody and perhaps travel to Holland to buy Jews their freedom. Or, if freeing them was impossible, to wash their feet and go along with them some of the distance, who knows how far .... Or sit in the cells with those under sentence of death.'

'The Pope has a totally different task,' says my Catholic brother. 'He is head of a world church.'

'Not so. Jesus Christ is head of a world church. Yours and mine. And with regard to the Pope: whosoever exalts himself shall be abased. Or am I now wrong?'

'No, that is in the scriptures. And the reverse.'

'In that case haughty, arrogant clerics who seem to be at home with God will be abased. For instance, here in Amersfoort. But which one of you will give us a good sermon for a change?'

One of them often did. And he did more. During the week in the evening and particularly on Sundays he was busily running Bible courses in all the barracks. He also had a Bible. He talked a lot with those under sentence of death. His whole being radiated invincible strength. When he prayed with you that strength enveloped you. He had been arrested for helping Jews, but survived the war and remained a tower of strength until he died recently.

The theologians' convention and I did not lose heart and continued the next day. I risked another remark: 'You're not only preachers and spiritual advisers but also theologians.'

This was confirmed.

'Did you ever wonder whether you haven't stifled the Christian faith for twenty centuries with theology? I seem to remember Christ saying that matters of faith remain hidden for philosophers but are revealed to children. But what are you doing? For 2,000 years you have written rows of books in all languages, miles long, libraries full, to explain the Bible, apocryphal and non-apocryphal treatises, church history, theses, doctrines, dogmas and documents of that sort. I believe that you've buried faith under words, as wall paintings in historical buildings are often hidden by many layers of dirty paint. Is that possible?'

The convention nodded, yes. I thought at that moment that essentially we all agreed after all. Still, now and again, throughout the peeling sessions, a remark or bombastic formula would roll off their lips, which astonished me. I thought to myself, secretly: 'My God, they don't understand You.'

WRITING

My emotions needed an outlet. I organized - one learned that art soon enough - some pieces of paper and a pencil stub and started writing. I wrote whatever moved me, haphazardly, as a letter to my wife. That letter eventually reached 3,000 small scraps of paper. The first quotation from my 'diary' reads as follows.

Here we truly have it under the influence of hunger. Exalted or humble, old or young, cleric or not, all become more or less equal, it unifies. Hunger is fear. What moves the world, what causes quarrels and fights and wars, is greed: I want to eat, eat more, eat a lot, I want this and that and the other too, I want to amass, to possess, to hoard. Instead of: I want to give, help, bring one more, to people instead of pull in like the croupier with his rake. Greed. Gluttony. And what else is greed but fear? One wants to have certainty, enough, even more than enough, more and more and preferably everything for fear of being left short. And why this fear? Because one does not appreciate that God is with us, loves us and takes care of us. God takes away all fear. Without fear there is no distrust and greed; once these have gone there will not be any more quarrelling and war. Incidentally: the sexual function has completely disappeared here. One of the most important forces that influence people's actions is here simply eliminated. Does this obscure my judgement about everything, or perhaps sharpen it? Is the disappearance of sexual passion caused by lack of food or by feeling distressed in prison? I do not know. I do know that its absence is a blessing. Only when you see some women in the new barracks built next door a recollection surfaces; it reminds you of another life, of something ardent yet tender, qualities that are totally lacking here.

Deprived of hairs on your head, of normal clothes, watches, rings and such like, uniformly clothed, the face of a *Häftling* told you everything, all the rest was the same. One day I spied an ecstatic face among the prisoners in a new intake. Soon after I saw it again in the potato-peelers' shed. I made the acquaintance of Dr H.B. Wiardi Beckman. He was deeply moved. When I asked him why, he told me about his elation at seeing people again after months of solitary cell-confinement, fellow human beings, and the beauty of nature and of the clouded sky. He did not talk about his 'crime'. For all of us this was a sensible custom. You never knew who was listening and why. You could only vaguely allude to what you were suspected of having done. Stuuf Wiardi Beckman had been caught on the beach at Scheveningen in temperatures of -12°C during the night of 17/18 January 1942, waiting for an English MGB to take him to London in order to join the Dutch Cabinet in exile as a future prime minister. He died on 15 March 1945 in Dachau of typhus. He had volunteered to help out in the typhus barrack against our advice. It was felt he was too important to the future of our country to endanger his life still further, and too vulnerable, but he felt it his Christian duty to help fellow human beings where it was most needed, and immediately.

I also bumped into our young client and one of his friends and they introduced me to other members of the Lion Guard. These contacts remained brief. As mentioned earlier I did not know of the existence of the Lion Guard and there seemed no reason in Amersfoort to assemble such a group. We had no connection with each other in the past. Being a lawyer they nevertheless approached me occasionally for legal advice on their case. Of course I could not give any sensible answers, but I began asking what they had actually done, a question that they wisely chose not to answer directly. Their answers were extremely vague, but it appeared that no one had actually done anything of any importance. I got the strong impression that they had been arrested for almost nothing. One of them claimed the SD had arrested him because he carried a picture postcard with an aerial photograph of Rotterdam airport in his pocket. Whether true or not, it certainly cost him dearly.

THE TWO BROTHERS

Amersfoort held two brothers who were not popular and generally avoided. They were nasty fellows, selfish, cantankerous, never willing to help, supremely negative. It seemed that they had only themselves, no one else.

One night I was lying awake in the utmost discomfort: tired, afraid, cold, wounded, without hope. Prayer did not help, God seemed to have decamped elsewhere. The dormitory was very dimly lit with a night light. In the distance I noticed a ghost on the move, a man had climbed down from his wooden bed, presumably to proceed to the lavatory. Throughout the night groaning, defacating, coughing, retching and furtive smoking went on continuously in the *Abort* (lavatory). The figure walked silently and carefully nearer. He wore rather too decent white underclothes, a vest with long sleeves, long pants. He sighed. He mumbled. He was utterly pitiable. A poor, helpless creature in white underwear. It was one of the brothers.

At that moment I experienced a miracle, the miracle of absolute neighbourly love. I passionately loved the hated brothers. And all the others in the barracks. Everyone in Amersfoort, in Holland, in the world. Even my enemies, the enemy. All my fellow human beings, all those whom God created, poor, desperate, whining and particularly wicked people, I loved them fiercely. So completely lost. So helpless and abandoned. So terribly far from any bliss. So lonely, in their white underwear. Never before or since did I feel the truth of the second commandment stronger and more purifyingly than that night. I offered it to God, Who had apparently returned from his journey elsewhere.

A GOOD SS MAN

After a time, I gradually built up good relations, especially with those working in the barrack where our own clothes were kept, and I succeeded in persuading a fellow inmate who worked there to rescue the photograph of my wife from one of my inside pockets. He did and handed me the photograph, which moved me intensely. After some time you cannot recall the faces of your loved ones exactly, and now, suddenly, there she was . . . . Occasionally I showed her portrait to one or other of my friends, surreptitiously, for the possession of photographs was, of course, prohibited.

One Sunday morning I was standing behind a barrack in the sun chatting to a friend about home and showed him the photograph. It was not he but someone else who reacted.

'What've you got there?' in German. 'Let's have a look.'

Rigid with fear, I stared into a face shaded by one of those high-peaked Nazi caps. The face had a not unfriendly look, which always meant you should be on your guard. Jumping to attention, I passed the portrait of my dearest to him . . . .

'Is that your wife?'

'Indeed, sergeant, sir.'

'Pretty woman. Well, haven't seen anything.' He returned the photograph and strolled away. It was Engbrocks, the good SS man.

THE LITTLE BIBLE

I had managed to smuggle the pocket Bible my wife had given me in Scheveningen into the PDA. It proved of incalculable value to many of us. The few Bibles in the PDA were in constant demand by people who could not live by bread alone and yearned for invigorating texts. The SS not only objected to the Bible but to all religious ceremonies. The walls in all barracks carried strongly worded bans to that effect, along with many other bans and orders. Once a guard told me bluntly that the Bible strengthened prisoners' will to resist.

One day there was another warning of a Bible raid, this time with the additional threat that offenders would be sent to a penal camp. Until then I had trusted that He whose word I so badly wanted to read would take care that this could be done with impunity. This time I weakened, impressed by the ominous penalty. I didn't want to lose my Bible either.

I found a compromise. I let my Bible slide under my shirt along my bare back until it struck the wire around my waist which I used to hold up my trousers. That same day during the evening roll-call we were all searched one by one. And so was I. Because no one thought of touching me around the kidneys they didn't find my Bible. I was as pleased as Punch. I had clearly taken the right course.

That night before 'closing time' I visited the lavatory as usual to relieve myself. I undid the wire, dropped my trousers and sat down. Once seated I felt something slide down my back .... Oh God! I jumped up but it was too late. With a light thud my little Bible dropped into the dung. As almost everyone in a KZ suffers from diarrhoea the book disappeared immediately from sight. I went down on my knees, rolled up a sleeve and started to search in the mass of faeces. In vain. I had lost my Bible. That was the reward for my fear and lack of trust.

THE ALDERMAN

During one evening roll-call, arranged in exemplary fashion according to the strict instructions, it struck me that the man in front of me did not stand absolutely still but swayed to and fro, an inch to the right, an inch to the left. I hissed to his neck: 'Stand still, man, don't attract attention,' - but he did not react. Then came the command, 'Caps off!' The man in front took off his cap, as we did, but slowly. I then noticed at the back of his head a considerable fissure, some 3 inches wide, full of clotted blood, some of it still dripping down into his neck. While the SS were rushing up and down our line counting us I had plenty of time to study the fissure. The edges showed up whitish. It was clear that he had been hit not with the shaft but with the blade of a spade.

The man complied with all subsequent commands but more and more slowly, and when we were dismissed, he remained wobbling for a while before falling down.

When I had almost reached my barracks and could risk turning round, I saw two fellow-prisoners were kicking and beating him with clubs. After our evening ration of bread had been distributed I took a walk and saw him again, lying against a barrack wall, his breathing a soft rattling. A strapping fellow stood next to him, hands on hips. 'That's how I like to see you,' he said. Two men arrived with a wheelbarrow.

They flung him in and carried him off.

This was the well-known Jewish alderman of Amsterdam, De Miranda.

THE AGONY OF CONSCIENCE

All inmates of the PDA are assembled to witness, in petrified awe, a prisoner being finished off with clubs for an escape attempt. As collective punishment the roll-call is continued until it becomes unbearable. When at last the guard screams, 'Return to barracks, quick, quick!' and we stumble into our barracks, on our infernal clogs, deadbeat, filthy, famished and disgusted with ourselves, I come across a friend who looks unusually depressed. He is a Protestant clergyman but had kept himself aloof from the potato-peelers' shed, and was therefore not one of the theologians' convention.

He looks exceptionally miserable. At last he is able to talk. 'I should have done something. We all looked passively on while a fellow human being was murdered. Myself included. Yes, I've prayed for him, but I should have stepped out to protest, in God's name.'

Several others, chewing breadcrumbs, have joined us. 'You're mad, man. If you had opened your mouth, vicar, they would have beaten you to death at once and another twenty-four of us as well. Keep your trap shut, vicar, don't be conspicuous, you damn fool.'

He stares at us, a face with clear blue eyes and a strong chin; a noble man, dismally sad.

'Who's to say that? Who's to say they would have done anything to me, to us, if I had done my duty and protested, supported by the invincible power of Christ? Perhaps they would have sneaked away, these Germans.'

'Come on, man, don't talk drivel. You've been here long enough, haven't you, vicar; these swine don't stop at anything, not even for your God. Leave it alone. You'd implicate a lot of others too, vicar. Keep quiet.'

He does not give up. 'That's human reasoning, but has anyone ever tried it here?' He starts crying. 'But I ... I've been too much of a coward.'

Some time later the two of us try to solve this riddle, entirely in vain. The vicar then says, 'Perhaps . . . the boys were right. Perhaps they would have murdered me and a few others as well. So what? Is that a reason for abandoning your duty? History is full of people who sacrificed their lives with open eyes in obedience to their conscience. But I, a servant of God's word . . . .'

Oh, that bundle of misery, that poor, poor vicar! After this he says, dreamily, 'Who knows whether we don't attach too much value to human life on earth, Floris. Tell me, is it really quite so bad when I give my life and that of others? Do you think that God cares that much for human lives? There's a war on, human lives are taken by the hundreds of thousands, on both sides. Maybe we value it too much? Perhaps .. . are you still listening?'

I am listening, but a horrible thought strikes me which the vicar himself expresses, very softly.

'Perhaps it isn't so bad after all, the loss of these lives. We are so very attached to life, but read the Bible. Don't you find there how little value our lives have? Perhaps there are divine plans more important than millions of human lives. . . .'

We then started to eat our bread. A few weeks later my friend was released. Once again he mounted the pulpit to preach the Gospel of Christ. He was better informed too. He was then, and after his release remained, President of the Dutch Reformed Church, the main Protestant church in Holland, to which our Royal Family also belong.

MORE THAN OTHERS

Häftlinge who were seriously weakened and emaciated could - with influential protection or by other means - get so-called extra food rations which in the PDA consisted of one slice of bread, one slice of sausage and a mug of skimmed milk. Those qualifying had to collect this after evening roll-call at the *Schreibstube* which had a separate counter for that purpose. Exceptionally tall people, like me, usually qualified. I was supremely grateful. When the hundreds of often soaking wet and mud-stained prisoners entered the barracks after the roll-call for the normal evening bread distribution on noisily clattering clogs, you could see some walking twigs shuffling across the parade ground to the *Schreibstube*, empty mug in hand, to collect their possibly life-saving treasure, and then returning some time later, step by step to avoid losing one drop of skimmed milk.

When you returned to the barrack, where most had already finished their meagre ration, you had to run the gauntlet. Everywhere on and between the beds and at the long tables piercing eyes focused on you.

'Well, Floris my boy, got your extra rations again?'
'Lucky chap. I'm still bloody hungry.'
'Hello, Floris, can I come and see you in a minute?'
'Did you get your normal ration as well?'
'Enjoy your special treatment.'

Hardly anybody could keep silent. Envy showed clearly on the faces of all my poor barrack-mates. As I shuffled to my place the bald skulls on spindly necks turned to follow me. Murmuring continued behind me.

Yes, that is how it was. You witnessed in the KZ what happens in a community as soon as inequality of property appears, plainly and without frills. As long as everyone has the same and gets the same, without privileges, the atmosphere is reasonably friendly. You are all in the same boat, you must try to survive together. Comradeship predominates, due also to having a mutual enemy. But as soon as one gets more than others - extra rations, a scoop, a parcel from home, etc - the poison seeps in: jealousy, theft, corruption, barter, intrigues, even fisticufs among outcasts. Not covered up, not clever or cunning, disguised or elegant, but entirely open, brutal, crude, primitive. The SS realised this and made use of it to increase the misery by sowing discord.

I recognised that our experience in the KZ was the same as in society outside, where it happens in a more concealed way, blurred, cunningly. Probably no one really objects to living soberly, modestly, simply and healthily, supplied only with the essentials. But when a new neighbour arrives with special riches, something extravagantly new, our eyes pop, the mouth pouts, the pulse starts racing: he has, I have not, I too must have.

We are all like that. Myself included. In the KZ I have known murderous envy. It reminded me of the last of my father's theses for his doctorate in political science, in 1899: 'The public display of excessive luxury should be made punishable by law.' Perhaps excessive luxury should itself be made punishable by law. . . .

ICH BIN WIEDER DA (I'M HERE AGAIN)

One evening during roll-call there was an atmosphere of growing confusion. Again and again SS men roared past the troops, each time touching the front men with a gloved hand: fifteen, twenty, twenty-five, etc. We just stood there, caps off, at attention. At the front of the troops endless deliberation appeared to be taking place, more and more nervously. Most SS men disappeared, some at the double. We remained standing. Murmuring started somewhere and news was whispered along the lines: someone is missing. An hour passed. Two hours passed. More hours. The strict lines became disordered, more murmuring. Bread awaited us in the barrack. It got later, dark, cold. We stood there numbly. I cannot deny it: all of us were hoping that the fugitive would be caught soon.

55

The faces therefore brightened up when far away the howling and wailing of the dogs was suddenly accompanied by human cries. The howling and wailing, and with them the crying, came nearer, changing direction with the curve of the outer fence. They were approaching. They had got him. He was brought inside and presented triumphantly to the troops. He stood utterly alone among those who were going to murder him. Round his neck he carried a noticeboard: 'Ich bin wieder da' (I'm here again).

[I personally know of only one successful escape from a KZ. In November 1944 only 140 men were still lodged in the PDA. Thousands upon thousands of *Häftlinge* had been removed to German KZs, the Jews to Polish extermination camps. It was expected that these remaining 140, all of them skeletons, would be *Umgelegt* (bumped off) whenever it pleased the Nazis. One of my friends, like me a member of our University Club, who had succeeded in obtaining a job in the kitchen, had no intention of ending his political imprisonment with a bullet in his back. The kitchen happened to have one exit outside the inner fence. One pitch dark evening in rain and storm he went outside with trays of food for the dogs. After arriving at the SS barracks, shuffling on his clogs, he deliberately made a lot of noise to attract the attention of the SS, intending if someone appeared, to explain his presence there with the dog- trays. However, not one soul appeared. He put the trays down and started to negotiate the first obstacle, a barbed wire fence; then a deep ditch; another barbed wire fence and another. He did not have pliers, it was a matter of struggling. As a result he lost almost all of his scanty KZ clothing. An hour and a half later he found himself outside all the fences and went on his way. He lost his bearings. After a while he saw . . . the entrance gates to the PDA; a ghastly mistake.

He returned to the wood, roamed about, spotted a villa, got hold of a strong branch to protect himself from any possible hostile reception in the villa and rang the bell, almost naked, soaked, covered in scratches, bald, emaciated and in the middle of the night. A woman with a lighted candle opened the door. She came, she saw, she understood. In a few hours he was delivered to a safe place.

After the war I asked my friend what had given him the courage to leave, in the full knowledge of the consequences a failed escape attempt from a KZ entailed. He answered that fear did not come into it - and so courage did not come into it. He felt the Germans to be so bad, so stupid and so ridiculous that he could not possibly fear them.

On another occasion one of the vilest SS men approached two

prisoners, my friend was one of them. The other was ordered to stand with legs wide apart. He did so. He was immediately struck down with a crashing kick between his legs. My friend received the same order. He refused, looking the murderer straight in the face with steely eyes, his contempt erupting into laughter. The SS man, for whatever reason, turned round and walked away.]

INTO THE BUNKER

One day it became known to the *Häftlinge* that a German train had been derailed by sabotage some forty miles away. The PDA itself was hermetically sealed off, the working parties were not allowed outside. The numbers of fifteen prisoners were called out. They stepped out of the ranks, were taken away, re-appeared shortly after in their own clothes, and were stood aside. Soon enough we knew: they all lived near the site of the sabotage. They did not have to tell us more.

That morning, afternoon and evening the atmosphere in the camp was electric. A terrible tension gripped the entire population, the SS included. It was the first time I smelled the danger of imminent death.

At evening roll-call all fifteen had disappeared.

We were lying on our bunks later that night when suddenly the lights were switched on. German voices, boots, the *Blockälteste*. Equally suddenly my name is called. 'Here,' I cry out. The *Blockälteste* approaches, followed by SS men.

'Get dressed at once.'

Frantically I try to get myself into the still wet, muddy Dutch army uniform, the leggings, the clogs.

'Come along, you, *Häftling*.'

From the bunks hundreds of eyes follow me as I walk past flanked by guards. Outside there are more SS men, with torches.

'Quick, man, get going.'

At a jog I am escorted across the parade ground, past the delightful flower garden, through the gate, to the SS office. My personal details are read out. Name, forenames, date of birth, place of birth, reason for imprisonment, profession. They take me to a concrete building, the bunker. Inside the bunker to a cell, quite small in the light of the torches. No bunks, only horse blankets. An iron door. I pass through it. Shut and locked. Pitch dark. God, don't abandon me.

I hear a voice:

'Looks pretty bad for us,' a shrill high voice.

Another one: 'New one, who are you?'

I reply. There are more voices: a clergyman, a priest, a public notary.

And a lawyer. In complete darkness a conversation it is hard to describe. Our fear of death incarnate. And whining: 'Our last night. We'll have to be strong.' Occasional prayers. I search for an explanation. I refuse to believe this. I use slang in order to crack the rarified web of menacing madness. 'You're crazy, vicar . . .' When I wake up on the concrete floor a tiny square high up in the cell is vaguely grey: daylight. In the distance we can hear the morning roll-call. We faintly hear the marching troops: 'Left, two three four.' For ages we do not hear anything else but birds. German shouting in the far distance, dogs barking and our own voices.

Towards evening: pounding boots, tinkling of keys and saucepans, shouting in German, unintelligible. Do we get food? Now a woman's voice as well. Murmuring, tinkling, doors creaking. And then all is quiet. The little square darkens, everything turns black. Evening becomes night. The second one. No food. No drinks. No *Abort* (lavatory). Hardly any talk between cells. The Catholic priest mutters prayers, I join him.

Another day. The bell, the commands, the dogs, the shouting, the summer birds. Towards evening tinkling again, pounding, croaking, swearing. The female voice. And again: silence.

Unexpectedly, when the little square has already become invisible, a key in my door. The door is opened. A torch, a female voice.

'There, eat. Quick. He's plastered in his room, I pinched the keys.'

I eat, stuffing the food into my mouth. Cold swede, as always. Ambrosia.

'Look,' she says, shining the torch on herself. I see a dark face, black hair, black eyes, lovely.

'I'm Jewish,' she says, 'I've been here for months. Quick, finish it. You've got to be locked in again.' She does lock me in. I am truly blessed. The third night follows, and the morning. It must be Saturday. Saturday? Suddenly I understand: we shall be released. Idiot that I am! Releases always occur on a Saturday. We are not such grave offenders. They wanted to keep us away, isolate us. We will be leaving.

'Boys, we're going to be released!' I yell. The others start yelling too. Talk, prayer, laughter, crying. That will be the bell for noon roll-call. Keys, rattling, footsteps, doors open, SS men.

'Out, but quick! Come on, man!'

We run outside, into divine sunlight. We are escorted. Past the garden. To the parade ground. To our places in the lines.

'*Häftlinge* - stand still. Caps off. Eyes left.'

Roll-call. Afterwards many friends rush to me.

'Thank God! Thank God! You're alive! What happened?' Some of them cry, I feel arms round my shoulder, they accompany me . . . . 'The fifteen have been shot dead, we thought that you too. . . .'
Then something rends my brains and the flood rises again along the canals once dug in Scheveningen, and I have to shout loudly: 'Thank God I'm alive. Oh God, I'm not going to be released.'

It was not until seven years later that I discovered what had happened. In 1949 in the presence of the Dutch prosecutor I came face to face with the SS man Berg, one of the most vicious brutes in the PDA. He had by then already been sentenced to death. I asked him why we had been shut up in that bunker for three days in September 1942. He replied that Berlin had given orders to treat the fifteen hostages correctly and give them spiritual and legal support. For that reason, though with no explanation, several clergymen and a lawyer had been isolated in the bunker to give succour when needed. Later on that sort of assistance had to come from outside the camp, as they forgot about the specialist *Häftlinge*. The fifteen hostages were executed in September 1942, their executioner in November 1949.

HUNGER

The three great powers at work in the KZ were fear, cold and hunger. As a phenomenon, hunger is so serious, so dominating, that I want to discuss it separately. Hunger, real starvation, disrupts body and mind. There are several stages. Everyone has at times felt hungry. When it persists you start yawning, you feel faint and hollow in the stomach. Next your legs begin to tremble. In a further advanced stage, obsession creeps in, you visualize food and meals, often accompanied by the secretion of saliva. The mind is then exceptionally clear, a process of mortification and spiritualization has set in. On the other hand, concentration diminishes.

The arrival of real famine is accompanied by various physical symptoms. Dizziness, trembling knees, general weakness. Water collects in the feet and under the eyes, then in the legs and elsewhere (oedema). The stomach seems like a loose organ in the belly, you feel it floating. Occasionally it feels like a cloth being wrung out and that can be painful.

Sustained starvation causes terrible emaciation, of course, especially visible in the upper arms, neck, thighs and buttocks. The knee becomes a fat lump of bone between upper and lower twigs. Hallucination sets in, you dream of food mountains and of gluttony, in daytime and particularly at night. Concentrating is impossible, you cannot collect your thoughts, discussions are suddenly suspended. When you sustain a cut, it will fester within an hour, and it will not heal or only barely. A combination of factors - dependent too on the sort of food you still get - causes chronic diarrhoea; many times a day you suddenly feel the need to rush to the lavatory and your faeces resemble dirty-yellow or light brown water streams. You feel as if life itself is draining away.

The body has gradually become skin and bone: a pallid, flabby, flaky skin draped round the bones like a sack. You are always cold, all internal organs now feel loose in your body: heart, lungs, kidneys, liver ... and cold surrounds them. Getting up calls for a great effort, walking even more; you feel faint, your appetite declines and can even fade completely. At that point you have already gone a long way towards death. You have become what was called a *Muselmann*, barely more than a mobile skeleton held together by a few tendons and ligaments and a bag of skin.

One of us from the tree-felling party in the PDA once spotted a batch of chickens, lost on the edge of the wood. He stalked them and grabbed one. He wrenched its head off, put his mouth at the neck and sucked the chick dry. On another occasion he ate one raw.

A prominent legal scholar on Sunday afternoons used to sit on his bunk in the PDA, third storey up. There he wrote recipes. Whoever passed by was hailed:

'Hello, you, d'you have some nice recipes for me? I've now reached cheese recipes. D'you know of any tasty cheese recipes?'

He was completely serious.

One day another prisoner was called away from the potato-peelers' shed. Fifteen minutes later he returned, desperately upset. We enquired. Sobbing, he replied: 'I'm being released today, will be free this afternoon, but I'll lose my extra ration.'

JAKE

My friend Jake, 22, was only allowed restricted movement in the PDA like many others with a red ball: a piece of red fabric sewn on the back of his uniform. This indicated there was a high risk of an escape attempt in his case as he had been condemned to death. He was not allowed outside the inner courtyard.

Jake, a Calvinist boy from The Hague, gentle, quick to laugh, impressed us all as a well-balanced person. Nothing seemed to hurt him. He mixed with the clergymen but also with me. He told me about his happy childhood, sheltered by a warm family. When I had come to know him well I asked how he could behave so calmly, even cheerfully in the face of almost certain death.

He replied: 'Presently I'll receive death from Him Who made me, has always accompanied me, is now also with me and will always be with me.'

And, after a pause: 'Nothing can happen to me without Him, who gave me so much happiness, knowing it.'

A day later I talked to a group of mortally frightened newcomers. They cursed heaven and earth, and seemed to be entirely lost to God. I went to get Jake and returned with him. Jake testified ardently to God's love, omnipotence and presence.

Jake was executed on 26 October 1942.

SKIES

Notwithstanding all their efforts the Germans could not deprive us of everything in the camps: They could not take away faith, friendship, love, nor memories, or hope.

Nor could they take away the skies.

To me it seemed a gross mistake on their part to take roll-calls around sunrise and sunset. Did they not realize that the glorious spectacle of the heavens in the light of dawn and in the approaching dusk offered much comfort to all those thousands of outcasts, standing like statues? The astonishing contrast between the marvels above and the filth below should have alerted even the most insensitive idiot. As long as such glittering scenes of clouded skies in many colours could be watched, we *Häftlinge* could not be lost altogether. Like trained marionettes we performed the ridiculous motions ordered by screaming guards - *stillgestanden*, etc - but our thoughts wandered through these far-away worlds of clouds, past the golden towers and silver milled edges which God conjured up at the start of an exhausting day, or a mercifully granted night. I quote from my diary:

Sunset

Last night's sky - Sunday evening 30 August 1942 - between 7 and 9 pm, after a warm, humid day with fantastic skies and a warm shower of rain: In the west the sun, going down, sinking, first white fire, then less white, yellowish, pink, red and again yellow , washy, just above the lead-blue, then dark leaden banks full of ominous light-grey masses, like cotton wool, coils. Those banks have watery golden edges, pure tinsel, sun-gold; suddenly one races along, threatening but far away, a golden chariot with twelve prancing stallions: Donar, the god of thunder. Electrical blue-white flickering light, with intervals, in the thick leaden banks. In the south thinner banks, silvery grey, tatters; in between those tatters, ethereal, infinitely far away, a vista of summery snow mountains, pink as a mountain chain in the Alps, very, very high: small clouds perhaps - yes, indeed small clouds! In the north, reddish, against sea green, no, pastel blue, no, sea-greenish-blue; mother of pearl: reddish towers of thick, distant cumuli with blue grottoes full of evil, full of power and passion, towering in solitude, northerly, like the North Pole; and alongside: the naked sky turning into evening: sea-green lakes, watery turquoise, in places delicate cotton wool ladders, rows of thin fleecy clouds and feathers, wind feathers - but those copper-red colossi, those heavenly castles.... In the east, yes, in the east the main events: misfortune, deprivation; where the low, grey rain-veils chase wind rags across the countryside, where tattered rain curtains are hanging, where it is disconsolate and terribly grey and gloomy, so gloomy.... Ouch! it rends, splits, hurrying along - and what follows behind is painful, it dazzles, it takes the breath away and over-whelms: over there, in the evening east, into the highest of heavens almost directly above me, towers the alto-cumulus, snow-white mountain range, an edifice with battlements, terraces, blue caves and silver pinnacles, violet caverns, golden depths: higher and higher, thinner and thinner, more ethereal, more heavenly. . . .

One day I was unfortunate - or fortunate - enough to be taken away from the potato-peelers' shed for *leichte Lagerarbeit* (light work in the camp). The reader can have no idea of the fear this generated when I believed myself to be safely stowed away amongst clergymen. Nothing was safe in a KZ. The job turned out to be the passing of a pile of bricks (four at a time) down a row of *Häftlinge* from a large pile to a new barrack under construction. The man in front of me, who would hand me a pile for hours on end which I would pass on to a third man, had an exceptionally friendly, even affectionate face. Soon I felt I wanted to address a few comforting words to him. There was an instant rapport. He turned out to be a Protestant clergyman. Rarely have I felt so strongly the great warmth, instinctive among the community of the faithful. I refer to an immediate feeling of close affinity between co-religionists. In a KZ this was unmistakable. The bond that faith produces, even between complete strangers, regardless of nationality, was stronger than the bond with non-believing fellow sufferers whom you had known for months.

ACCLIMATIZATION

In October, having climbed to the high function of assistant clerk in the *Schreibstube*, I became alarmed that I was getting accustomed to the status quo, something one should never accept, a sensation vaguely felt earlier. After a few months, many prisoners - myself among them - began to get accustomed to the occupier, his behaviour, his campaign of lies. Goebbels had proclaimed that in the end a lie, if repeated often enough, will be believed. For us too it became progressively more difficult not to get accustomed to the poison of daily life. That included Amersfoort. My diary for October reads - the reader will remember it was written as a letter to my wife:

> It is awful but I find it continually harder in my thoughts to be with you, in a physical sense. It is so completely unreal: outside. I have adapted so fearfully, I must try hard mentally to take myself home
> . . . .

For instance I started drawing. I made an accurate drawing of our home in Pijnacker. I made plans of the rooms and drew all the furniture. I indicated what hung on the walls and where. I drew plans of town districts. I drew a map of Holland, of our sailing boat, of our houseboat, of a villa where we went for our summer holidays. These were threads with which I attempted to bind myself to the normal world. A little later I started making illustrated alphabets: objects, concepts, places, people, beginning with A, with B, then C etc., all from the 'past'. They were mental gymnastics. Another quotation:

> In here simple people usually know how to behave, aristocrats often disappoint: they are not accustomed to want and humiliation; contentment, simplicity and truth are unknown to many of them. They are accustomed to being spoilt, to greed, good manners, complexities, convention, antiquated slogans and false views. We must never forget this, never.

FAITH AND CHURCH

In this realm of hell, the PDA, there were many debates about faith. During these discussions 'Christian faith' was repeatedly equated with 'Christian churches and clergymen'; also, it was assumed that whosoever is not for is usually strongly against. Emotions soared. Some with whom I talked about faith immediately pulled a face, even showed a dislike in advance.

'Don't talk to me about Christians, church, pastors and priests; all hypocrisy: countless crimes have been and are being committed in the name of Christianity', etc. etc.

First of all, the fault of this widely held view lies in confusing faith with church. To this should be added something else. It is supposed that those who say they believe, and particularly the servants of the faith, the vicars, must be supermen who do not do any harm, never sin, and generally lead saintly lives. When a clergyman acts badly, or at least fails, it is very easy to point at him with a sneer: 'And he calls himself a man of God!' The same applies to anyone who openly confesses to Christianity: 'Look what he's doing, listen to him. So that is a Christian!' It is thought unacceptable that Christians sin. It is assumed that anyone who calls himself a Christian is an exalted being, who never yields to temptation, renounces the flesh, loves all neighbours unceasingly and does good without fail.

I wonder how this misapprehension could have occurred. Usually the opposite is true. A Christian is deeply aware of his own imperfections, his depravity; he only hopes to be saved from his lamentable state by Jesus. Simplified: a Christian is all too often perceived to be pretentious, haughty, and a perfect human being, whereas the Christian himself knows the reverse to be true. Examples are often given of people, usually clergymen, but also statesmen and other important people, who committed villainies in the name of the Cross. One forgets that these people are considered to be Christians only by themselves, not by others.

Other opponents are irritated by humiliation, especially self-humiliation. It maddens them. Why kneel, why incriminate oneself, why be defenceless, why abase oneself? What is left of human dignity? What about proper self-respect? Is no one allowed to be proud of, or at least satisfied with, an achievement? I find this a more difficult problem.

Anyone is entitled to be annoyed by the moaning, the almost inhuman self-denigration, the masochism of some believers. I cannot solve this problem unless one accepts several levels of assessment: a worldly, social level and a super-worldly level aimed at eternity. Perhaps we do not have to denigrate ourselves socially. Perhaps, in ordinary life, some commandments and prohibitions of Christ simply cannot be implemented, as for instance in a time of war. Perhaps on occasion we are allowed to be proud. Perhaps at times we can judge our fellow men; there have to be legal judges after all. Perhaps once in a while we may return a slap. Perhaps? Is this fair?

It is tragic yet true. If the directors of companies, politicians, civil servants, judges were to behave exactly as the Bible requires society would be disrupted. But perhaps this is in fact the intention.

FAREWELL

On 13 November at roll-call, many numbers are called out, including mine. 'Prepare for transport. Prepare for trial. Come on, bastards, *los, los* (get going), get your things.' The numbers are those of the men of the Lion Guard. I've come to know some of them but there are still many unknown to me. Each time I am surprised anew that I should belong to their organization.

The metamorphosis in the changing room is unbelievable. Suddenly we can be distinguished one from the other. Boys in overalls, a man dressed as a vicar with a dog collar, some with leggings, some in decent suits, me in my smart coat and black hat. Of course the clothes do not fit any more and hang loosely, sloppily round our bony bodies, while from our collars rise thin necks like plucked chickens. Suddenly, because of the clothes, there is class distinction. Whether you want it or not.

Heavily escorted we march to closed lorries, after giving all our camp possessions to friends who must stay behind. Beside and inside the lorries are Dutch policemen. As usual the SS men run around shouting, counting, lists in hand, railing at us and each other. We take our leave of Amersfoort.

As soon as we are outside the PDA the policemen turn out to be splendid fellows. They give us bread, cheese, apples, cigarettes.

'Boys, you're looking awful!'

'You're going to Utrecht, to Gansstraat (Goose Street).'

'Who has letters for home? Listen, only small letters, with a clear address.'

'The war is going well, the Nazis are getting bogged down in Russia.'

'Keep your pecker up, boys, everyone sympathizes with you.'

'You'll be home for Christmas.'

And soon, early in the evening of 13 November, these fine fellows deliver us at the Remand Prison in Utrecht's Gansstraat.

4.
KRIEGSWEHRMACHTGEFÄNGNIS UTRECHT
(German Army War Remand Prison)
13 November 1942-7 July 1943

THE GANSSTRAAT (GOOSE STREET)

In Utrecht, the remand centre - used by the German Army - was, *mirabile dictu*, an oasis after the PDA, though one fraught with an ominous prospect. Unlike the Orange Hotel at Scheveningen, the prison in Utrecht was not under the command of SS, SD, Sipo, Gestapo or whatever else they were called, but of the Wehrmacht, which made a world of difference. The commandant was a captain named Wöllhardt, the warders were soldiers who had been given this soft job because, according to what they told us and indeed to their outward appearance, they had been wounded physically, or equally likely, psychologically and were excused frontline duty for a period. This engendered a totally different atmosphere.

Moreover, the German authorities had retained the services of part of the regular Dutch prison staff. Not only was this staff completely on the side of the prisoners but it did not hesitate to render assistance including smuggling messages into and out of the prison. Some even helped with escape attempts. Invaluable services have been rendered to my wife and me by 'Cousin Jan', an assistant warder, who for months on end made possible an intensive illegal correspondence between us. Clearly such activities could easily have cost him his life.

COUSIN JAN

By profession a butcher, 'Cousin Jan' had responded to an invitation from the deputy governor of the prison to join his staff as assistant warder in order to provide a courier service for the new prison population. Cousin Jan was hardly an assistant warder at all; he was a messenger! And in constant and considerable danger for his life. He received not only correspondence from both the prisoners and their families, but occasionally also 'tools': saws and files. In the kitchen or scullery where he worked, an ever increasing number of letters were crumpled into his hands, and he smuggled more and more letters into the prison. At his home, after hours, there was an incessant to-ing and fro-ing of spouses, sons, daughters, fathers to deliver and receive 'post'. Often the visitors were not permitted to meet each other.

He puzzled over ways to facilitate contacts. He even took a course with a dentist and when he had grasped the basic principles of dentistry, including the construction of crowns, he reported to the German commandant that he was also a dentist. They took this up, and Cousin Jan started to treat prisoners with 'toothache' in their cell. He carried all his own equipment and the German warders took it for granted and locked him up with the prisoner as long as the treatment lasted. That way Cousin Jan had every opportunity to exchange views with his 'patients'.

One day the Germans felt the remand prison needed an extension. Building materials were stacked near an exercising cage: scaffolding, trestles, planks. This did not escape the attention of some members of the OD, an important semi-military Resistance group whose future looked extremely bleak. With Cousin Jan's help they devised an escape plan that made use of the scaffolding. External help was organized and on the day before the escape the OD men were taken to the kitchen to collect potatoes for peeling. Among the potatoes a file had been hidden. On the day itself it had been arranged that they would be exercised in the cage nearest the scaffolding.

The file was never used. There was no sawing. There was no escape. Returned to their cells the men let it be known to Cousin Jan they had abandoned their escape plan in order not to endanger his life. All of them were later executed.

Later on Cousin Jan got assistance from a German soldier warder, who had proved to be reliable. He even took the German home. Other visitors were terrified when they came face to face with a German in uniform. Four months after the end of the war the German committed suicide, in Holland.

Initially Cousin Jan also helped a prisoner whom he later came to distrust. The man soon turned out to be an *agent provocateur*. He was 'released' and visited Cousin Jan's home in order to draw him out. One evening after that the bell rang. Cousin Jan thought, 'Here come the Gestapo!' Armed men did indeed rush in, but they were not Gestapo but men of the Resistance who intended to bump Jan off because of his association with a traitor. He had a lot of trouble changing their minds.

Later still a prisoner's relative who frequented Cousin Jan's home was arrested. He carried an address book with masses of names and addresses, including Cousin Jan's. Jan too was arrested, and spent six weeks in the Scheveningen Orange Hotel before being released. If only they had known!

Cousin Jan survived. He did not get the VC, nor any other decoration, not even the Resistance Cross. What he did have was bad health - and a good conscience. He died in 1979.

THE REMAND PRISON

Under the circumstances, our care in Utrecht was definitely good. Our hair was allowed to grow. Several times a week we could shave; razorblades were handed out and then taken away after use, for security reasons. Once a week we had a bath. The food was scant but reasonable. Those who, like my cellmates and me, were allowed to clean vegetables received extra food as wages. There was a library. There was a *Sanitätsgefreiter* (medical orderly) who could be summoned with a prisoner-assistant to the cell for small medical complaints. Occasionally there was even a real dentist.

But, much more importantly, we could get in touch with home. At regular times we were allowed to write and receive letters - an additional bonus for those of us who corresponded illegally via Cousin Jan. Also, parcels and clean clothes could be sent to us. In this respect most prisoners were unbelievably fortunate. We could barely hold back our tears when a German warder entered our cell with much rattling of keys, called out a name and added, 'Dirty washing'. That implied your wife was downstairs to collect dirty washing and bring clean clothes together with food and cigarettes.

Once again we had names instead of numbers and enjoyed a little respect. The governor was a fairly decent bloke. He looked gloomy but behaved in a markedly friendly way. You could make a request for an interview. On one such occasion he said to me, 'But, Herr Doktor, we are after all in this world to help each other, aren't we?'

Those parcels from home - we felt almost embarrassed when displaying the contents in the presence of others. It was pure love turned into food. The Dutch population already suffered from meagre rations and it was clear that most delicacies had either been bought after paying through the nose or with coupons saved from a hungry family. The parcels my wife brought were splendid works of art, imaginatively composed.

Of course, parcels from home also created tensions and quarrels. Day and night we were together in communal cells, six or seven of us, and nothing could escape anyone. Sometimes it also happened that a cellmate did not receive anything, or something quite modest, and then one had to share, of course. For hungry men sharing with others was an immense moral undertaking.

Letters, parcels - once in a while even a visit. I do not know how this was arranged, but in Utrecht it did happen that a prisoner would receive a visit from his wife. That befell me too.

In addition to all this there was something that to me proved of inestimable value. The Remand Prison in Utrecht was a pleasant, cosy, typically Dutch institution compared with Scheveningen or Amersfoort. The November season contributed to this atmosphere, as did old copies of magazines from the library (it escaped the Germans, of course, that these contained reports on the Royal Family and also of the rise of Hitlerism). The building, constructed in the 1870s, was properly heated and lit, guarding was good natured, a lot was permitted, and you could read. When you hit it off with your cellmates - as I did later, though not in the beginning - and all were well supplied with parcels, it was really quite bearable, especially when you considered what it was like outside where one suffered from hundreds of restrictions and every moment risked being caught either in a police raid or in some other way and dispatched to Nazi-land. In Utrecht prison we felt we were safe . . . .

But, of course, that was an entirely false impression because soon enough we discovered that the remand prison was the seat of the *Feldkriegsgericht des kommandierenden Generals und Befehlshabers im Luftgau Holland* (the field court-martial of the commanding general and commander-in-chief of the administrative air force district of Holland), a court-martial which pronounced death sentences on an assembly line principle. That gave our stay a most sinister twist. I shall return to this later on.

In any case it began to dawn on us that we had been transported from the PDA to a prison in order to stand trial. You were left to guess things like that, the Germans never told you. As soon as we understood, the joviality of the governor and the soldier guards acquired a distinctly sinister aspect and caused extra suspicion and extra fear.

My personal life in the cell improved as I could now write at will. It was my fault that our cell used unbelievable quantities of lavatory paper. In the corner of all communal cells stood a *Kübelton* (literally: clay bucket; in military jargon: a thunderbox) behind a wooden screen with a low swing-door. My cellmates got accustomed to my disappearance for several hours each day behind that door, when I sat down on the *Kübelton* and covered a pile of lavatory paper in my scribblings using a chessboard as support. I made them believe I was writing a novel. Inquisitive German warders were told the same when they looked through the spy glass in the cell door and counted one prisoner less. They swallowed my explanation readily.

Cousin Jan came to fetch us almost daily to collect vegetables - especially turnips - in the kitchen downstairs which we had to clean in our cell. I always had a pile of lavatory paper with me. We clumped down the many iron stairs. Next to the kitchen was a barred inner yard. Not without gruffness, Cousin Jan would order me into the yard to pick up a case of turnips. When the accompanying soldier looked elsewhere my pile of paper disappeared with lightning speed into his white coat, from which he produced a letter from my wife that went into my trouser pocket. He also hissed the latest news from the BBC.

My prison diary is voluminous: 1,600 pieces of paper, more than half the total, were written in the period of nearly eight months at Utrecht. Another peculiarity in Utrecht was, again, the noise, similar to that in Scheveningen. Strange. A factory making aircraft engines was not far from the prison. These were tested round the clock. Day and night we had to live with continuous heavy engine noise, from close by, sometimes a fifth tone higher, at others a fifth tone lower. This booming reverberation was the macabre accompaniment of the death sentences in the *Kriegswehrmachtgefängnis* in Utrecht.

The 'Trial'

At the end of November, in the church hall of the Remand Prison, the trial of the Lion Guard took place before the *Feldkriegsgericht im Luftgau Holland*. We were provided with German solicitors. Mine was called Albrecht, from Hannover. Initially he could barely hide his distaste for me: resistance to the German occupying power, how could I? Hoping to tempt him into some positive activity on my behalf, I told him we were colleagues. This surprised him and he let himself be seduced into a discussion. I had regained some ground and drove him into a corner. He had not been allowed to see any documents of the case. How then could he decently take on my defence? *Bei uns* (with us, i.e. in Holland) this would not happen, etc. . . .

We also came to talk about faith. I told him that ultimately no occupying force could have any power over me other than a derivative one. I quoted a line from the Bible: 'They will haul you before the authorities...' His mouth sagged and he said, 'Really, Herr Doktor, for a lawyer you are very philosophical.' He regarded it as subnormal tittle-tattle. Despite this he took some trouble on my behalf.

The day of my hearing before the *Feldkriegsgericht* arrived. I had worked myself into a state of nervous tension in advance. What would be dealt with during the session in court? My original statement, which had been put in writing or the later one, much more damaging, which was not recorded?

I appeared before my 'judges', the members of the court- martial, who were dressed in full military attire, watched by their Führer from his portrait above them. I noticed at once that my Sachbearbeiter Heyduck and Walthes were present as well. I was taken to sit next to them. The 'president' read out the official report of . . . my first statement, occasionally raising his voice in indignation. He asked a few inane questions. A lawyer should have known better! Did anyone else have any questions? Sachbearbeiter Heyduck, playing with a pencil, gazing at his papers, did not have any questions. My solicitor pleaded for a few minutes. Did I have anything to say? No. I was returned to my cell.

This was one of the strange phenomena that befell me during imprisonment (and afterwards). Why did Heyduck not say anything? His mistake in not making a written statement of my second 'confession' could have been redeemed at this session. Was he afraid to admit his mistake? Had he forgotten all about it? Or, perhaps, did he want to save me? The mystery has never been resolved. However, when I heard the sentences a few days later, it struck me that God had indeed responded to my prayers. And in a sense, a completely different sense, answered them. . . .

The day for sentencing arrived. The behaviour of the judges, the public prosecutors and the defence lawyers was so asinine that we asked ourselves whether they took themselves seriously. This often happened when confronted with German officials. Was it really possible that generals, judge-advocates and lawyers actually meant what they said? An ostensibly impressive occasion turned into a grotesque, even farcical joke. Did they really believe in it? Yet human lives were at stake.

All of us appeared at this session together, hair cut and clean shaven. The gentlemen put on their caps, the chairman rose and read the sentence. It was given 'im Namen des Deutschen Volkes' (in the name of the German people). In view of its excessive length it must have been composed long before the session.

Thirty-two of us stood trial as members of the Lion Guard. Twenty-one received the death sentence. Against the remaining eleven 'das Verfahren wird bis auf weiteres abgetrennt' (the legal proceedings will be set aside). I was amongst them. I would certainly have been among the other group if my second statement had been raised.

[In 1976, to my utter surprise, I received extensive details of the trial. The sentences had had to be confirmed by the Chief of the German Army in Holland, General F. Christiansen, who had also had to decide whether to accept petitions for a reprieve. Thirteen members of the Lion Guard were executed on 29 December 1942 at 2pm. Reading the eighty-two pages of the verdict leaves a feeling of uneasiness. They had certainly been resisters and they died for freedom and justice. Our only tribute can be silence and respect. On the other hand - what pitiful resources they had used to attack the German occupying force! They had a few pistols, a few rifles, a little ammunition, some explosives. They had marked on plans of harbours and maps of towns which installations the English should bomb; but nowhere in these eighty-two pages was it suggested that this information had been sent across the North Sea. This was all these men had to pit against the Wehrmacht, Luftwaffe and Kriegsmarine, men who in the autumn of May 1940 shot with pistols at dive bombing Stukas. The military impact was nil, the moral one incontestibly inspiring.]

Back in the cell after sentencing, we found that emotionally we had been split into two groups: those sentenced to death, and the others. Suddenly there was a world of difference between us. We *Abgetrennten* - incidentally, we did not know what it meant, it was never explained - could not possibly show our delight freely in the presence of the others. In their turn they felt that, regardless of the terrible threat under which they lived, some congratulations to us would be appropriate. Then again, we badly wanted to comfort them, though not too ostentatiously as that would then have given the impression that we thought there was no hope of a reprieve. An electric tension separated the two groups. We were fellow sufferers, we meant well for each other - but suddenly we belonged to two worlds: the realm of the living, the realm of the dead.

PRIDE

When one talks about the unbelievable humiliations our torturers meted out to us, I must make one reservation. More often I felt that the Germans humiliated themselves to a greater extent than they did us.

With one exception, however. As soon as we had been arrested and were at the mercy or inhumanity of the Germans, almost all of us tried to ingratiate ourselves with them. In that sense our imprisonment was indeed most humiliating. As it was also for our families when they tried to obtain privileges for us or even release. Our pride was badly hurt. Attempts were made to obtain permission for parcels, letters, even visits. Various officials were cultivated. Acquaintances of friends always knew a 'good' German somewhere in a government directorate. Our wives, in their prettiest finery, would go there to try their - our - luck, usually to no avail. In the KZ you would try to earn a place in a better working party, a privilege, a concession, all aimed at saving one's life. This necessitated a respectful, even servile approach to the enemy. In their contacts with German authorities - big and small, outside as well as inside prison and KZ - many squirmed with the humiliation of achieving this.

One is reminded particularly of petitions for pardon by or on behalf of those sentenced to death. All this was morally acceptable, indeed imperative. It was also humiliating. To ask these villains for a favour! My respect for the few who did not take any part in this was and is considerable. Above all for the heroes - the correct word this time - who were too proud to ask for a pardon.

How would it be?

Connected to every large communal cell in Utrecht's Remand Prison was a cell for sleeping consisting of a narrow corridor off which were four separate barred cages, roofless, each with a little iron door and a bunk. During our sojourn there were usually more than four prisoners in one cell, so as many extra bunks were put in the corridor as there were additional inhabitants.

Every evening the sergeant opened the gate to the sleeping cell and the doors to the four cages. We were then granted some time to prepare for the night. Some brushed their teeth and changed into pyjamas. Others took some treasure to the bunk: a photograph, a slice of bread, a sweet out of a parcel from home. All, without exception, took some cigarettes, smuggled from the exercise yard. One had a few matches, another a surface to strike them on. Each bunk would be meticulously arranged - as prisoners are wont to do.

Half an hour later the sergeant would appear again. We entered our cage, the supernumeries lay on their bunks. Each cage was locked, followed by the grills. With his studded boots the sergeant clanked through the now empty living cell, loudly called 'Good night', flung the cell door closed, shot the bolts - and turned the lights out, whereupon his footsteps would fade away.

He had barely gone before we started our furtive and utterly perilous bed-time treat: smoking. When there were men on the bunks in the corridor it would start there: one match struck on the strike-surface would light the first cigarette. The men in the cage would receive the light through the bars and before long you saw luminous points everywhere in the dark, accompanied by sighs of contentment. It was much more dangerous when only the four cages were occupied.

The man who produced the light had to stand on his bunk and stretch over the concrete wall between the cages to pass his lighted cigarette to his neighbour who would light his cigarette, return the original to its owner, and then supply his neighbour in the same way, etc. Our mattresses consisted of straw. We had blankets. Apart from the glowing cigarettes the cell was pitch dark. The doors of the cages were locked, as was the gate to the living cell. If something went wrong with the match or the lighted cigarettes we would almost certainly be roasted alive. We were all very much aware of this and consequently the entire operation was carried out with the utmost caution.

Sometimes, unexpectedly, there would be an inspection. Invariably the sleeping cell, and through the barred gate, the living cell too, was blue with smoke. In my experience this was never punished. Presumably the Germans only came to see whether a fire had to be extinguished.

After smoking - I always held the portrait of my wife close in order to see her face in the glow of every drag - we prayed, aloud. A general prayer befitting our situation. Then the Lord's Prayer. Then a Hail Mary. This prayer was said aloud by a Catholic, invariably with the soft 'g' prevalent in the accent of the southern provinces near the Flemish border. We Protestants willingly joined in, also out loud. Usually also, finally, the Apostolic Creed.

Every now and then we chattered a little while or ate, inaudibly to avoid annoying others. Subsequently silence prevailed. Deadly silence reigned, especially in the cells of those condemned to death by bullet because they had followed the dictates of their conscience and resisted the occupier.

Autumn turned to winter. In the distance the engine factory raged. This caused some of us to be gripped by supreme desperation. It was then that quiet comfort was called for - quietly, for somewhere else snoring had already taken over. The only comfort could be found in some words Jesus had reportedly used: 'He has sent me to proclaim release to the captives.' 'Do not fear those who kill the body but cannot kill the soul.' That consolation proved entirely sufficient. Finally we floated beyond the walls, in our thoughts first, then in our dreams later, as free as birds, set free by the God who guards prisoners.

But there is always another man lying on his bunk in pitch darkness, completely alone, with a death sentence hanging over him, pronounced by an enemy to whom all offences, however nominal, are serious; a man who is considering how it will be, and where, and when; whether a clergyman will be in attendance, whether he will be handcuffed, blindfolded; whether it will be early in the morning, outside, so he can still see the sunrise. He thinks: 'I shall never see this sky again; I have to take leave for ever of everyone and everything', and, 'How many will there be in the firing squad, which weapons will they use, and all will of them be loaded?'; and he wonders, will he be tied to a pole, and finally, will he notice it, will he feel it when the bullets smash into his heart, one bullet, or ten or twelve? Will he still be conscious for a moment and what he will then think? Will he call something before they start shooting, 'long live the Queen!', 'long live my Country!' or alternatively, 'have mercy upon me, sinner'? Will the order be *Feuer* (Fire)? Will he be dead at once or will there be a *coup de grace*, and where? He feels his neck, he feels his chest. Will they cremate or bury him, and where? What will they tell his family? He asks himself whether his resistance activities were really worthwhile, worth his life, *his life*! Yet still, in desperation, he clutches at the thought that it might all be one grotesque mistake, a nightmare from which he will awake. But this is fantasy. What will they do with his clothes, his belongings? What is his wife, his beloved wife to do now? What are his little children to do without a father, fallen for his country? Perhaps he will, after all, be weak, crumble, scream out in fear.

'Do not fear those who kill the body but cannot kill the soul.' Christ said this, God Himself as Man! Do not be afraid of the German firing squad, says God, it cannot kill your soul. It cannot kill your soul! Christ says your soul remains alive.

It is then that Christ shows Himself, clearly visible, in the utmost glory, to the man under the death sentence on his bunk in the cage in the pitch-black cell in the prison in blacked-out Utrecht in enslaved Holland during the Second World War, 1,942 years after His birth.

THE LAST CHANCE

When death looks you straight in the eyes you will sometimes become quite serene. This can only be envisaged by those who possess strong powers of imagination, courage and concentration, and who can accept at the profoundest level that death is unavoidable.

You are utterly alone. There is no way out. Not one. No more people to see. No stay of execution, no diversion, no last appeal, no mercy. Nothing is left but a creature, alone, naked, without anything, with nothing, before an empty ocean and above it a star-studded sky, where shortly you will be heading.

One should not conceive of God as a good wise Father, neither as an image of brotherly love. God is love, but, in such circumstances, it is a terrible love. God is infinite, impenetrable, incomprehensible, glacial. You might say steely, tough, unyielding. 'It is a fearful thing to fall into the hands of the living God.' This is . . . not fearful: you should embrace the idea. God is love, we are His creatures, He has made all the glorious things, nothing in Him is terrifying - but He is majestic, glacial and unyielding.

You are in a cell, deserted by everyone and everything, in a vacuum, trying to see eye to eye with God. You say to yourself, 'these are probably my last hours, the last ones, my last ones. There is no reprieve, no alternative. I have to see eye to eye with God and this is my last hour. This heart will shortly stop beating and I am on the way to an unknown Kingdom, perhaps one I knew prior to my birth. . . . I shall not need any clothes any more.'

At that stage you perceive Jesus Christ, a human being, a human God, a mediator who understands us, who understands God, who is us and God. That is how it was. In that way God came to us through Christ bringing the mercy of faith. By making us completely uncertain, by having everything smashed out of our hands, by allowing us to be made outcasts, we will fully understand the Gospel. By taking us to this ultimate condition we truly appreciate faith.

LOVE YOUR NEIGHBOUR

The first commandment is to love God, the second, your neighbour. That is what it is all about. The first never caused me any problem, the second all the more so.

Of course you can love many neighbours with all your heart, without any trouble. When people are nice to you it is not difficult to be nice in return. The great art is to love unpleasant fellow human beings, those you loathe. Enemies. This is almost impossible to achieve. Nevertheless it is one of the essentials of life. It is worth taking a lot of trouble to acquire this art. You should imagine facing an enemy, not just an annoying person, but a really nasty one, an evil one, a malicious one who is after you. For instance, a *Kapo*, or an SS man. First of all, look at him closely. Remember that this enemy was once a helpless baby, that he had a mother and father who probably loved him. This approach already does away with many sharp edges.

Next you should recognize that you do not know what circumstances, what pressures, prompted your adversary to become evil. Perhaps you would yourself have turned evil in similar circumstances.

Thirdly - and most importantly - you have to assume that he will not have become your enemy for the pleasure of it, nor from having an evil character. He cannot possibly be happy with it. He is unhappy and deserves to be pitied.

Fourthly, he is, in some sense, possessed. A destructive demon has taken hold of him. For him this is frightful, much more so than for you. You will have to look at him as someone who has to be redeemed. You should not hate him but his demons.

Finally, it is pertinent to exercise some degree of self-criticism. The enemy is bad, but are you yourself entirely good? Not many will in all honesty think so. Nobody is entirely good. It is for that reason that we pray, 'Forgive us our trespasses as we forgive them that trespass against us'. We too are bad. Who determines whether our enemy is worse? How bad would we have become given his circumstances, his past, his character, his upbringing, his physical and psychological make-up? Who are we that we not only judge but even condemn someone else? Judge not, that you be not judged.

When you have weighed up all this the enemy looks altogether different. He should not be your enemy anymore. Rather, he will have become a poor afflicted soul, like you. Now you must try to take one more step. You must endeavour to help the former enemy, bearing in mind that what you do to him, you do unto Christ. You must try to deliver him from Evil as you ask God to deliver you from Evil. Perhaps he will not accept that. It could be that he starts cursing. This is no reason to give up. You never know whether he will not repent afterwards, perhaps even years later. You should never refrain from trying to do good to your fellow human being because you doubt that it will help. You can never be sure. The point is that your attempts at help will be supported by divine power. There will be a formidable force to sustain your attempts. Perhaps you are its vehicle. If everyone lived like this what a different place the world would be!

THE MOLAR

One of my cellmates was in a bad way. He had been a member of the Lion Guard in the northern provinces of Holland and in his capacity as a surveyor had been allowed to climb church towers with all manner of optical instruments to take 'measurements', under the watchful eye of the Germans. In reality he would photograph German installations with a telelens.

He was a cheerful person, but after our trial - where he too was sentenced to death - he developed a toothache. When this got progressively worse he asked for a dentist's appointment. A few days later he was collected 'Zum Zahnartzt!' (to the dentist). He was away for a long time. Back in our cell he explained having been taken, under escort, in a prison van to a dentist somewhere in Utrecht. Had the ache abated?

'A bit. I've been given a drug to alleviate the pain. They drilled a molar. It's in a bad condition. Needs a gold crown, which will cost 90 guilders. The dentist asked whether I would be able to send him this rather large amount. Well, it's a huge amount for my wife. I'll wait until they've decided about my request for a pardon. I think the answer will be no. A crown of 90 guilders would be pointless. A bit of toothache on top won't make any difference.'

This was said in a tone so matter-of-fact that it sounded as if he were giving a trivial business report. Shortly afterwards he was executed with twelve other members of the Lion Guard.

MORTAL FEAR

A middle-aged evangelist shared our cell. He too had been sentenced to death, he too had petitioned for a pardon. Most hours of the day and some of the night he was exceedingly excited, which proved to be contagious. His tension communicated itself to us all. He talked loudly, sometimes for hours on end.

'Sentenced to death! Who would ever have thought so? And really for nothing. What have I done to them? Nothing. I had no intention, I walked into a trap. Who denounced me? Probably X, but could have been Y. I've got to find out - but perhaps there won't be time. Who decides on pardon? My lawyer didn't do badly but he did not say anything about my many children. Oh God, sentenced to death. What will happen? And where, boys? Here in the prison? Or outside? They usually do it early in the morning, don't they? Come on boys, stiff upper lip, we'll not be left in the lurch. The Lord is our Shepherd, isn't He, boys? We'll want for nothing. What will my wife have to live on at home? But they wouldn't be that stupid, would they, and shoot us dead for nothing, eh, boys? A few photographs, a few bottles of chemicals, a map, hardly anything, I've never done anything with it, never, I was too afraid. You'll see, they only want to frighten us, the Germans. They are after all our brother-race, they treat us well here, the *Hauptmann* (captain or prison governor) is a decent chap, so are the soldiers, old fellows, very different from Scheveningen. The trial might have been worse, I've been treated correctly, perhaps I worry needlessly. You'll see, it'll be alright in the end. Lord, I believe, help my unbelief. And that wonderful Psalm 23: 'Yea though I walk through the valley of the shadow of death I will fear no evil, for Thou art with me.' That's how it is. The valley of death, yes, I'm certainly in there, suppose they really would... and I expected to be home for Christmas, never see Christmas again, and you see the sky for the last time and never again. Boys, I'm hungry, it's time for a parcel from home, I hope they'll put sausages in it again and sugar, butter, cigarettes. They condemned me *Im Namen des Deutschen Volkes* to death. You too. Death, the scoundrels. They're bastards! That this can still happen, and for nothing at all. Well, I've done something of course, and they didn't even know the half of it.'

He would pace up and down, face flushed, mouth drooping. He would walk to a shelf where there was a piece left over from his bread, pick it up, start eating. He would resume pacing up and down, picking up the crumbs with a wet finger.

'We would never have thought it, boys, bread without butter, without anything. At home we did a lot better, really great, all gifts from the good Lord. Oh, how well off we were, and such a marvellous large family, all healthy, and Saturday evenings, and Sundays at church. Is that all past? Will we still be allowed visitors? Aren't you allowed to eat what you want, and smoke, and write a letter? There'll be a clergyman, surely. And then . . . they come to take you, early in the morning. And then, I haven't really done all that much, they only found a few photographs and they call that spying, sabotage, *Feindbegünstigung* (aiding and abetting the enemy), or something like that. Let's see, the sentence was twelve, no sixteen days ago. A petition for pardon may have to go to Berlin, takes a long time . . . or will it be Christiansen who decides? It was a court-martial, therefore army, therefore the general decides, but in Holland the Head of State decides, true? Therefore perhaps the Führer himself. . . .'

His mouth would twitch violently, his lips drawn back from his teeth. He would finally sit down and rest his balding head on his arms. His back would then start shaking, time and again he would wipe first his left cheek, then his right cheek on his arms, tears streaming from his eyes.

'God, oh God, sentenced to death, boys, they're going to shoot us!'

A few days later they arrived, decked out like butterflies, in uniform, gold braid, medals dangling, peaked caps, documents in gloved hands, briefcases under arms. And our friends left us, the middle-aged man with them. Only three of us remained. It was 29 December 1942.

THE LIMITS OF EMOTIONS

In both prisons and all the concentration camps where I was interned I found it difficult to digest emotions. If I want to pick up a pen from my desk, an impulse originating in the brain, my brain communicates this to the muscles of my hand, which then lifts the pen up. When I see beautiful flowers, my eyes communicate this through the optic nerve to the brain where an emotion occurs: How beautiful these flowers are! These processes occur all day - also at night - with the speed of light and in vast quantities. In prison these processes are severely disrupted. This contributes considerably to the unreal character of imprisonment.

When someone is told abruptly that his child has just been killed in an accident, the shock is of such magnitude that the accompanying emotions of terror, grief, despair and misery will initially fail to materialize and will only gradually grow to become overwhelming. When such vehement emotions become a regular occurrence, for instance when one good friend after another dies, or one murder follows another, they seem to lose their force. Death becomes commonplace. One catastrophe is thrust onto another. Catastrophe becomes a part of daily life. One learns to live with it and a regulatory mechanism comes into play.

In contrast, other affairs, especially of a sensory nature, could produce unusual, even amazing effects. The world of the KZ and even more of the prison is mainly grey and brown, with elements of black and white. Red, yellow, blue, orange and green hardly appear. Everything is grimy, grubby, pallid, of a sickly colour. When suddenly a bright colour comes into view it can stir up emotions out of all normal proportion.

In the Utrecht prison, just before Christmas 1942, my parcel from home contained chocolate wrapped in red foil. At the first glance I was completely transfixed. The colour reached my brain via my dazzled eye; my entire world of thought was filled with the idea of Christmas: Christmas trees, candles, glass bells, silver trumpets, Christmas baubels, Christmas carols, Christmas reunions, Christmas dinners. For hours on end I could not think of anything else, a long train full of images raced past.

In prison, notably in solitary confinement, I discovered another curious phenomenon: when there is nothing new happening, and one's very consciousness gets emptier and emptier, progressively older memories appear on the screen of the imagination. Clearly the mind yearns for activity. If nothing new, then something old, older, oldest. Memories of events, moods, even those when I was ten, eight, six, four - and earlier - emerged. Concentrating a bit more I could go back even further into the past.

If solitary confinement lasted a year, would you then perhaps remember your birth? And if it lasted even longer, would pre-natal memories crop up?

Back to the Big Emotions. Take pain. When you are in a lot of pain it is difficult to keep quiet. In my experience it is impossible. You start groaning, complaining, sometimes even screaming and yelling. I do not know of anyone who was able to refrain from making a noise when tortured during interrogations or at other times. When pain becomes unbearable one loses consciousness. Apparently the nervous system has a mechanism that brings about unconsciousness, perhaps in self-defence. Another comparable mechanism turns out to exist and comes into operation at a different kind of unbearable emotion: not of pain but of happiness, supreme delight, a superhuman perception. You can indeed lose consciousness not only from pain but also from a feeling of adoring bliss. A sudden shock as a result of either an unfathomably profound happiness, or on receipt of a calamitous message can also cause death by heart attack. Perhaps man is simply not allowed to cross certain barriers of misfortune or good luck. Perhaps the organism of the human body cannot cope, is not constituted that way. Perhaps a direct confrontation with pure divine power has to be paid for with death: the organs are just not up to it. Furthermore perhaps - and it is difficult for me to write this down, for which I ask God's forgiveness - it causes the clinical picture called the KZ-syndrome: we have crossed the barriers of the permissible, albeit marginally, and remained alive 'by accident'.

VISIT

It was 29 December 1942. Long practice enabled us to work out which cells were being exercised from the single blow on the bell. Still only the second floor. You never knew where they would start on the third floor, our S cell, or T cell directly opposite. A single blow, down below, deep sound on the bell. Shabby shoes stepping up and down the iron stairs, one row after another. The gloomy soldier-guard whom we called 'the stove-pipe' shouts something downstairs. He shuffles in front of our door, though still without keys. We have already put on our coats and the others stand virtuously waiting in a group, like cows ready to be milked. I never join in, feign independence, want to keep some pride and sit ostensibly reading, without actually seeing the page before me.

The keys now rattle loudly, the door swings open, the stove-pipe silently stretches out his arm, holding it out horizontally, like a schoolmistress keeping a flock of children from crossing the street because of the traffic. Creaking, leather on iron, pallid heads above coats, a column of men climbs up the stairs, they gesture to us, crazy, it is meaningless, we return the gestures. 'Also' (You next), says the stove-pipe.

We move. We walk down the stairs. On the way we notice major things, as always, but thank God nothing exceptional, no memorable faces, no open doors that should have been closed. Thank God, the gates to the lobby too are closed, as are the two main front doors behind these gates. All is safe and sound, and we proceed through the small door at the end into the large central exercise yard. Now I will have to do my best, my very best.

I have got the photograph with me. I isolate myself at once, at the front on the right. The others are standing near the door, waiting for the cigarettes to turn up. Stay there, wait, I have to be alone. But first the sky, what is the sky like? The weather is clear, just above freezing, somewhat hazy. The slate-grey gutters are the same as always, so is the yellow-brick top floor. That is all right then. I expand everything, nostrils, eyes, ears. The engine factory bangs and booms, higher, then lower, all right too. The photograph. I take the photograph out, upside down. First eyes closed. Turn the photograph over. Eyes open. Eyes wide open, very wide. They are smarting. That is the last thing I need, but they are smarting. I am borne away heavenwards by the sight. . . .

'Hey, Floris, aren't you smoking?'

I start.

'Well, all right, thanks, I am allowed to smoke, smoke!'

'Day and night He heaps favours upon us', that is what she wrote and I may therefore believe it. But there are no more cigarettes for me, the guard pinches them, but one mate has a spare one and also gives me a light. The first drag makes you feel sick, blessed nausea. I grip the bars with two hands and pull myself up, smoking, and again take out the photograph. Now it gets better, a mighty wave with silvery fringes, that is her. An angel, an archangel. She is the air, she is the bird above me, the frosted-tinged grass in the piece of soil in front of the wall, she is.
. . .

Inside, in the immense boiler house, the single bell strikes. 'Na!'

(well), the guard says. I look up, four floors up, towering, the little windows of S. This is what she will see when she comes, but she cannot understand how safe and sound it is behind those little windows. All of us have our smuggled cigarettes, upstairs we also have two matches, this evening we will be smoking again. How marvellous God is - today it would be twelve steps without holding on to the banisters, twelve of the first flight of stairs up, but try not to grip the banisters, it can be done, it must be done, one day you will have to go home - fifteen are achieved. You see, it works, I am improving, getting stronger. He wants me to become stronger in order to go home, calm down, calm down. . . .

Upstairs on the landing is the guard, known as the 'bawler'.

'Bakels,' he shouts.

'Yes, Herr Wachtmeister,' I say, happy that I am able to reply firmly and briefly, military fashion.

'Mit!' (come along) he says.

This is bad. It was so quiet. I do not want anything, only to go back to S cell. I walk ahead, down the stairs.

'What is it about, Herr Wachtmeister?'

Oh, dear, this supplicant voice of mine. He does not say anything. We are downstairs. He nods: the big gates. I am mortally afraid. The gates, leading to other gates, the lobby, the main doors. . . . Gracious God, they are about to release you. What date? 29. They are releasing you. We have passed the gates. There are three familiar sergeants, they should not be here, like me they belong behind the gates, the sergeants are not allowed in front of the gates. We turn left, up a few steps, straight on, turn right, a dark corridor.

'Wait!'

Chattering teeth. Everything above my heart is shaking upwards because of the pounding of my heart. I hear a woman's laugh for a brief moment. There is the bawler, I can see him, he is normal, let him stay, let him take me back, snarl at me, beat me up.

'Besuch' (visit).

There she stands. The Goddess stands there.

GOD EXISTS

Those first seconds will always be secret, intensely secret, for me as well as for her.

'Hello, darling,' was what she said. Seconds pass. We are allowed to smoke. Someone gives us a light, a sergeant, a handsome, sympathetic chap. She does not say anything, or perhaps she does but it is all the same. What I am saying remains unknown to me, the mouth utters words, only a few. I gaze at her. She is wearing the black coat, the ugly one, and a white scarf I do not recognize, and a headscarf I do remember, which I gave her. On her cheek is a plaster presumably to cover a boil. Her face, her sweet face is afflicted with boils. Be strong, be manly, it is not important that she has boils. God exists and He wants it. Everything is different, you have died, you now live elsewhere. I notice in her handbag sandwich paper.

'Is that bread?' Oh! is it bread? Would she have bread?

'Darf er?' (is it allowed?) she asks.

I am allowed. I get the bread, her bread, and eat it, her bread.

'I've got more,' she says. She displays it, the handsome sergeant looking on. He looks a bit resentful.

'Time's nearly up,' he says.

Far away I can hear a cow, a bull, a roaring bull. I look at her and eat her bread, both smoking at the same time. Where could that bull be? At the other end of the room are two people, a fat woman and a man, a labourer, and another sergeant. This is where the sound is emanating. The man is roaring loudly. All three are standing.

'That one,' says our sergeant, confidentially bending our way, 'has been sentenced to death, be glad.'

We continue talking. Behind us people are moving, at first two, then another one. The bull has gone. We continue talking. Presently, in the quiet of my cell, I shall reflect on what we said.

'One more minute.'

I take her hands. Our Father, I say, who art in Heaven, hallowed be Thy name - and she says the same, and a divine force turns up, rushes in, and we are laughing, just like that, nothing special, normal, normal.
. . .

'That's it,' the sergeant says.

We move. It is not bad, not really, not the plaster, the black coat, the bread, not at all. She stands there, at the end of the corridor, in the open door. She waves. I wave.

I am upstairs, the bawler lagging behind, I have climbed the steps too quickly, am hanging over the railing. A single blow on the bell brings eight men shuffling down the staircase. The engine factory bellows. German aeroplane engines on their trial run, higher, lower, higher, lower. I should not fall, must keep alive. I hear someone cry 'Oh my God, Oh God,' and he begins to weep, he is sobbing, and it is me! This is not permitted, there is no reason for it, not one, but it is me.

'What's wrong?' shouts the bawler, 'What's wrong with you, man?'

The door swings open, there they are, frightened, together, my cellmates, creatures from Mars.

'What's the matter?' asks one, his hand round my shoulder, 'what is the matter?'

The bawler shouts at me, 'I'm homesick too, you know,' his swarthy face twisted. 'You idiot!' and he bangs the door making cell S boom. When I quieten down I notice that my cellmates are sniffing the air. 'You smell of woman,' they say. Which is when I too smell it. It is 'Soir de Paris', her perfume. My clean laundry also smells of it. One of them approaches me, his eyes closed, breathing heavily. 'Your wife,' he murmurs. That evening we do not wash ourselves, nor the following morning. We all want to hang on to the scent of my wife.

From My Diary

The Spider Weaves

In the exercise yard today a performance uniquely for me: a small spider with a great many hairy legs was busy weaving its web in the morning sun. For a full fifteen minutes I watched it, mouth open.

It is not quite clear how it works, even a spider has its mysteries, spinning away with lightening speed and infinite complexity. Approximately as follows:

At a particular moment there are suddenly a circumference and a centre. From the centre one thread reaches out. The spider now sits in the centre, like a miniature version of Amsterdam's centre on account of what follows. First of all it doodles a bit and gropes around, then incredibly fast it dashes down the existing thread. This dash miraculously results in a second thread, spun from its abdomen, as quickly as the first. Once out on the circumference it quietly walks with the new thread a small distance to the right, ties a knot (it is not clear to me how) and then hoists itself up the first thread to the centre again, where it fastens the new thread.

More doodling follows, I do not know to what purpose, though without any doubt the spider has a purpose. But suddenly, it dashes outwards again, this time, of course, along the recently spun thread; again a short distance to the right, another knot and back again.

When hoisting itself up along the old thread trailing the new one behind it, the first one sags perilously under its weight - even a spider has a weight. You might think: you silly spider, that thread has now been stretched, you will never get it taut again . . . but look, nothing of the kind. Once the spider has arrived at the centre the entire net has tightened like the strings of a tennis racket.

This continues unceasingly, one radius next to another, Leidsestraat next to Vijzelstraat next to Utrechtsestraat, extremely fast and evenly. When the radii diverging from centre - say, Amsterdam Central Station - are ready the spider makes an inspection trip. Occasionally the distance between two radii is too large; quickly another is spun in between, rush, rush. From time to time there is a gust of wind; dammit, the whole work of art will be torn to shreds... but no, not at all! It sways with the wind and, afterwards, is just as tight as before.

What next?

Well, the concentric circles - the four main canals: Singel, Herengracht, Keizersgracht, Prinsengracht - around the centre. This takes place at even greater speed. The spider tears round in progressively wider circles and at each crossing with a radius a knot is made. Sometimes, when a tiny irregularity occurs in the spaces, she derails briefly in a desperate swarming of legs in open space... hurray, it has got hold of a secure thread and it zooms around again. At last it has reached the circumference.

The spider has finished.

It climbs back and seats itself in the centre; the spider has completed its job and waits ... for whatever flies into its web.

REFLECTIONS OF A MONK

On Saturday 2 January 1943, only three of us left in cell S after the four condemned to death had departed, strengthened by the visit from my wife and all those treasures she had brought, among them a French Bible, with gilt edges in a leather binding, I find in my diary:

1. Man is often unhappy because he is ungrateful. He is ungrateful because he does not appreciate that what he has got derives from grace alone and not from his own deserts (he does not deserve anything). Here we have learned that everything comes by grace; but we have also found that everything can be taken away.

We have noticed how extraordinary it is to be able to wash in clean cold water with real scented soap. Similarly with clothes, we know how it feels to be dressed in rags and thinly too. Only now do we appreciate wool on our bodies and comfortably fitting clothes and the smell of the linen cupboard.

The daily bread: some pray for it every day and take it for granted. But in Amersfoort we discovered that this was a false assumption. When you have to do without bread you feel constantly hungry and truly appreciate the inestimable value of receiving your daily bread. The same with sugar! What longing for pure sweetness develops when you have not tasted anything sweet for four months.

So, too, we learned the value of shelter. We know now what it is like to have to get out of your bed, suddenly, without warning, in flimsy clothes, and stand straight without moving for three or six or nine or twelve, even fifteen hours in wind, rain and darkness with your back slowly bending and with teeth clenched to resist the onset of fever.

To have a Bible and to be able to read it! If you are accustomed to this and it is suddenly taken away, what a barren, empty, miserable situation!

Friends: imagine being locked up for weeks with unpleasant people with whom you cannot unwind, to whom you cannot give, from whom you do not receive! Then you meet a friend; you perceive the blessings of tenderness, you dissolve, you can sleep secure. Therefore we realize all the time that what you see, eat, smell, feel, experience, read: this is grace. Remember continually: it could be different! Whatever I receive is God's gift.

* * *

3. Hubris, the classical, rich word for exaggerated pride. The man who fails to heed this advice becomes spoilt and ungrateful, and naturally wants more and more and expects these needs to be satisfied automatically, he becomes reckless. According to the Greeks a man like that challenges the gods. The gods will destroy such a man because he is becoming too dangerous for them as a rival. There is a lot of truth in this: all his good fortune is only a matter of course, and, equally, all his needs must be satisfied. That man feels safe, wrapped up in his riches, and embarks on raids from this fortress to grab more. More and more, who can touch me? I am safe.

This is hubris, conceit. A man like that, who does not gratefully acknowledge grace, will indubitably be destroyed: 'whosoever shall exalt himself shall be abased'. It is also a good reason why one should never be envious of someone blessed with earthly goods: in one second all of it can be wiped out, in one second too that man might be hit by a heavy blow, in which case all his earthly goods will have lost their value.

* * *

5. Sin. The mole in someone else's eye, the beam in your own. Remember, however, that it is quite possible that someone who commits a small offence may well sin more than a murderer. All sorts of factors play a part: the nature of one's conscience, class,

education, background, maturity, character, temperament, motives, experiences, intention, incentives and many other matters. It is very possible for a Papuan head hunter to sin less than I when refusing someone a slice of bread. 'Whosoever is without sin, let him throw the first stone.' And: 'Judge not that you be not judged.'

* * *

7. Imagine you can do something well, have done something exceptional. Take a genius, for example a pianist who has played Rachmaninov in a masterly manner before a large audience, or a hero who has saved a child from a fire in front of a multitude, a surgeon who succeeded with an impossible operation - add any other example. The world looks on breathlessly and thereupon cheers success, showering the hero with decorations, titles, marriage proposals, parades, tributes, statues and so on and so forth. Woe betide the man who now becomes proud, throws his weight about, struts like a peacock and boasts of his achievements. Nonsense: it was God after all Who worked in that man. When the pianist has finished playing his concerto to the rapturous acclaim of his audience, let him accept that fame, not for himself but for God.

8. Charity. I do not mean *l'amour* but *la charité* as meant in 1 Corinthians 13. However, this general love, or charity, the love for God and one's neighbours, includes, of course the love between man and woman, parent and child, *l'amour*. But charity is such a comprehensive concept that it becomes infinitely difficult to comprehend. Love your neighbour like yourself. When you enter deeply into the concept of charity, I see someone with arms stretched out and hands turned upwards, left and right, helping hands; someone who offers helping hands, not one but both; someone who is charitable, is radiant with helping hands stretched out, someone who wants to draw one in to cherish, to give, to embrace, to warm.

* * *

10. Talents. When you know you are able to do certain things, that you possess particular talents, remember constantly: your duty is to cherish them, to honour them, to develop them and to use them for the benefit of mankind and the glory of God. You do not receive these talents for nothing. Talents are like shining pieces of gold or like unlit fireworks, light them and they will sprout wonderful gold and silver fountains and those who watch them will rejoice. Neglect to light them, store them away, and their force will disappear, they

will perish and decay. Those who have talents should be constantly feverish, in a fever to light the fireworks, to warm, to lighten, to work, to show the beautiful God-given treasures to all men. Talents compel one to have the fever of work.

* * *

12. Artificial Distinctions. I believe that one of the causes of the present world catastrophe is artificial distinctions. In the first place, class distinction. We have now seen how curious this distinction really is. It is absolutely irrelevant whether someone is of high birth, practices a more distinguished profession, has more money than others. We have been able to establish that the percentage of people in distress and hardship who carry on behaving decently is lower among so-called distinguished men than among those considered simple. Mannerisms, conventions, decorum; they could often commit offences in secret, protected by their wealth, position or, sometimes, the public authorities; they have not been tested as often and as profoundly as the poor. They had it so good and most of their necessities were satisfied. They have not, like the poor, been toughened up. The rich are covered with frills and finery which prevent you from seeing their own true faces. We have seen them deprived of all these. And there it was! The only difference capable of truly distinguishing one man from another is between believers and unbelievers. Other differences do not really exist or are irrelevant or can be bridged. What does it matter to me whether someone's accent is flawed, whether he has dirty nails or is the son of a labourer, has other manners or none at all? Fundamentally we are exactly the same; that became evident in Amersfoort where everybody had the same, lived in the same circumstances, faced the same fate. There the plain man, toughened, never having put on airs, always having had to fight for his life, often prevailed over the distinguished man.

Yes, fundamentally the same: also the furious desire for wife and children, also the appetite for work and the love of work (all work deserves to be honoured, good workers are worth the same regardless of the nature of their job), the same too when hungry or thirsty, all bodies have the same needs, reactions and desires - all elementary things are the same. Differences are only on the surface. And what do we care about the surface, the semblance, the transitory, the frills, all of which, as we have witnessed with our own eyes, can drop away in emergencies?

Of course this does not mean that your friends should not come from the same background, the same class. Why not? It can hardly be otherwise: memories of youth, upbringing, language, acquaintances, ambitions, plans, these will all be related; if only for that reason and because of your similar and like-minded culture, you feel attracted to one another. But this does not mean that one cannot mix with someone of lower birth, even be friends with him. Class distinction is one of the causes of war: people do not know each other, do not know each other's circumstances and way of life, do not know either that they are fundamentally the same; and those who do not know each other, fear one another. Here too: act normally. Talk normally with people, ask, draw the other out, enquire, have a look, and show yourself, tell them, inform. Build extensive contacts with each other. You, especially the rich man, should put on overalls and join in, you are welcome to share a meal with your workmen, sit at table with their family, you can learn a lot, just as much as the workman can learn from you.

13. The distinction between nationalities is equally fantastic and artificial. There is no fundamental distinction between Englishmen, Chinese, Germans and Italians: one is first and foremost a human being. There are differences, of course, but so there are between Limburgers and Groningers, between Amsterdammers and Rotterdammers. The development of the world will not only make these differences less relevant but will also in fact diminish them: the world is becoming progressively smaller.

14. The Life of a Monk. Locked up in a cell many a prisoner comes to God. Not only have I heard that in peace time prisoners are religious, as long as they are in prison (unfortunately they often let go of God once they have regained their freedom), but I have experienced it myself and have had it confirmed by others in similar circumstances. How does this happen?

First of all, anyone who finds himself in distress and fear reaches out for God. When distress and fear disappear, God is suddenly redundant: one can cope on one's own again! But, secondly, life in a cell, the life of a monk, is very closely knit, so there is no distraction, no relaxation. Nothing can be blurred, everything is naked, bare and lonely, one cannot clutch at anything, seek diversion, delude oneself. Life in a cell is divorced from life outside, one has been taken out of the world, obliged to rely only on oneself, thrown on one's own resources, one must try in this hour of need to make something of one's life and to spend one's day as usefully as possible, make it fertile. Remarkably one then starts automatically to lead the life of a monk, the life of a pious person, a life similar to the one the Bible prescribes; at least one should aim at such a life. For if we fail in this attempt, life in the cell is absolutely unbearable. Unmitigatedly intolerable! Gluttony, gorging, lechery, vanity, swearing, selfishness, laziness - you name it - all of these provoke immediate vehement reactions, high tensions, and burden the conscience to such an extent that life becomes instantly unbearable. Whether one wants it or not, in a cell one is almost forced to live as a Christian in order not to succumb.

15. Fear. At this moment I am afraid. Yes, fear, let me admit it bluntly. I am afraid and lonely, notwithstanding countless gifts! God, Bible, you, your letters, your photographs, especially your last letter of 18 December, letters from others, the delightful visit that inspired courage and confidence, all the care you put into the parcels and clothes you gave me - yet, fear. Do you know why?

Because all the delicacies you brought me have gone, because I am cold, because outside the wind wails and because I assume that next week I shall be carried far away from you, for months, perhaps years, to a camp abroad, in the freezing cold, with cold roll-calls and illness. Fear! And whatever I tell myself: all the beautiful things, the full power of faith, all those strong comforting proverbs we shared; all your love, all your letters and photographs; however much I rebuke myself and preach to myself, however much I pray: my fear remains, fear from lack of delicacies (a feeling of unsafety), from being cold (also poverty: a feeling of uneasiness). This is an ordeal: at the moment I feel I am being put to the test. This test comes from God. It has a purpose, and I have to try and be aware of it as a test by fighting and by making the most of it. Perhaps this is the purpose: that I am aware of it, that lack of comforts, therefore poverty, creates a feeling of insecurity and consequently induces fear, as does physical uneasiness, which is why the poor must be afraid of material poverty; unnecessarily, because material shortages are irrelevant.

Complicated! In any case I realize that it is difficult to rejoice, 'at all times', when one suffers from poverty. And I understand this too: that I do not listen to Jesus' words: 'do not be anxious about your life, what you shall eat or what you shall drink, nor about your body, what you shall put on' and all that follows. How slow of understanding is a man!

HE SPEAKS ON YOUR BEHALF

We have been transferred to cell T and have acquired new cellmates. One of them, Luigis, is impossible to put up with today. He has accosted all of us. Now it is my turn again.

'What would they know? My Sachbearbeiter says he knew. Knew what? From whom? Jan says he didn't say anything. I'm sure of Jan. But Wim? Would Wim? If the Sachbearbeiter knows, why didn't he talk about Paul? Because Paul told me that one bit, only that. Man, I don't know anymore. I don't know whether they know what they say they know and what I know and Jan and Paul, but Wim doesn't know. Man, I'm so afraid.'

Luigis, bright red, eats the last remaining remnant of his sugar. He resumes his trudge. In five minutes he will accost us again. In reality Luigis is afraid of death. Mortal fear for the *Feldkriegsgericht im Luftgau Holland* which will try him for sabotage and *Feindbegünstigung*. Laughing exuberantly he now accosts another cellmate in the corner of cell T.

'I don't know what they know, man. . . .'

I take him to a bench and seat him next to me. I ask him whether he believes in God, in Christ. He assents, his teeth chattering, laughingly. I take my Bible and read in a low voice: 'And when they bring you before the synagogues and the rulers and the authorities, do not be anxious how or what you are to say; for the Holy Spirit will teach you in that very hour what you ought to say.'

I want to continue. I grit my teeth and give Luigis, the petulant abusive cellmate, a piece of my bread, at the last moment a slightly smaller piece than intended, which, hopefully, God will not hold against me.

The cell door swings open. Two sergeants.

'Luigis! Zur Vernehmung!' (For questioning).

Darkness has descended, we are reading a magazine from 1936, breathtaking. Suddenly keys rattle. Luigis stumbles inside. He looks pale, serious, happy. He speaks as he walks over to me:

'I don't know what has happened. They've been busy with me for hours on end. Hours and hours. They asked questions, I've talked. I've been acquitted.'

I ask him, 'What did they say? What did you say? Jan? Wim?'

Luigis, very pale now, says, 'I don't know who has said what. Kill me, I really don't know. Someone else spoke with my mouth.'

From my diary again.
6 January 1943

As if stung by an electric shock I jumped up: our signature whistle! You whistled, outside! I leaped up, my cellmates got the fright of their lives. I threw open the ventilation shutters, which enabled me to see outside, though only a bit of white snow, but also the legs of a large black dog. I could not see you. I too whistled our signature tune, you shouted, 'Hello, darling.' I heard your beloved voice very, very clearly, it penetrated right through to my heart. I called out: 'Have a good journey!' and then 'See you soon!' I did not really have time to think what to say. Therefore I whistled once more and you whistled in return. All this in complete silence and to the utter surprise of my cellmates, to whom I said: 'Well, so now you've heard my wife'.

The warders here are exceptionally decent and allow almost anything. The other day one of them jokingly remarked: 'Tomorrow you'll want the key as well'.

I quote the following passages after much hesitation. They were written while under the influence of our executed cellmates and accurately reflect our feelings at the time. Later on during our imprisonment we came to feel differently, much later completely so, but honesty demands publication of the actual contemporary text.

What I'm now about to write may sound defeatist, perhaps even dishonourable and extremist - 'red' - but I will say it nevertheless because it is my true opinion and I consider it to be the truth.

What do I care about my country, our national honour, when my freedom, the happiness of wife and children are at stake? What do I care about 'liberty' when my head is at stake? Where does this leave our artificial hatred of each and every German when a German delivers me a parcel from you, with a smile? When a German gives me a salute? When a German, almost crying, shouts at me, 'I too am homesick!' And what do I care about our so-called ally, England, with all its incitement and zealotry from the safety of its shelter, when here I observe the consequences: the mortal fear of those sentenced to death as 'saboteurs', 'spies', etc. Fellows who have hardly committed any crime', and the untold misery of those left behind? All this is nonsense. In life the real issues are much more profound. Keep your commonsense; bravely face the truth, do not be proud.

1 Corinthians 13, verses 4-8:
'Love is patient and kind;
 Love is not jealous or boastful;
it is not arrogant or rude;
Love does not insist on its own way;

it is not irritable or resentful;
It does not rejoice at wrong,
but rejoices in the right.
Love bears all things,
believes all things,
hopes all things,
endures all things.'

I see the world outside from inside my prison. But because the outside world is normal and imprisonment abnormal, I see it as something strange, and I see myself as even stranger. After all, after nine months, imprisonment has become normality. I am now going to withdraw. I detach myself and at times creep into my wife's mind, then into my mother's, also into my senior partner's, or my clubmates'. That way I see myself from various points of view and as a result I obtain a better picture of my normal self. It is a bit like playing chess.

I have been summoned by the *Hauptmann*, our governor, for a business discussion: proxy, salary, rent. He says, 'After all, we're in this world to help each other.'

I suggested to one of my cellmates that he ask his family to send him some text books. This was allowed.

He replied, 'No, because books are heavy and parcels should not weigh more than one kilogram, and there wouldn't be any food.'

Ninety percent of their thought processes centre on food. I am being threatened by proletarianization.

A new parcel from you has just arrived. I have been provided for in abundance. It is sufficient to know that abundance is there for the taking whenever I want. This shows that we prefer possessing things to actually enjoying them. Man is like that. Particularly the rich man, I believe, who often behaves like a Scrooge. He knows: I have, and when I want I can enjoy it. But he does not enjoy it. Enjoyment is a great art.

Matthew 6: 27-34

And which of you by being anxious can add one cubit to his span of life? And why are you anxious about clothing? Consider the lilies of the field, how they grow; they neither toil nor spin; yet I tell you even Solomon in all his glory was not arrayed like one of these. But if God so clothes the grass of the field, which today is alive and tomorrow is thrown into the oven, will He not much more clothe you, O men of little faith? Therefore do not be anxious, saying 'What shall we eat?' or 'What shall we drink?' or 'What shall we wear?' For the Gentiles seek all these things; and your heavenly Father knows that you need them all. But seek first His kingdom and His righteousness, and all things shall be yours as well. Therefore do not be anxious about tomorrow, for tomorrow will be anxious for itself. Let the day's own trouble be sufficient for the day.

COMPASSION

Being imprisoned can scarcely be defined. An invisible girdle encircles you, a kind of astral body. Others are reluctant to touch you; you yourself hesitate as well; you are hermetically separated from non-prisoners. Your freedom of movement is tightly restricted (even to zero in a *stehbunker* = standing-up bunker). Your every move is directed, centimetre by centimetre. Whether you are told to walk or stand still, it is all dictated. Life is being organized for you, there is nothing you can bring up against it. You have become a kind of adult baby. Someone who has lost his liberty can be compared to someone castrated. Very fundamental faculties have been taken away. However, 'He has sent Me to proclaim release to the captives.' I experienced this particularly in the Utrecht prison. The Spirit cannot be castrated (although, occasionally...). When the cell door has been slammed shut behind you and bolted, the Spirit does not oppress you anymore. God permitted the German to lock you up. One more step: God locked you up. This had a purpose. And it could be fathomed. Once you grasp its purpose, suffering becomes a blessing. One can suffer and be very happy: when one suffers with Christ.

SHE TOO

Rattling of keys. The door bursts open. The soldier known as stovepipe stands in the opening, behind him the *Kalfaktor* (prisoner-assistant) who usually brings parcels from home. 'Gentlemen! Parcels!' Names are called, everyone rushes to grab them, the treasures from home are handed out. For me ... nothing, even though it really is my turn too. Three days later this is repeated. Again nothing for me. Now what? This cannot be true, it is absolutely out of the question that she has forgotten me. Is she ill? Is something wrong?

The next day: 'Bakels! A parcel!'

It looks different. The label is different. I recognize the handwriting of my brother. The parcel is smaller. The contents are exquisite but impersonal - different from the usual. Is she ill? But in that case she could have written the address, could she not? Unless she is seriously ill!

95

A week later I get my answer when the letters for cell T arrive. A letter from her for me: sender A.M. Bakels-Gunning, Zelle 324, Deutsches Polizeigefängnis Scheveningen.

[Not until after liberation in 1945 did I hear the full story. On 16 March 1943 'German gentlemen', acting on a tip-off, appeared at our Pijnacker home where they found only our maid Nita. She gave the Sipo-men the address in The Hague where my wife was staying. After their departure she at once rang my wife, who was then sheltering a resister eagerly hunted by the Sipo. Within five minutes the resister had been moved to a safer place. Within twenty minutes the Sipo arrived at the house of my wife - who lay in bed with a serious inflammation of the ear - and took her to Scheveningen, where she remained in *strenge Einzelhaft* (solitary confinement) for three months, suffering from lice, eczema, hair loss and a throat infection. She had many contacts in the Resistance, some of whom were executed while others who also played influential roles, survived. However, the Sipo only knew about the resister who had been hiding with her. My wife was treated 'properly', i.e. not molested. *Einzelhaft* incidentally meant: no cellmate, no books, no letters, no exercise, no parcels, nothing. In mid-June she was suddenly released. Outside the prison gates, totally confused, ill and dizzy, she was spotted by a greengrocer who offered her a cigarette and then took her on his horse-drawn cart to the home of my parents in The Hague. Hiding a resister and the many other resistance activities could easily have cost her her life. Fortunately it only cost her three months. I, however, suspected of much lesser offences, served three years. The resister escaped altogether and Nita served six weeks.]

A COMMUNITY

The Utrecht diary contains 1,600 pages of lavatory paper - more than half the total. Lack of space in this book and lack of interest for the general reader have forced me to be selective. The following extract is, however, fairly extensive because it covers passages from the last weeks in Utrecht before the horror of the concentration camps and because they provide an insight into a special kind of community.

29 May 1943. I'm lying in the sick ward. I boast a fine fiery red tree on my hand and lower arm with all sorts of branches: blood poisoning. I might as well confess: I thank God that I am here. There are five of us. I'm being looked after. My carefully bandaged arm is hung up in a sling. A very full bowl of cold porridge. Eating creates warmth, as a result my finger and hand ache more and more. The windows - of frosted glass - are very big and not blacked out, fresh

air comes in through small open window-lights at the top, a well-furnished ward, 6 x 8 meters (20 x 27 feet), a cat, a rose in a vase, a made-up bed. Two Germans and one Dutchman are nursing me in a brotherly way. My cellmates were miserable because of my departure. It is said that pain disappears when praying. This is not quite true. The pain does not go away but God lifts you beyond the pain so that you almost don't feel it, mentally. And when you feel it, you bear it patiently, remembering Christ's wounds.

Everyone smokes during the day although it is prohibited. One of my neighbours is partially paralysed; he has been confined to bed for eight years. He went to his trial on a bed, he was sentenced to death on a bed. Inspite of this he is cheerful. His son, brother-in-law and mother are also in prison.

30 May. Returning to my bed after washing I found a big bowl of stew. Sated, one changes one's entire thought processes and one's world of feelings. No wonder that those who have to toil all day for their daily bread have no room in their minds for any art or anything beautiful. My finger is improving.

31 May. Once again I was dying a bit. Thick fog - hiding the future - makes sad. Man wants and has to make plans, but when there is only fog how can this be done? That is why my thoughts like birds fly back to their nest. To everything that is beloved and past. Anyone who 'has his feet firmly on the ground' is outside reality. He is tied to what passes away. Here we are exiles. We are only here for a short while. Anyone who dreams, creates works of art, has a spiritual dimension and feels himself a stranger on earth, far removed from his native soil, he belongs to reality. The sergeants tell us that the effect of the bombing raids is terrible. But how does one win a war? On the battlefield, by defeating armies: Not by bombing cities. Look at London. I am opposed to this. One of the prisoners here is a woman with a baby of two months. Her husband has been executed, but she does not know. Another woman here is pregnant, but she does not get any extra food. I have seen epileptic, paralysed, mad, stunted prisoners. I know of a family whose husband has been executed and the wife and children killed by English bombs. They stop at nothing. I saw a Jew who had been mauled by a dog, pieces of flesh torn out. Abcesses. When they started smelling too much he was put in a shed, alone. There he was doomed. Another Jew is being beaten up and half-dead. He then gets a rope and is ordered to hang himself. Which he actually does. Five in one evening. Another had his arm knocked

off with a spade. Another one: an eye knocked out. A Jew is kicked until almost dead, loaded on a wheelbarrow, and tipped into a ditch. Head kicked under water, after which they threw sand on top. Never forget: this is the truth. We have seen it ourselves. The world must be told. Half of the German people are insane.

1 June. Am reading the Bible at the crack of dawn. You don't know what hits you. I washed, my fellow prisoners felt I was too thin and I don't like getting remarks about my body. All those who don't want war anymore should fight against greed. How? By putting more women in government. Why? Because greed is less deeply rooted in a woman than in a man. I'm now bursting with food, there are some ten fellows who seem to take pleasure in fattening me up. The sexual drive immediately starts to flow again through all thoughts and feelings as if through delicate veins. A little while ago I saw . . . a woman, behind a frosted window in the corridor. I could watch her when she passed the door which is always open. She looked young and wore a yellow sweater. I think she smiled at me.

Cell D has received smokers' requisites. That implies that inmates will be executed early tomorrow morning. A woman whose husband is waiting for his pardon arrives with a parcel. As she reaches the gate her husband is headed for the car that will take him to the place of execution. Yelling, the woman grabs hold of the car and has to be pulled away.

There is a cell with six prisoners, among them one sentenced to death. He gets the message that he will be killed the next morning. That night no one sleeps, all are praying. Except the one who is sentenced to death: he sleeps like a log. When later I come to give testimony for Jesus, I will meet one formidable enemy: mockery. Mockery is a terrible weapon which only one weapon will be a match for: mockery.

2 June. Today at 3pm my fifth meal: two deluxe rolls with plaice fillet and sole as well as a chunk of rye bread with butter and sugar, homemade shortcake, pink candy and nuts; meat soup from the Wehrmacht, bread and cheese and a fried egg with ham, followed by . . . strawberries and custard pudding. The five of us laughed like mad. Five prisoners, among them three sentenced to death, doubled up with laughter because we imagined meeting each other in the future, should this be granted, when together we will repair to a corner of the room to squat down and shit, just as we are doing here.

'Even a doctor of law,' cries one of them and he laughs so much that he wets himself. Heroes they are, real heroes.

3 June. Outside, behind the prison, a train full of prisoners-of-war passes by, they scream and shout, that happens every time they pass by this building. I read three newspapers, which are strictly prohibited. Crazy articles by Goebbels about the Jewish-pluto-demo-liberal-Anglo-American-bolshevik war-waging. Most Germans are simply bonkers. They take it seriously! What is the street for? Marching! A prisoner sits on a thunderbox. Having finished he wants to wipe his bottom with a newspaper. Before wiping he scans the paper. He reads an announcement of his mother's death. He had no idea about her demise. Why should one only prepare for death when one receives the death sentence? All of us should live in such a way that we are ready to die at any moment. Doesn't that possibility always exist? The wife of one cellmate sends her husband ever more glorious parcels since she knows of his death sentence. As I have eaten enough during five days, everything has become more normal, less profound, less fearful, less perplexing. More superficial. I am becoming complacent, it won't come to much, don't make a fool of yourself, behave naturally. Has therefore my entire religious evolution been induced in my brain by hunger, spiritualized by starvation? I am waking up. I have had visions and will hold on to what I saw. When it was night, I saw stars. Now it is daytime, I don't see the stars but I know they are there.

4 June. I look upon God too much as our Father. He is also the Father of Hitler, Himmler and Goebbels. We are brothers! It is quite possible that God puts swine in our path in order to make new men out of them with God's word. You've got to pray for people you don't like. Saul turned into Paul, and St Paul became Christ's great apostle. The same could happen to Himmler.

One of my fellow patients, 29 years old, was caught a year ago by the Gestapo for very serious political activities. Seven interrogators, one after another, questioned him continuously for thirty-six hours. He is put on a chair, head down, one man keeps this head between his legs, two others hold on to his legs, a fourth flogs him until he loses consciousness. When he comes to, more interrogation. Next more flogging. Four times he is knocked unconscious. He pleads, 'Kill me.' Answer: 'That's what you want, isn't it?' All this for one long week, sometimes with a pause of an hour and a half. Serious injuries, a lot of blood, kidneys damaged, blood in urine. This is followed by several months in Amersfoort, again maltreated (dogs!). After that this prison, for trial. Sentenced to death. Arrives with his thirty wounds in this hospital ward, lies next to me. He is cheerful. He is a pious Roman Catholic. I go downstairs with him for a bath, have to support him, he can't walk. We come across sergeants, most of them feel embarrassed, they all know that he is an invalid as a result of the bestial behaviour of their compatriots. If I were German I would feel ashamed all my life.

5 June. The medical orderly, a prisoner, is prepared for release. My fellow-patients tell me: try and take his place. I write a petition to the *Hauptmann*. A quarter of an hour later he arrives, followed by three other Germans. 'Do you want to be Sanitäter, Herr Bakels?' 'Yes, please.' 'Alright then.'

Sanitäter, that is the choicest job one can get here! I now look after the patients, in this ward, in the cells. I nurse them, do the washing-up, have four assistant cleaners, wear a prison uniform with a red cross on the chest, can freely walk around in the building, am allowed to exercise twice daily, to smoke as much as I like, and eat as much as I like. As regards the nursing: I simply told them with a straight face that I could do it. I am smothered with bottles, pots, bandages, have studied everything. It'll be alright. Have cleaned everything here and cleared up. Am now sitting in a large armchair at a table with a tablecloth. Am smoking a pipe. Read the forbidden newspaper. For the first time since November I can see a landscape. Below us is the sewing room, it doesn't have frosted glass. I can see everything! Houses, trees, meadows, a railway track, a windmill, the river where some men are fishing from a little boat. I feel reborn. My perspective has suddenly widened to such an extent that it engulfs me. Dear brother, don't send me any more parcels, send everything to her, in Scheveningen. But give me some medical advice, list some medicines and what they can be used for.

7 June. I spend my free hours in the library. Have become high and mighty (a VIP). I found the complete Racine. This afternoon one of the boys sentenced to death will be married here in our prison. It will be followed by a meal for thirteen members of the family in the boardroom. I don't know whether the newly married couple are allowed to be together tonight, reflect on the possibility, however. I am allowed to have a bath every day. I am a free man but not allowed to meet my family nor leave the building. I often have to summon up my courage.

8 June. Have just heard she may be allowed home next week. God be praised and thanked. I can't do anything. I leave everything to you. Don't let her immediately start toiling for me! My medical orderly - very polite, you go first, no, thank you, after you - is a German hairdresser, I am a Dutch lawyer, together we care for the sick. I am subordinate to my hairdresser. I, who belong here, have to do what he, who doesn't belong here, tells me to. He is aware of the lunacy of this situation. I feel more or less like a Russian grand duke transformed into a valet in Paris.

9 June. The gentlemen in England keep on calling: 'Sabotage! Sabotage!' Sabotage yourself. What can one achieve with a small revolver, a little fire, a tiny organization, against the German Wehrmacht? Mortal fear, torture, concentration camp, death sentence, crushed wife, desperate children. They then call me a defeatist who is allowing himself be cheated. But I can beat them on points in any debate. You've simply got to want to see the truth and boldly tell the truth. All of us are accustomed to the lie. The whole day we are lying without batting an eyelid. My medical orderly superior tells me, 'In Germany there are no people without arms or legs anymore. They get an injection.'

The Allies are rumoured to have landed in Italy. Made a tour of the building. There was a plain, common woman of about 35 in a pink dress with bare legs (a warder), but I couldn't trust my eyes, kept gawping at her. Went to exercise alone, with the cat on my shoulder.

10 June. I read out the pastoral letter of 12 May from the Dutch bishops. What brave fellows! On my round past the cells I noticed an ex-SS man, a malingerer who lay crying and reeling off a lot of nonsense. I can identify malingerers unfailingly. The Germans here are decent chaps, you can talk with them, provided it is not about the war. Then they suddenly become completely mad and mendacious. Their eyes glaze, their mouths twist and they echo Goebbels' nasty lessons *ad nauseam*. What ghastly disenchantment awaits these chaps!

11 June. When you enter a communal cell, inhabited by six, seven, even eight men, you're astonished by the strange behaviour, nervous giggling, crowding around you, pulling your sleeve, whispering, 'Any news? Could you use me? Do you get more food?' I've been a bit like that too. Hunger and the cruelly restricted horizons make everything into an occasion. The bars before the windows don't harm me. Wherever the spirit of the Lord is, freedom can be found.

When I get 'outside' there will be bars too. But eventually nothing will separate us from the heavenly beauty, a glimmer of which we see at times.

13 June. Whitsun. And what a Whitsun! God be praised. Let me try to behave normally. My love, my own darling: you are free! Cousin Jan, I arrive at 7.50am in his kitchen, he stands there, I collect milk for the patients, he shakes my hand, radiant, and says, 'Congratulations!' I don't understand. He: she is free, yesterday morning; yesterday afternoon he received the agreed telegram. I'm doing my Whitsun morning round. Have just been handed a new patient: captain of the Dutch army, in full uniform. He cut his own pulse-artery while trying to escape, I have just taken out the stitches. Cousin Jan, busily filling teeth in the kitchen, has taken our photographs. In this prison everything is possible. But when will the time come when one gets answers to one's questions?

14 June. I have carried your portrait in my hand and looked at it all the time. 'Heroine,' I thought, 'heroine'. You have been persecuted for righteousness' sake. I am proud of you, as proud as a peacock. One thing patients - but almost all healthy people as well - love is to be able to tell something to someone who listens. Few people listen. It is already a bonus when they don't interrupt you and start talking about their own affairs. Cousin Jan told me that 4,000 planes flew for forty-eight hours above Germany. He had also read an advertisement offering 1,000 guilders for whoever found a stolen bicycle. Imagine! A used bicycle is therefore worth 1,000 guilders now (it used to be less than 100).

15 June. There are prisoners here who make ladies underwear for the sergeants, in secret: in exchange they get bread and beer. If they refuse they are returned to their cell. I ejaculated. It was not nice. I am longing for you. Will I be deported this Saturday? Will I be allowed home for a change? I have been looking out of the window downstairs. It does not look like reality to me. More like a painting, a photograph. I cannot imagine myself walking out there - not in any way.

16 June. In the same way that our house in Rotterdam shook on 14 May 1940, so I shook when I received your first letter after your release, dated 14 June. Those vile bastards. You write: 'It was really very bad.' I can't do anything, I'm not with you, I can't see you, can't rock you in my arms, press you against my breast, stroke away all the terrible memories from out of your head. . . . I'm changing my

opinion. Perhaps they are after all God's enemies, perhaps we do have to rejoice when thousands of tonnes of bombs rain down day and night on this people who bring such endless misery and horror on the world, time and again.

17 June. A *Kalfaktor* shouts, 'Bakels! Dirty washing!' Downstairs a sergeant asks, 'Are you Herr Bakels? Where's your wife?'

'In Scheveningen prison.'

'No, she's here.'

Besides simulated joy - I'd known, of course, for four days - there was violent emotion: because you did come yourself after all. After only five days you've come. Was summoned by the *Hauptmann*, 'Herr Bakels, your wife has been here with a little parcel, she was released the Saturday before Whitsun, I congratulate you!' His name is Wöllhardt; I shall never forget Wöllhardt.

18 June. I was deeply emotional. I went to the library and read Matthew chapters 5 to 14 in one session, the Sermon on the Mount etc. One of my patients has serious wounds on his genitals (as a result of kicks in Amersfoort), it is strange to have to bandage them, but one can get accustomed to anything. The cook here is in reality captain of a tug, the assistant-cook a builder, the 'dentist' (Cousin Jan) a butcher, the tailor a gardener and the *Sanitäter* (me) a lawyer. I'm not stirring up my case any more with the military court or the Sipo, for it won't help, they will hold on to me until the end. I don't tell anyone how well off I am here, *Abgetrennten* aren't allowed jobs! The Germans here say that 10 million German civilians have been killed in bombing raids. There are rumours that all death sentences have been shelved as a result of the situation. Twice I have been barked at, undeservedly, by Germans. I fumed. Some are quite decent but they remain strange fellows, you've got to be damned careful. They are all really unreliable, and ungodly and immoral as well. Let us resist being honoured for 'having suffered for our country' when we get out. Help me not to be tempted and accept such honours. I have done too little for my country.

19 June. In the door of the women's section a young girl suddenly appeared, with a blue sweater, sailing trousers and blond curls. She moved her head and the curls danced about. I was deeply moved, I nearly choked. I've been so completely estranged from everything female. Patients are difficult people; what you clean and clear up is

dirty and untidy again within an hour. I feel I'll never be a lawyer again.

20 June. On one leg alone, his right one, a new patient has got fifteen large wounds, kicked and beaten by an infamous murderer. I shaved the entire leg before cleaning it with ether. I put on an emergency dressing of ichthyol and notyol as I haven't got anything else. I'll leave it on for four days. It took one and a half hours. Afterwards we were both exhausted. 'You are a born nurse,' he said. I'm now allowed to be alone in the sewing room to boil my instruments. I fill up the disinfectant kettle to the brim in order to make it take longer to boil, enabling me to sit down and look outside. They are canoeing on the river, a record player offers real American jazz. In the past I was all for it, now dead against. Jazz music is out of place on the Dutch waterways, especially on a Sunday, and in wartime, and certainly in front of a prison full of people sentenced to death. The patients want me to read from the Bible. Sicily is supposed to have been conquered.

21 June. Speech by Goebbels about the bestial British *Luftterror*. Warsaw! Rotterdam! Coventry! Belgrade! A German naval officer passed by, tall, handsome, young, arrogant. Let these fellows enjoy their power now, they will soon sing a different tune. In the cells prisoners are still very hungry, now and again I deliver some extra saucepans. I put on a Prisnitz water dressing.

22 June. Here there are still Germans who believe they will win. I feel very sorrowful. The most important cause is that I'm writing almost nothing. I'm pretty well stocked with material but it won't come out. No time, and when there is time, tiredness prevents it. I need courage too in order to write down some of my opinions, for sometimes these are diametrically opposed to the usual ones of people in our situation. Some of them have no experience of what people are really worth when in distress.

24 June. It turns out not to be true that executions have been shelved. This morning all doors of all cells were locked, everyone inside, no exercise. By chance I stood downstairs (prohibited) and could see everything. The *Hauptmann*, followed by two airforce officers decked in silver and gold, entered cell U. They carried dossiers. No one was supposed to see this. At this moment German clerics are in two cells. There's dead silence. Some of the sergeants could not hide their emotion either. The effect on my patients is devastating. Father, forgive them for they know not what they do. Father, please deliver

this insane, misled, wretched people from their satanic delusions. Deliver all of us from evil. The war has already lasted four years! Millions are dead, millions more will die. In one night, in Krefeld, 120,000. At night the star-spangled sky is full of the roar of these murderous weapons on their way to wreak destruction. We know we deserve this. We fail to do what You in Your infinite love have told us to do. We are Your enemies, our Father, who nevertheless overwhelms us with benefactions. Your Fatherly hand is always stretched out to us - we continue to push it away. Now we get what we deserve. Now we know where we end up without You. Now the gigantic monster holds us in its claws, it squeezes us like a lemon, blood spurts from all sides, and tears, tears. Be merciful, O God. Give us another chance, give us Peace.

25 June. As many as three German 'doctors' arrived, each one even crazier than the last; they brought me two more patients: one with an inflammation of the bladder, the other with angina pectoris. It has become madly busy. At 4pm suddenly there is commotion: tomorrow at 3pm a large transport will leave with all the chaps from my Lion Guard case except three. I am one of the three! When they called the names I thought, Floris, now it's your turn. I despatched my *Sanitäter*-soldier to find out. He returned with a happy face: 'You'll just stay with me, Herr Bakels.' Some have suggested that we three may perhaps be released! I don't believe it but anything is possible.

26 June. The boy with angina pectoris has been transferred to the University Hospital. I helped him put on his shabby rags. He had an accordion with him. I weigh 73 kg (11 stone 7 lbs), as against early November 1942 when I weighed 55 kg (8 stone 9 lbs). The transport has left for Amersfoort where they will be distributed to other places. If anything is unpredictable it is the Gestapo. I have learnt that it isn't at all sufficient to toil for your fellowmen. The point is that you've got to do it in such a way that they don't notice your efforts, how tired you get, how much energy you spend. If you don't do it this way you put a burden on them, and they won't dare ask anymore from you. If you're really at the end of your power you must disappear from their sight.

28 June. Now I'm ill myself and in bed with a fever. The medical orderly proposed not to mention it to the *Hauptmann* because I would risk losing my job and being replaced. The forty-year-old medical orderly is called Ittermann, his health is weak; while

walking with his nail-studded soles on the stone floor he fell down with a bang, cried out from pain, his cap had fallen off. So heartbreaking that I had to cry.

29 June. Prince Bernhard's birthday. This morning temperature down to normal. I opened the Bible at St John, 8: 11: 'Go, and do not sin again'. It couldn't be clearer. I got up and started work. The curse of this century is overloading. There are too many possibilities, everything is big, strident, too much of everything, also anger. Museums should be prohibited: there is far, far too much. It isn't possible in one morning to enjoy fully even two sculptures by Rodin. One sculpture alone, like *Le Baiser* (The Kiss), holds enough joy for hours. We wrong artists abominably.

1 July. Another German doctor turned up, a heavy man of forty, with a tanned face full of duelling scars, steel blue eyes, a uniform loaded with gold and decorations. In his wake a boy of about seventeen in white naval uniform, a handsome boy with dark, curly hair, an impudent face and with all sorts of glittering weapons, watches and instruments. Both correct, military, pugnacious, dominant. The doctor acted decently. He diagnosed pneumonia in one, inflammation of the bladder in the other. As my vitality and physical strength grow so does my susceptibility to humiliation and my capacity for hatred. These guys, strong and handsome, sleep with women, make war, are armed and unassailable. One patient, stripped and emaciated, is examined. Another, a perfect example of misery, deathly pale, sentenced to death. Another, helpless, paralysed, sentenced to death. A fourth, covered in foul wounds. All of them first-rate Dutchmen who belong in this country. Contrast them with these two beasts, in radiant health, vigorous. I was boiling with rage. Those who have never experienced an occupation can't understand this. That young chap, I could have crushed him. Enemies, enemies! Occupation! Humiliation! What business is it of theirs to be here? Death! And I am as stupid, slow of learning and unChristian as all the others. I now realize more than ever that our government in England cannot return in its present composition. It cannot be alive to the significance of the occupation. Therefore it will not be able to understand us. Here we need fellows who have gone through everything that happened. There is a wide chasm between us and the allied peoples and governments who are fighting. They don't know what it is like. This is clear from the senseless and irresponsible incitement of Radio Orange (broadcasting from London). Let me

ask forgiveness of God for my nasty, reckless words. We discussed the bombing of cities with one of the sergeants. They are nonplussed to be experiencing something of the war even in their own country.

2 July. Several patients have given me instructions intended for their wives and children in case they are suddenly carried off. For hours at a stretch I'm administering pills, emptying urine-bottles and bedpans, giving injections and enemas, helping with washing, distributing meals, applying bandages, cleaning wounds, taking temperatures. I'm learning a lot about medical matters. Again two new doctors. Why don't I get any more letters from you? Cousin Jan thinks that you've become very careful after being in prison: you are afraid.

3 July. I'm damned if I'll continue to wear the very dirty brown jacket with the red cross. The *Sanitäter*-soldier now salutes neatly when he sees me and says 'Guten Tag, Herr Bakels' every day! Rumour has it that 3,000 doctors have been carried off to Amersfoort because they refused to assist in the sterilization of Jews. On my table I now have a heavy, glittering percussion hammer. As we are about to eat, five pairs of eyes from the surrounding beds look at me full of expectation. I then lift the hammer, strike a blow on the table and command *'Oremus'* (Let us pray). Oddly surprising.

4 July. St Luke 8:39: 'Return to your home, and declare how much God has done for you.' God lets me read this again and again 'by accident'. A prisoner came to see me who said that his wife doesn't love him any more and wants to start divorce proceedings. However, he loves her and believes he can bring about a reconciliation in a private conversation. I therefore wrote a request on his behalf to the governor. Great debate about religious affairs. What I warned myself about is threatening to happen as predicted. God is good for us and we grab hold of Him when in distress, but we let go of Him when prosperity beckons. We predicted that when peace has broken out and we return to normal this distancing from God will accelerate. We agreed on two ways to avoid this cooling off and weakening: (1) by constantly immersing oneself in the terrible things we have witnessed, remembering that the sacrifices should not have been in vain, and (2) by regularly retreating into solitude. Pascal said that two things prevent man from coming to God: his pride, and his lust. I don't quite agree with the latter. In theory only monasticism is right, but what about marriage and children?

6 July. I, I, I, all the time I again, who am I, really? What does it matter whether I am sad? As long as you are reasonably comfortable, my darling. Who knows where you are! I don't know, I know nothing, absolutely nothing. I'm only asking questions, questions, questions and never receive answers any more. Write! Please write! Has something terrible happened again? The war is now waged on a gigantic scale. We can't take it in any more. What agreement will the USA and the USSR reach? Germany is fighting *for England* against Russia? Where will there be revolutions? When will Germany start gas-warfare against England? Will the French people go to rack and ruin? Will America return the Dutch East Indies to us?

Stop! I am being informed that tomorrow morning at 8am I shall be transported. I've got to digest this. I already had a premonition. I've got to reflect.

I've been busy packing and taking my leave. Where are we going? Possibilities: Amersfoort and Vught (another concentration camp in Holland). It is said that these camps have been greatly improved lately. Or Scheveningen. Perhaps there are now others in Holland. Alternatively: a prison, a concentration camp, a factory in Germany. Should we now have doubts about God's grace and protection? As something is happening again, after eight months, God took hold of me again, and firmly by the hand. For I am, of course, deeply moved. He tells me, 'You're now ready here. We're now going somewhere else where it'll be better than here. Trust Me, I am your shepherd, you shall want for nothing.' All my possessions were returned to me, including a bunch of keys. When will I be allowed to use all these keys again? There they are: our front door, two garage-doors, wardrobe, linen cupboard, money box, office front door, office bicycle shed, office vault. Oh keys! My God, it's getting too much for me. It's now really all over here. Your portrait stands on top of the open suitcase in the full glare of the evening sun. It talks. How proud I am of you, how happy with you! We've had a farewell meal: eel, mackerel, peanut butter, butter, berries, prunes, and a food parcel and shag tobacco for the journey. They are very sad I'm leaving and are more deeply moved than I am. Will I ever see them again?

[Only one returned after the war.]

We have put up the blackout, both lamps are turned on, I'm sitting at the table smoking. May God now give me the strength to write my most beautiful words to you. Tomorrow I'll be travelling to an unknown destination. Perhaps to the centre of government in The

Hague in order to be released after a brief hearing. But perhaps to a German concentration camp or munitions factory. This looks bad and dangerous, but all remains essentially the same. How marvellous God has been with us, all this time! Re-reading everything I've written, I stand by it. God gives us all the strength we need, that has been proved. He knows better than we do what is right for us. Our day will come, not a second too early nor a second too late. Support all those in need, be a Christian. Be good. Never be afraid. I will survive. God has promised it, really. When you are in trouble, pray and read the Bible. That will always - always - give deliverance. Don't weaken in your faith, hold on firmly. Don't let anyone confuse you, whatever happens: God's guidance and plan run right across everything, knocking away every obstacle: He can do anything! And let us now pray together: 'We thank You for all we have received in this prison. We don't know why we have deserved this. We humble ourselves before You and ask forgiveness. God, give Peace! Teach us. May lovely fruits grow from us. Be with each and everyone. Give faith to all, destroy the devil. Tomorrow I'm leaving. Travel with us. Give us confidence that nothing will happen to us without Your permission. May Your loving plan be fulfilled through us. Give us strength to pray wholeheartedly: Your will be done. I have a dear, great treasure. Preserve her, give her more faith, hope and love. Hold her hand, Father, I can't take care of her, only pray for her. I leave her to You. You have said that all we pray for in the name of Jesus, You will grant. We pray to You for Jesus' sake: re-unite us at the right time, chastened and magnified. Amen!

I'm taking you in my - once again - strong arms. I'm with you, always. Don't be afraid: the Almighty Himself is with us. He cares and keeps watch. We are safe now. One day our day will come. I love you.

Utrecht, 6 July 1943 Your husband, Floris

HANDCUFFED

On 7 July 1943, a little after my mates from the Lion Guard and more than half a year after the trial, I was carried off from Utrecht, together with a small elderly man who often laughed sadly. He and I were chained together with handcuffs, he on the left, me on the right. Our escort consisted of two loathsome Dutch policemen, called *Schalkhaarders*. These were Dutch policemen trained or re-trained in the 'German spirit' at a special training school, set up in an old barracks in Schalkhaar, in a word: Dutch Nazis. Although it was July, both of us were wearing winter coats and suits that had become ridiculously big for us, and a hat and a soiled shirt. We went to the station in a carriage. At the station and on the platform we created quite a stir. Of course we probably had a haggard look in our eyes after eight months in prison. There were revelations, albeit painful: the traffic, the people, the noise, houses, women, girls, towers, a station, the platforms, trains. Where were we going?

The two *Schalkhaarders* cleared one compartment, sat us down and took a seat on each side of us. We could not utter a word. My mate and I laughed to each other instead. The train moved off in the direction of Amersfoort and when it stopped there, we had to get out. It then became clear. We walked along the platform, the people made way for us.

Then I noticed him, one of my oldest friends stood there, one of my club-mates. I gave a sign of recognition, he recognized me, glowered at me, followed us with his gaze, fixed, shocked, while we walked on between the two traitors again on the way to the PDA.

Together with many others we were put up in a new brick barracks. We kept our clothes, did not get a number, did not work, did nothing. We were told we would be transported again shortly.

5. NATZWEILER CONCENTRATION CAMP 10 July 1943-2 September 1944

NACHT UND NEBEL

The transport of over eighty Dutchmen from Amersfoort, destination unknown, took place by D-train. A special carriage had been attached for our benefit. The escort of SS officers and *Grüne Polizei* was hardly irksome. The PDA-Commandant himself, Heinrich, accompanied us in person. We sat like ordinary passengers on seats. We were given food. It was 9 July 1943. Among our group was prisoner no. 1400 of the PDA who had already achieved some notoriety in Amersfoort. He was said to have been a member either of the Dutch SS or the Dutch Nazi Party, ending up in the KZ for some misdemeanour. During the journey he repeatedly got up, walked to other compartments, then returned. He behaved restlessly. After some time he came swaying along the carriage to us for a chat, holding on to the luggage rack and bending down.

'T've talked to the transport chief. We're on our way to a camp somewhere in the Vosges. You'll be working in stone quarries.'

'We? Not you?'

'It's a bad camp, an NN camp.'

'What's that?'

'NN stands for Nacht und Nebel (night and fog), your family won't be informed, no contact with home anymore. You're going to disappear without trace.'

'We are? What about you?'

'Not me. The transport chief told me I'll be the only Dutchman to survive the NN camp in the Vosges.'

Successive thoughts came to us: he's gone mad - NN camp sounds really bad - stone quarries - the Vosges are west of Strasburg, in France, temporarily German - disappear without trace - but not him - he's talked to the SS - something smells - we must be careful with him.

Agents provocateurs, traitors, *Spitzel* (informers), *Zinker* (secret agents) often penetrated prisons and KZ. It has even been established that SS, disguised as *Häftlinge*, entered camps to put their ears to the ground. They sacrificed their hair for it. Usually it was not difficult to identify these rascals: they were too stupid to tackle it shrewdly. By way of the 'Lagertelegraph', i.e. by word of mouth, everyone would be rapidly warned. It was generally considered not only morally acceptable but desirable to eliminate them. Which happened sometimes. It was incredibly stupid of no.1400 to lay himself open in this way. And his bad luck that he fell ill. In the sick-ward they knew how to deal with him. . . .

After a stationary night at the Mannheim railway yard our train went west on 10 July, and crossed the Rhine into the low mountains of the Vosges. The landscape was beautiful and reminded me of pre-war holiday journeys to Switzerland. Amicably, Heinrich pointed out rivers, farms, factories - 'ist alles jetzt Deutsch' (it's now all German). We passed small stations without stopping, the train gently swaying as it wound its way through a valley, past Schirmeck station. The train started braking. Rothau station. The train stopped.

On the platform we saw SS, rifles cocked; outside, a row of vans, neatly parked next to each other. Our escort got out, the transport chief talked loudly to an SS officer wearing a mountaineer's woolly hat instead of the usual peaked cap. Papers were handed over and checked. On the other side of the train where there was no platform more SS stood guard. As always the officer took an eternity to study the papers. Head bent he pored over them, then gloved hands pointed, mouth shouted, everyone jumped to attention, saluted. . . .

Then, suddenly, the German became a kraut again. We had to rush out of the train between a line of armed SS with dogs. 'Los, Mensch! Los, los! Schneller! Immer dalli dalli, los, los. . . .' We ran to the vans, at the double, punched, kicked. We were pushed into our van, crammed on top of each other until no one else could fit in except one SS man. The door closed, we could not see anything anymore. The van started, lurching forward with a jerk, throwing us on top of the SS man who cursed, shrieked and punched. Second, third, fourth, third, second gear. Clearly we went up steeply around hairpin bends. The driver drove aggressively, at every corner we were thrown all over the place. Our ears popped. Higher and higher. My pulse indicated too that we were rising several hundred meters. Nobody said anything, we held on tightly to each other. Second, third, fourth gear - reducing speed, changing down a gear again, wild barking of dogs in the distance, next loud voices nearer, then close by. The door opened. The SS man jumped out. A large number of SS with dogs on leads stood around our van and other vans which kept arriving. We were driven into Natzweiler, beaten, flogged, cursed, screeched at . . . like cattle to the slaughterhouse.

NUMBER 4381

The *Empfangzeremonie* (reception ceremony) was far worse than at Amersfoort a year before. I realized: this KZ is deadly. Undress naked, hand over everything except spectacles and dentures. Head hair, armpit hair, pubic hair, all gone, with ancient cut-throat razors and blunt clippers, which tore hairs out and inflicted wounds. Lysol is applied to them. Camp clothes: some sort of shirt or vest, some sort of underpants, a coat, trousers, rags for our feet, wooden sandals. Two red triangles stamped with an H (for Holland), two pieces of cloth with a number; mine was 4381. Triangles and numbers had to be sewn on by ourselves, on the left breast and the right trouser leg on the thigh. Our clothes were painted with red stripes, on the back a cross, with NN on each side as well as on the front of the thighs.

All these formalities, lasting hours, were accompanied by the usual shouting, punching, cudgel-beatings, kicking. Profoundly miserable, our scalps spottily close cropped, our shaved genitals smarting from lysol, underwear torn with holes, the coat too tight, too short, the trousers double width, far too short, without belt to hold them up; the rags wound round our feet as best we could, stumbling in the far too small, usually defective, sandals, barely able to recognise each other, we hurried to the roll-call sites where we were taught drill: 'Häftlinge - stand still! Hats - off! The eyes - left! Correct: eyes - front! Hats - on! Get a move on!'

Many of us already knew this ritual from Amersfoort, but here in Natzweiler it was much more brutal from the start. Woe to those who still had to learn German drill .... After hours of standing and exercising and *Hinlegen - auf!* (down-up) we were lined up for the mass evening roll-call.

Through *Das Tor* (the gate), far above us, we saw the outside work details march in: marionettes, fabulously in time, the hundreds of bald heads directed at the *Schutzhaftlagerführer*, little finger on the seam of the trousers, the arms swinging not against the movement of the legs but with them: 'Left, two-three-four, left, two-three-four' - endless columns, here and there bloody pates, dirty bandages, some with a fellow-*Häftling* on his back - a hideous phantom crowd from another world.

And the last column - the wasps. Men whose clothes were not painted red but yellow. Everywhere. From top to bottom horizontally with yellow circles. Not one of them was undamaged. Many walked with a limp. Bloodspots on the trousers, especially the thighs, the back, and on the sleeves. Blood on faces, on bald pates. Many carried on the backs of their comrades. They marched badly, tottering convulsively. We heard the cudgel's dull thud up there.

After the roll-call we received instructions from our *Blockälteste*, the Viennese communist Franz Gutmann. He told us how to act and not to act in order to have a chance of staying alive. He taught us the house-rules of the Block, getting up, washing, collecting food, 'Betten bauen', behaviour when the SS appeared, which commands were used, etc. At the end of all this we were allowed to ask questions. Someone began, 'Herr Blockälteste . . .' but got a friendly rebuke: 'You fool, have you gone mad, or what? My name is Franz, understood?'

'Well, Franz . . .' He asked about the *Häftlinge* who were painted like wasps. Silence descended. Franz then explained they were French maquisards, just arrived, mostly communists, from Marseilles and the surrounding district. He did not say any more. Shortly after we heard that all of them had to be *fertiggemacht* (done in) within six weeks. This was pretty successfully accomplished.

We were dog-tired and miserable when a man with hair on his head, impeccably dressed in an ordinary blue striped suit, appeared after our *Blockälteste*. His look was tense, he made an effort to appear friendly. He spoke Dutch!

'I am Wim Roessingh, one of three Dutchmen in Natzweiler until now. Welcome, all of you. Together we'll make the best of it. Keep your chin up. Don't be conspicuous. Being at the right place at the right time is of great importance. Observe all rules precisely. Anyone caught stealing will be disposed of at once. I'm planning to come along every evening to keep in touch. At the moment there's grave danger. You've seen the French, painted yellow. I work in the *Revier* (sick ward), I have contacts. As yet it isn't known how they will treat the Dutch. Let's hope it'll be like the Norwegians, not like the French. I'll try to find out. I'm going now. Keep your pecker up.'

To us Wim appeared like an angel of light, sent by God. The first human-anchorage in this hell. . . .

[Wim Roessingh was allowed to correspond with his family, who were also allowed to send him parcels and did so. For some of us, including me, he accomplished something that earned him our ever-lasting gratitude: he passed on to his family the names of his fellow sufferers in a sort of code or cryptogram in ways which eluded the, fortunately immensely stupid, censors. This meant inventing riddles for his family to solve - in this case Wim's mother. In the letters from Natzweiler he mentioned places, events, characters, from which it could be deduced which other Dutchmen were in Natzweiler and how to reach their families and report their presence. This involved quite a lot of research and detection work, almost always with positive results. Such work continued on a large scale throughout the war for prisoners in various prisons and concentration camps, with information circulating either encoded in officially sanctioned letters or in illegal letters without any code. The homefront was thus kept extremely busy. Parents, spouses, brothers, sisters and children spun webs of contacts all over Holland. My relationship with Wim continued after the war with an extraordinary and delightful result: on 5 May - liberation day - 1979 our only daughter married Wim's elder son. He and I - both survivors - now share two granddaughters and a grandson. How it is possible!]

Lying on our wooden beds, full of fear for the morrow, the light was suddenly switched on again. Voices, rumbling. In the distance stood Wim, clearly choked with emotion though smiling broadly. 'Tomorrow you'll all go to the stone quarry, with the Norwegians. Not like the French. Sleep well.'

Not like the French - not like the French - that is how we passed the message on from bed to bed. Meanwhile that evening it was clear to us in Block 10: we now found ourselves in a most perilous KZ. By comparison the PDA had been child's play. The next morning we marched out to the *Steinbruch* (stone quarry) with hundreds of others.

[The pieces of paper from my diary between 10 July and 8 November have been lost. From then on I gave them every week to a friend who had an opportunity to hide them. Just before our evacuation I hid them all in the rafters of Block 10.

In early June 1945, soon after the liberation, I wrote to the burgomaster of Natzweiler, asking him to send someone to Block 10 to retrieve my diary fragments and return them to me. A detailed plan was enclosed. Not long after I received a letter from a French military commander and judge in a military tribunal at Strasburg, stating that the papers had been found and would be sent by courier. Soon afterwards a French diplomatic courier did indeed kindly deliver the well-preserved parcel of papers to me in Amsterdam.]

THE WASPS

A special work detail has been set up for the maquisards (Gaullists as well as communists) who are painted like wasps. Every day they march out to the very steep muddy slope just outside the gate. This detail has the special attention of SS and *Kapos*. The SS keep trained police dogs on leads. The dogs whine softly, they yawn, their ears pricked up. The French get wheelbarrows. They have to fill them with stones in record time and then push them at the double up the muddy slope. Their tormentors stand alongside. The Frenchmen slip, they stumble. Wheelbarrows slip, tumble. Stones roll down the slope. On top of the Frenchmen following behind. There are collisions. The French curse, '*merde!*'. Cudgels rise and descend, rise and descend.

The SS let the leads of the dogs run out as soon as a Frenchman with his awful load runs up the slope. The dogs snarl and tear pieces of flesh out of the thighs and buttocks of those Frenchmen who are still walking. Some, slipping in the mud or felled by repeated beatings, topple down the slope. At the bottom is a barbed wire fence, behind it a watchtower with a machine gun at the top, an SS man behind it. The machine gun rattles briefly: another Frenchman 'auf der Flucht erschossen' (shot while attempting to escape), another special leave for the brave marksman.

The muddy path is now littered with red spots and pools which turn brown red. Anyone who becomes unconscious is thrown onto a small flat area of ground next to the slope, in the burning sun, in torrential rain. He does not work, therefore he will not eat later.

When the detail returns in the evening those left alive carry the dead and nearly dead on their shoulders. They too have to attend the roll-call, lying in long rows behind those standing, or reeling.

After roll-call the Frenchmen carry their comrades who are still alive on their shoulders down some granite steps to their barrack, separated and fenced with barbed wire. SS and *Kapos* take care that this is done quickly: regularly the condemned are kicked from behind down the steps. Visits to the *Revier* are prohibited, as is attending to wounds in the barracks. The large jagged wounds get infected almost immediately. Red bleeding slowly stops, yellow festering replaces it. The infection comes alive, maggots feed on it.

After the first few days some Frenchmen would deliberately throw themselves down the mountain and roll onto the barbed wire fence. Another extra ration and three days leave for the marksman.

On Sundays, Zeuss - what a name - an SS man of exceptional viciousness and a real killer, and Ehrmannstraut, nicknamed Fernandel, played havoc with the French maquisards on a platform in the camp. There was drill with *hinlegen - auf* while the cudgels hammered down on backs, loins and heads. Systematically skulls were cracked. That anyone survived this inferno must be deemed a miracle.

I found out later that under cover of darkness a group of *Revier* staff sneaked to the French barrack every evening to treat the worst off in the washing room with potassium permanganate and dermatol powder, among them Wim Roessingh. Wim pointed out to the SS doctor Rohde that an epidemic would otherwise break out in this barrack which could spread to the SS-Mannschaft. Later all sick and wounded were admitted to the *Revier* (some had already been hidden there) where most of them succumbed.

FERTIG

One could write a handbook on beating. The beating of human beings by other human beings. The facial features of the sadist. The sound of a cudgel touching flesh, or bone. The fantastic sounds made by the recipient. His movements. Perhaps there are incidents that should not be described? The arm and shoulder movements of the sadist who hits and keeps on hitting are horrible. The beating motion starts in the eyes and the forehead, almost visibly it travels from the brain, via the shoulder to the arm, mostly a very muscular arm, a sort of living tree-branch extended by the deadwood of the cudgel. At first the movements are still fairly personal, blow upon blow still to be seen as separate. But a little later it becomes a machine. The sadist becomes an overwound machine that cannot stop anymore.

The arm rises, the shoulder rises, the shoulder comes down, the arm whizzes down bringing with it the arm-extension: the piece of wood. Up, down, up, down, numerous times. The sound of wood on man changes into the smacking, wet sounds of wood penetrating inside man, into the flesh, into muscles, into organs. A little bit of red becomes a lot of red, overwhelming red, blood everywhere. The machine pushes on, and on, and on, does not know how to stop.

The yelling has died down long ago. The beating has become independent of purpose, an issue on its own. A systematic exercise for its own sake. The human element - one man murdering another - has been lost. The muscle-machine smashes flesh, makes mincemeat of it. It has become a butcher's tool. When the muscle-machine runs out of fuel it stops. Slowly it takes on human shape again. That of a murderer.

The Nazied call it *fertigmachen* (doing in).

117

ERNST JAGER

In Natzweiler the work details are formed after morning roll-call. The largest, the stone-quarry party of 1,000 men, assembles on the highest road, near *Das Tor* (the gate). They are divided into hundreds of *Häftlinge zu Fünfen* (five abreast), the red NN on their back. The SS stand at the gate, groups of ten with carbines and dogs on leads. The *Kapos* run alongside the rows, beating and kicking.

'Häftlinge - stand still! Forward - march!'

The columnn marches through the gate, passing the *Schutzhaftlagerführer.*

'The eyes - left!' ['The' before 'eyes' warned us that eyes had to be turned left; otherwise eyes had to be turned right.] Hundreds of bald heads jerk to the left as a salute to the ruler. The SS with carbines and dogs arrange themselves alongside the column which turns sharply left, up the road to the stone quarry: on the right high barren hills, on the left a wood and a ravine. Separate small groups of prisoners drag the large containers full of bread along.

The road climbs fairly steeply, it takes more than twenty minutes to reach the battlefield. Talking is now allowed, though not, of course, too conspicuously. Most are in too much pain and too afraid to talk. Some know this to be their last day on earth: they will be *fertiggemacht.*

Softly I say to my neighbour: 'Golgotha. But He was innocent, we are guilty, though not of anything against the Nazis. And He was almost alone, we are hundreds. And He climbed that day to His murder, we may well survive today. And if all of this is not true - He is climbing with us.'

Kapo Ernst Jager was a lot more dangerous than Kapo Jack Schreuder, imprisoned for vice offences with a pink triangle on the chest. Jager was a *Grüne* (a green triangle), a professional criminal. Jager's physique was that of a dockworker, which is what he seemed to have been. During the work in the stone quarry, in summer 1943, he wore only trousers. His boxer's body, obscenely tattooed, gleamed with sweat. Where we have eyes, small dark orbs like raisins shone from his bald muscular skull. When work on the granite, with pick-axes and spades and the tip-carts on the narrow gauge railway had started and the quarry was lined with guards, Jager sprang into action, the shaft of a broken spade in his blood-thirsty hand. The whole day Ernst Jager rushed alongside the hewing, jerking, shovelling, cart-loading *Häftlinge* to make sure they worked. Jager has *fertiggemacht* many in the quarry. But not Arie van Soest. And that is quite remarkable. Because Arie is the prisoner I know for certain who has physically assaulted one of our executioners. In addition to pick-axes, spades and tip-carts work in the stone quarry also requires big hammers. Provoked beyond endurance Arie lifted one of those hammers and attacked Jager. Then I heard a sickening blow of ash-wood on spinal column. Arie, I could see out of the corner of my eye, slumped forward on the small gauge railway line between the carts and Jager was exercising his gigantic force, wielding the spadeshaft energetically and rhythmically. Arie started shrieking. Arie shrieked across the rubble, the steel, the granite, the field, up the mountain, down the ravine, to heaven itself. Until Ernst chose to resume his walk, shouting: 'You'll work! You'll load the cart!'

Did Ernst forget on purpose or by accident to throw Arie's pummelled body on the tip-cart filled with granite and dump him with the stone into the abyss? For that is what he did occasionally. He probably did not have any formal instructions about Arie.

A week later it was almost my own last day in the quarry. That morning fog had come down, as often happened in Natzweiler. We should have assembled for the job but were marched instead to the halls and locked up. A voice in the fog shouted: 'Guards dismiss!' For hours we sat waiting in the halls. At noon our ration was distributed, two sodden slices of brown bread. I was sitting next to the empty bread chest. Behind it lay Ernst Jager, dozing, in his arms one of the little prominent Poles, 13 years old at a guess. The little Pole's hands were busy exploring between Ernst Jager's legs and he was kissed in return with nauseating smacks.

In the afternoon the fog lifted and we marched out again. I was then already broken down. I was assigned to a tip-cart. 'You'll load that cart, and quick!' Ernst had shouted. Like everyone else I had struggled as quickly as possible to the pile of tools to look for a small spade instead of the new large ones. With the others I loaded the cart with small pieces of granite. My back began to ache, my arms sagged, my knees trembled, pause a moment - the spade was then pulled out of my hands and I smelled sweat and perfume. The Jager monster stood next to me, the raisin-like eyes fixed on me.

'You'll come with me.'

From the pile he took a beautiful new shovel, a very large one. We went back. Then, quite softly, almost politely: 'And now I'll teach you what working means.'

The shovel fully loaded with the damned stones could barely be lifted. Some five times I succeeded. Then half of the stones fell beside the tip-cart. And at once, I was beaten ferociously on my loins. And again. And again. Jager, sweating profusely, finally retreated with ominous promises for the next day.

That next day I was in mortal fear. Walking uphill to the quarry these words echoed in my mind: 'Do not fear those who kill the body, but cannot kill the soul.' And I heard: 'Why do you have such fear? Do you not have faith?' I was afraid to be *fertiggemacht*. God was preparing me for the ordeal.

Ernst took me for a *Staatsanwalt* (public prosecutor), his arch enemy; he could not distinguish it from *Rechtsanwalt* (lawyer, solicitor). I set about work. I saw him leering from a distance. He had not forgotten me. And he slowly walked towards me. Jesus Christ approached with him. I thought: 'What can this man do to me? What can he undertake against God, his Creator? This is a child of man, like me, though alas possessed by the devil. This man is powerless when God does not give him power. I should not fear. I should pray for his deliverance.' I stopped work and waited. The 1,000 stone workers also put down their tools and looked on.

Jager came up to me and shouted something, probably: 'You'll load that cart, man!' I have never been able to remember what I then said to him. Perhaps something like this: it is not right that you treat me as an enemy. We are all in the same boat and must help each other. You can see that this work is now beyond my capabilities. You are not on this earth to beat me to death but to help me.

That started a discussion. Jager showed an almost bestial stupidity. He asked me, for instance, to explain the meaning of the word *Freund* (friend). What did it mean? After that - we shook hands. Ernst wiped his forehead and neck - it was very hot - and walked away. I have not had any trouble with him since.

If you consider this proof of superhuman bravery I must shatter such illusions. It is not false modesty when I tell it precisely as it happened: it is a clear example of the power God grants someone in need who believes in Him and asks Him for support. Angels had been standing around me.

BROTHELS

Our immediate ruler was the *Blockälteste*, a *Häftling* responsible for order, quiet, *Sauberkeit* (cleanliness), when assembling for roll-call, etc., in his barracks. The *Blockälteste* was a powerful man. He was often a German or Austrian communist, less often a professional criminal. In the barrack the *Blockälteste* had a sort of room of his own. There he received his *Stubenältesten*, *Stubendienste*, comrades and little friends, often young Polish boys. Several young Dutchmen were also invited to become 'little friends', although as far as I know none accepted. Those rooms looked like bordellos in the evenings after food distribution. There was whispering, also of course shrieking, petting, making love. Sometimes there were pink lampshades. Pictures graced the walls, there were cloths on the tables. Invariably there were jam jars and saucepans everywhere full of food 'left-overs', soup, porridge. And bread rations. Sometimes the smells of baking and roasting penetrated our barrack. They were snake pits.

Once in a while an SS man arrived to check. 'Achtung' (attention) was shouted. Everyone shot up at once, rushed from the beds, spirited iniquities away. Within two, three seconds all stood motionless and deadly quiet to attention. The *Blockälteste* reported *gehorsamst* (obediently) the number of his flock of slaves to his master. At that moment the *Blockälteste* was the model of the true slave. Well-fed, bald pate shining, jaws shaved, clothes impeccable, triangles and numbers clearly visible, shoes - yes, shoes - brushed, standing bolt upright to attention, the slave shouted his clipped answers into the face of his master. Thereupon, clearly content, the master magnanimously cried out, 'Weitermachen!' (carry on).

WEAVER

After my first *Revier* stretch (from 29 October to 3 November for a serious flu) I was granted another *Schonung* for an indefinite time. In the PDA this had meant peeling potatoes, in Natzweiler it was weaving. I, as a *Weber* in the *Weberei*, became a worthy heir to the tradition of my Twente textile family.

The morning roll-call finished, a large number of us feet-stamping, hand-rubbing, limping and nose-dripping rejects were assembled, and we shuffled through the snow to the *Schonungsblock* to sit down to work at a number of prehistoric wooden weaving looms. Others sat down on benches along the walls. What did they do, what did we? It has never been explained. There was a pile of cheap coloured waste linen. Those who sat on the benches cut that waste with very old razorblades into small strips and regularly took a stock to the weavers. The weavers wove them into a sort of ribbon, fourth-rate cords. We made ourselves believe - but maybe it was even true - that the linen came from aircraft that had been shot down, and that the ribbons were earmarked as straps for parachutes. It gave us great pleasure to accept this explanation because it provided an ideal reason for making the stitches between strips so poor that the ribbons would fall apart at minimal pressure or pull. With this in mind I pictured *Fallschirmjäger* (parachutists) jumping from their planes and whizzing down like a stone. This can in no way be considered a Christian thought.

The *Webereikapo* was Max, a professional criminal who had murdered his father. Max had the face of a clown, a sort of Grock, but had an unmitigated cunning. When not in his corner eating with his 'little friends', he would storm around checking on us. However, when one was virtuous and could show long strips of woven ribbon, an extra slice of bread could be earned.

The tearing and cutting of the linen caused clouds of dust which mixed with the foul smell of the filthy *Häftlinge*. When the atmosphere full of coughing cutters and weavers became unbearable Max would throw himself at the windows on one side and open them all. Then he would do the same on the opposite side. The biting winter wind, sometimes accompanied by snowflakes, whizzed straight through us all, while Max called out, 'You'll have to work hard to get warm, you nasty bastards!' Some of us did indeed find our temperatures rising after a few hours of cold wind, but not as a result of hard work.

Nevertheless, I gratefully spent many weeks as a workhorse in the *Weberei*. You could quietly let your thoughts wander while the weave rolled out on the other side of the loom.

Intelleltuellen sind wehleidig (Intellectuals are soft)

My diary, written in the *Revier*:

8 November 1943: Have had five days *Schonung*. Have begged, was thrown down the steps. Three days great suffering, bare swollen foot. No coat, icy wind at roll-calls. I've had to be carried. Any moment I'm about to cry. Sick with hunger too. Taken in after prayer. Operation, thank God under anaesthesia. I counted to 43. Then disappeared. Woken by blows, palpitations of heart, pain, vomited. A lot of pus came out. Now have crutches. Dutch friend came to comfort me. It's been snowing, the ceiling is white, the stove's at full blast. I'm now thinking too much about our past, getting sick of it. I'm wasting away, it's all too much. Have just been bandaged, on the way to the loo I slipped with my crutch, all damaged again, I'm moaning, being scolded. Insult, harshness, injustice. God, how long will You allow Yourself to be mocked? Christ, let me suffer martyrdom for You, for You, for You. Give it to me, I'll take it, I'll join the thousands of martyrs who suffer for You. Let me have it for it is blissful.

9 November: Everything here now maximum of hatred, harshness,

cynicism, is intended to infect man with hate viruses until he has been corrupted for ever. Persevere bravely. I wasn't brave. I was in mortal fear. I'm here to unlearn fear and to learn to love.

10 November: How many men on earth are allowed to lie in a warm bed on this day, 10 November? Here there is groaning and crying from pain. What more sacrifice will God demand from us? The ultimate as well? Will I fear it? No.

11 November: Oh God, have mercy upon this sinner. I can't pray much else. It is very bad again, very, very bad. Furious, desperate longing for you, for love, warm words, warmth, quiet and beauty. I cry out like a deer for the water of the river. Mortal fear on top of it all, fear of dying. What's this? Where is my faith? Also, why fear of death? I have no more words. But if I don't write I'll suffocate and might as well die. I've got to. Blue glittering crystals, green waters, pearly piano concertos, very soft animals, silver and log-fire, pink, orange. And lovely smells. And many mountains of delicious food.

17 November: Doctor Leo, the *Häftling* doctor, has been visiting. Another twenty-four hours safety here. Visit from the SS. 'You've been run down. How do you feel now?' Compassion from them!

20 November: I've got hold of Plato's *Gorgias* in French. How is it possible? He says: someone who satisfies his hunger loses two contrasting feelings: craving and unease; the craving for food is lost together with the discomfort hunger causes. And: dying is the separation of spirit and body. And: after death one is judged naked. And: there are more important things than life.

23 November: Doctor says new bandages. There's a new abcess on my foot. *Kleine Inzision* (small incision). Asked for anaesthetic none the less. 'Intellektuellen sind wehleidig' (intellectuals are soft). I counted up to 55. Then gone. Fourth operation. Debated with Leo about the New Testament on the operating table. Glad to be back under my own steam. Moaned a lot, cried a lot, burning hot wound-pain.

25 November: This morning bandaged. Two sizeable holes in my foot with a drainage tube through them. The healing is both gratifying and frightening: may have to leave.

3 December: Moved. Am now lying between Norwegians and French. We describe to each other our normal working day. Am now teaching my Norwegian neighbour Dutch.

4 December: Have eaten almost two litres of barley soup with meat, how grateful my stomach is, the belly once more becomes a sort of fortress where one is safe, not anymore a rumbling cavity as in Rembrandt's *The Anatomy Lesson*.

7 December: Am now weighing in at 57 kg, quite a bonus. My neighbours are: a lecturer in history from Oslo, a teacher from Cherbourg, a student from Béthune, a student from Christiansand, a farmer from Luxemburg, a farmer from just outside Amsterdam, a labourer from Leningrad and an engineer from Paris. All are quietly lying and breathing and meditating about home. They're waiting for the food saucepan at noon. Why all this idiocy?

8 December: Discharged, not recovered. *Schonung*. Weaving-hall. New large convoy of Dutch arrived.

I left the *Revier* after exactly one month. The chilly society outside. . . . Meanwhile a large group of Dutchmen had arrived. My own transport, of July 1943, consisted chiefly of 'ordinary boys'. This second group was entirely different: officers, high civil servants, lawyers, a few businessmen, students, etc. I found the atmosphere among the Dutch changed. My new *Blockälteste* was Hermann Kobold.

JOSEF ULC

One evening I received a *Meldung* (report) because my 'shoes' had been found dirty in a cupboard. Our Czech *Stubenälteste*, Ulc (Ooltsj), probably on orders from Kobold, had me squat on a stool for punishment with a second stool in my arms stretched forward. A grotesque sight for everyone present, a most awkward situation for me. Con Broers, who came in to finish drawing a portrait of Ulc's daughter from a photograph, saw me in this position and flew into a rage. He took photograph and drawing in both hands gesturing as if to tear them to pieces and ordered the Czech to get me off it or he would destroy both. That worked miracles.

'Hau ab, Mensch,' (piss off, man) Ulc grumbled and I stole away to the sleeping quarters.

A little later the Czech improved. He had a violin. He picked it up once and played us Chopin, quite excellently.

KOBOLD

The Blockälteste, later Lagerälteste, Hermann Kobold, deserves more attention. This communist, a butcher from Düsseldorf, was not the worst. Now and then he went 'Lagermad', rolled his eyes, shouted himself hoarse and ran round with a cudgel, though without using it to any great purpose.

Months later, when I too had become 'prominent', Kobold sometimes sought out my company. He did indeed turn out to be slightly mad, but was a great idealist and a man of character. Repeatedly he took endless trouble to try to convince me of the devilish nature of the capitalist system and the blessings of communism. This he did so capably and with such conviction that occasionally I was impressed by his world view. His strongest argument ran as follows: 'Where are your friends the English and the Americans? Where is the invasion? The capitalist imperialists will only come when the soldiers of the Soviet Red Army have cut the capitalist Nazi-fascists to pieces and not a moment sooner. The Anglo- Americans will throw bombs on women and children but beyond that they prefer to sit back and hope the communist and fascist armies will wipe each other out. Only when the Germans and Russians are lying stricken in their death throes will they come. Two birds with one stone. Don't ever be mistaken about that.'

Later again Kobold began to treat me in a particularly friendly way. It was then that we had this remarkable talk:

'You remember when as Blockälteste I had you given a hiding?'

'Of course, Hermann. I thought it a dirty trick, I couldn't take any more.'

He raised his voice, Lagermadness on the way. 'When I saw you couldn't take any more I let you off the hook, man!'

'Yes, but . . .'

'Now, listen. I've now been imprisoned for ten years, I'm a real old Lager hand. I can see who stands a chance of surviving and who doesn't. As you were then there was a good chance you would have had it. But I saw too that you had the potential to get out of here alive. That's why, my friend, I provoked you deliberately. I wanted to wake you from your reveries, man. You were running a great risk. Now, because of me, there's less danger. Verstanden (understood)?'

No, Kobold was not a bad sort.

BEGGAR

One evening that winter with persistent snow falling vertically, an unusual uproar started in the Block of the Luxemburgers. In Natzweiler they were the super-capitalists. They were *Häftlinge zweiter Stufe* (second-class prisoners), had retained their head-hair, were well dressed, received parcels from their families, farmers' families, and were assigned the best jobs. The Luxemburgers received loaves of bread, bacon and sausages from their wives and the fat built up on their bodies.

That evening a consignment had arrived for the Luxemburgers and already we could smell the frying from a distance through the curtain of snow. Automatically I walked in the direction of the smells. Inside it looked like a restaurant with music playing and spots of light from the windows on the snow outside.

I was not the only one who climbed the flight of steps to the entrance of the barracks. Several ghosts stood already on the steps, hands in pockets, stamping from one foot to the other, or their arms held out towards the noise and the smell of frying. I went higher up the steps and saw the striped capitalists walking to and fro with saucepans and parcels and plates in the light of the evening. I was standing at the top of the steps when two Luxemburgers appeared at the door to get some fresh air and smoke a cigarette after all that eating. They laughed and chatted in their curious German-French language. I asked them to give me something from their plenty; behind me other ghosts came nearer. The laughter and chatter changed to abuse and cursing. I got a kick and stumbled down the granite steps into the snow.

At that moment I was my Mother. I saw my son prostrated, I saw a beggar and outcast lying in the snow. It was not I, but my Mother who cried out of hunger, poverty and disgrace.

CHRISTMAS 1943

Christmas arrived in Natzweiler. The Germans actually gave us a day off, we were not bullied, got proper food and Russian cigarettes, Bregawa brand, and in one barrack a Christmas tree had been set up where we were allowed to sing Silent Night. Was this an unexpectedly sensitive kindness of the Germans? I believe rather that it formed part of the devilish game plan. One Dutchman (who would succumb on my birthday, 19 July 1944) read the Christmas story from an 'organized' (i.e. stolen) Bible and recited a Christmas poem. After that I wanted to be alone.

Secretly I stepped outside with my precious cigarettes into the thick snow. It was icy cold and some stars already sparkled in the sky. However, the sun had not yet set and glowed dark-reddish in the western sky. I walked down, to the plateau next to the crematorium beyond which stretched enormous woods. At that point you also had a magnificient view of the valley. The valley was full of a violet haze. As I stood there in solitude, lighting a cigarette and slowly regaining my sense of self, faraway beneath the haze in the hidden

126

valley church bells started pealing.

Not long after a huge silver cross appeared to me in the sky to the north, where Holland lay. 'The people who lived in darkness saw a great light; and light dawned on the dwellers in the land of death's dark shadow.

I did not imagine this. It was reality, so help me God Almighty.

But on the day after I read in my diary:

Our meal arrived early at 11am, thick macaroni soup which actually tasted of cheese. Followed by roll-call and . . . a check-up for lice. At Christmas they check whether we have any lice. Everyone had to appear stark naked before the *Stubenälteste*, who messed around with a little stick under the genitals. Strange world. At 4pm we got half a loaf and jam. Then two men were hanged; they had made an escape attempt. Murder at Christmas. The entire camp had to assemble and look on. It gives a certain satisfaction to watch the German beast in his perfection. We soon forget it: a defensive hardening process. Next we get potatoes with minced meat, not much but delicious. Ten minutes after an atrocious, horrible execution - the way they squirmed - we are eating potatoes.

NEVER ALONE

Fear as a result of terror, hunger, cold, maltreatment and the total lack of news from home; these have been mentioned as the main components of the severe suffering in a KZ. But there are more.

The forced and uninterrupted communal life, never ever being alone, was also a real plague that could have grave consequences. We were seriously put to the test with regard to the commandment: love thy neighbour as thyself. We had not chosen our neighbours in the KZ ourselves; there were, of course, people who did not suit us. Escape, however, was never possible. Day and night, even in the beds, the lavatories, on deathbeds we were together. Sometimes you could, depending on the circumstances in a particular KZ, try to go for a walk alone in the 'Lagerstreet', but soon enough you were accosted by people who were desperate for a chat. And when you were walking and smoking you could not be alone for even one minute: scroungers would find you soon enough ('can I have a puff too, Floor?'). Thus you were hampered and irritated by the physical, but especially psychic, presence of others, sometimes driven to frenzy - if you could still summon up the energy for frenzy.

You could not even think alone. All your thoughts, fantasies, notions were influenced, infected. This had been quite clear in the communal cells at Utrecht, with six or seven men together day and night. Within a few weeks a psychological network of influences had been created. When one cellmate left the community the change in atmosphere, for better or worse, was total. That single person had not only influenced each of us directly, but also indirectly so that his leaving changed our relationships with each other. When the web was torn, a new one was spun imperceptibly. People who had got on well with each other could now become almost enemies. Irritations arose about next to nothing: the shape of a nose, a piece of clothing, an expletive, a repeatedly whistled song, a sniffing, coughing or itching habit. Someone who drummed on the table in a communal cell could provoke thoughts of murder.

I have to make another confession: differences in social background and development could in fact endanger a friendship. On the one hand, I can truthfully claim to have judged the characters of fellow prisoners from humble homes and without education more highly than many from my own milieu. On the other hand, the difference in development could sometimes result in serious rows over ordinary vulgar class struggle. The quarrel was almost always started by the man with the humbler background, not by the more educated one. To my knowledge an academic or more socially elevated person almost never showed ill feelings for an uneducated man even if he was sometimes difficult to understand. No, on the contrary: it was the latter who would start the fight, shouting abuse, ranting about haughtiness, snobbishness, accent, the appearance, nose, pretentions.

That was horrible. Nothing could be done about it. After all, we were of course different. And we were all tightly packed together. Upbringing helped, of course. Those of us from privileged backgrounds had learned good manners, not just formal ones like fork left and knife right, but also sensitivity to others. You had to be friendly and polite, and as little burden as possible to someone who might feel at a disadvantage. Do not trouble others - that was the fundamental rule of civilized behaviour. The humble man, though often endowed with a heart of pure gold, did not always grasp this principle: he did not even know how much he could annoy you in all sorts of ways. For a time you could control yourself - that too you had been taught - but after several weeks, sometimes days, the explosion would come: 'For God's sake, stop that damned whistling!'

Irrational, desperate, irredeemable. It seems that too many animals, together in too small a space, finally attack each other and even eat each other. Sometimes we came close to a fight: fortunately we were too weak.

In a KZ community you were also cured of any embarrassment. A gathering of stark naked men - fat, a bit less fat, skinny or skeletal - would not be felt as something special. When bathing or at medical examinations or disinfections you had lots of time to study each other's bodies. This was of little interest unless someone had no earlobes, or had legs with feet pointed backwards instead of forwards, or strawberry marks on his face, or the most obscene tattoos on his chest, or a penis of really absurd length, 25cm (10ins) hanging loosely downwards - all of which I have seen. I have also seen a *Häftling* with a tattoo on his upper arm of a woman's head with real hair. But in the end we were almost all filthy sexless semi-skeletons. And when, at roll-call, we were examined, stark naked like slaves, by some krauts sitting at a table - you had to turn round like a contestant in a beauty contest - that too did not do anything to us after a time. The humiliation was no worse than any other; you did not feel anything different any more.

[Many years after the war, however, the Germans found a way to really humiliate me. One morning a letter arrived from some authority informing me that the German Federal Republic had awarded me an amount of Dfl 2,715 (at the time £271.50 shillings) in compensation for harm inflicted by its legal predecessor. At first I could not believe my eyes. I showed the letter to my wife, who was similarly stunned. I then remembered many years earlier having completed a form. . . . The letter said that the amount mentioned could be collected at the post office; bring along letter and identification. Happy as a child, yet deeply disappointed and humiliated I cashed in the compassionate allowance of Dfl 2,715 (those Dfl 15!) alotted to me condescendingly by the German Reich as compensation for the 'damage' suffered, receiving it from a wooden functionary at a counter in the Bussum post office. It was a wicked joke and a miserable pay-off, and yet I was absurdly happy with the money. That was the worst thing about it.]

SCHEISSEREI

It was rather different with defecation, in particular diarrhoea or *Scheisserei*, called *Durchfall* in high German and always everywhere part of the proceedings of day and night. It is unbelievable, the immense amount of shitting that went on in prison and KZ by thousands of men who lived continuously with starvation. Where did they get the raw materials?

Not being alone when defecating was and remained a horror. When there was a sort of lavatory, *Abort*, it was a communal one, and outside working hours it was continuously occupied by four, eight or twelve men, their trousers down, often two on one bowl producing a veritable concert of wind instruments: flute, oboe, clarinet, especially bassoon and trumpet, sometimes even trombone and tuba. It kept on gushing and gushing from dirty men with contorted faces: the foul smell of the pigsty compared favourably. And there was no lavatory paper. But sometimes there was not even an *Abort*. Sometimes there was only a pit with a pole laid across it and - what luxury! - a roof above. It then sounded like an open air brass band fanfare given by ten, fifteen, twenty men next to each other like swallows on a telegraph wire. Even there fights broke out, in the mass of shit in front of the pole, when a man came hobbling along, hands on crotch, who tried to push himself into the row on the pole because he was bursting. In this department our humiliation knew no bounds.

Once at roll-call I found myself next to an extremely tall, extremely thin doctor, who stood quietly crying. Asked for the reason, he pointed down to his sandals. I then noticed that the diarrhoea was slowly dripping through his trouser legs onto his feet. But I do not think that he was crying because of the humiliation. He was crying for fear they would discover that he had dirtied the precious roll-call yard.

STRUCK OFF

One day during roll-call my number was called: 4381. This never did bode well. In Amersfoort it could still mean that you were going to be discharged, in Natzweiler this did not happen, as far as I know. After roll-call you had to report at the gate: 'Häftling 4381 meldet sich gehorsamst' (prisoner 4381 reporting obediently), at attention like a wooden doll, woollen cap in hand, in a loud voice. It turned out that I had been summoned to the *Politische Abteilung*, the office of the SD and/or Gestapo in a KZ. This authority, outside the jurisdiction of the camp commandant, was especially feared, because among other things it received orders from Berlin about executions.

I reported at the office, 'gehorsamst', my heart in my mouth. They rummaged through some papers. At last a paper was produced and passed on to me after I had signed a receipt. Back in the *Lager* I read it. It turned out to be a decision of the *Reichskommissar* for the occupied Dutch territories to strike me off the list of lawyers *mit sofortiger Wirkung* (with immediate effect). This was a splendid example of German bureaucracy: someone had taken the trouble in The Hague to serve a writ by way of Berlin which could have no importance for a Häftling somewhere in a KZ in the Vosges. On the other hand, they did not take the trouble to explain to me such sinister terms as *Schutzhaftbefehl* (protective custody order) and *Vom Verfahren abgetrennt* (excluded from legal proceedings). Considering the unusual circumstances it arrived fairly quickly: it took only three and a half months.

For the rest, I have kept the document and even framed it. Seyss-Inquart signed it personally; he considered it that important.

BREAD

The significance of bread is enormous. Christ mentions bread in the prayer He taught us. Give us this day our daily bread - enable us to feed our body and thereby continue physical life on earth. The bread we received from the Germans was insufficient, pitiful, by human standards. We tried to make changes, reflecting that Jesus had the power to feed large masses of people with only a few loaves and fishes. What could be done then should also be possible today. We did not simply pray, 'Lord, bless this food,' but used the somewhat more elaborate: 'Lord, the bread received from the enemy is insufficient, but if we receive it on behalf of You it should be sufficient'. Naturally this prayer was answered as long as we believed in it.

When you are stricken by starvation the effect of food is physically palpable after only a few minutes. As an emaciated person, suffering from starvation, you could sit almost on top of a stove and still remain icy cold inside. The moment you had eaten bread, you literally felt the food inside you converting to warmth. As you ate more bread, for instance when you had received or earned some extras, that warmth lasted longer. However, that was not all. Just as starvation at first stimulated a heightening of spiritual feeling, even a desire to become a monk and experience the dying-out of the world, in a further phase it led first to the 'softness' described earlier, then to stupefaction and in the final phase with a gradual disappearance of hunger, it at first led to a rather more realistic view of things and of people from the safe entrenchment of the belly, and subsequently to a partial (never a complete) return of the intellectual faculties.

The bread in the stomach generated warmth there. More and more bread made that warmth spread through the body. A continuous and sufficient supply of bread directed that warmth as strength, energy, almost literally upward, by way of the neck to the head, to the brain, which became more active, less clouded. You started thinking again and exchanging views. You woke up from a semi-consciousness.

This was one of the reasons why the Dutch community, after half a year in Natzweiler, having achieved resignation, adaptation and a good job, became much more lively. Many of us - me too - ceased to be the half-dead, shivering, terrified wretches of the past but came to resemble human beings again; people who could talk, sometimes even laugh. Many never reached this phase.

I remember roll-calls where this could be seen clearly. The SS were still the SS and the roll-call was still the roll-call - but we had changed. The Dutch section looked less miserable - yes, we did - more conscious, martial, manly. Even more defiant. A strange sort of pleasure was evident in the way the roll-call orders were acted upon. At the order 'stillgestanden' many stood to attention like warriors, chin up, chest forward, motionless, eyes fixed to the front. With a little imagination you could visualize this battle-order in uniform, and armed. The Germans must have noticed that we improved in strength of mind and self-confidence in inverse proportion to the worsening of the war for them.

In this period too internationalism increased, a sort of mini-Europeanism. It now became clear what an enormous advantage those of us had who knew several languages and could associate with the French, Norwegians, Poles and even with Russians.

When describing Amersfoort I have already mentioned that among the Dutch being a Christian ensured a much stronger bond than equal social status or intellectual development. It now became obvious that the 'community of saints', the community of the believers in Christ, were bound by a stronger bond than a national community. In addition, on an international level a similar education also proved to be a common spiritual denominator.

This could create frictions in our own ranks despite national bonds and that was undeniably awful. In the evening in the *Stube* or afterwards on the 'Lagerstreet' or in the work details the believers and intellectuals sought each other out regardless of their nationality, while some less educated people, unable to speak a foreign language, huddled together, disconsolate and grumbling. This was clearly a genuine example of class distinction and that was both a relief and a pity.

It also became clear that intellectuals of the same kind not only sought each other out because of the common enemy - compare the monstrous alliance between Americans, English and Russians against the Germans - but also because they genuinely had common ideas and values. With Belgians, French, Luxemburgers and Norwegians you could discuss such subjects as Debussy's compositions, Rembrandt's life, the Italian Renaissance and even Plato's *Politeia*, as well as democracy versus dictatorship or the politics to be followed after the war. Even a 'United States of Europe' was discussed.

Now and again we were startled - yes, really - by the presence of the SS and the *Kapos* who reminded us of their presence by their animal raucous screams - poor backward devils as they had now become. Thanks to the increased amount of bread we could make merry about the postwar *Erziehungslager* (approved school) where we would take command. . . .

ECUMENICAL

At Natzweiler we tried to get together occasionally, especially on a Sunday evening. This was our church. There was no protestant vicar, but there were a few Roman Catholic priests. However, now and then it fell to me to lead the assembly. At that time we did not have a Bible. Rumour had it that there was a Norwegian with a Bible. I found the Norwegian. As he did not speak any language other than Norwegian it took some time at first to allay his suspicions and then to persuade him to lend me his Bible. At last I got the Bible - a Norwegian one, of course. I then searched for another Norwegian who knew some English. I indicated, in a general way, a text which I wanted to use. The Norwegian turned over the pages, reading aloud pieces in faulty English. This? No. This? No. Perhaps this? Yes.

He and I sat down somewhere in a corner of the barrack. He read the text jerkily in English, I wrote it down at once in Dutch on a scrap of paper. I thanked him and returned the Bible to the other Norwegian. All this had to be done discreetly.

I returned to my Block. If our current *Blockälteste* was more or less all right, like Franz Gutmann, I notified him. He thought it was crazy but we did not meet with any trouble from him. We had to set up lookouts, however. Two were nominated. We sat in the sleeping hall between beds: ten, twenty, sometimes sixty, eighty ghosts seated on the lower bunks. One lookout stood guard at the entrance to the sleeping hall; the other at the entrance to the barrack. There followed a church service.

The Bible text was read. A relevant dissertation followed. The text was usually chosen to be relevant to our cursed situation. A prayer followed. There were men of various denominations, and after prayer some always added a 'Hail Mary', or someone said the creed. Some crossed themselves, including a few protestants. Sometimes a Roman Catholic priest blessed us, mumbling in Latin.

During these gatherings we kept an eye on the lookout at the door, and he in his turn on the one at the entrance. Rough chaps attended these meetings too, and malicious ones. There were also non-believers, and sometimes communists.

During such gatherings on Sundays in Natzweiler a constant stream of strength could clearly be felt. The strength flowed into us, and bound us together as if we were holding hands, this strength flowing from man to man round the circle and back and to and fro. For Christ was in our midst.

Afterwards we would disperse one after another, or in twos, in order not be conspicuous. The men who had been lookouts went their way. Outside, in the snow, we looked at the world with different eyes. We were entirely happy and completely provided for.

HELP MY UNBELIEF

One Sunday evening my discussion partner was an educated man of about forty.

'You believe in God, don't you?'

'Yes.'

'And in Jesus Christ?'

'Yes, almost always, sometimes a little bit less.'

'I don't believe in it at all. How can you believe in God with this animal herd around you? In the past I too believed in God, not anymore.'

'In my case it happened more or less the other way round.'

'How did you come to that belief?'

'It has been given to me by grace.'

'That is a conversation stopper. I think that fear made you suddenly believe. It is a distress-belief. When you get out of here, you'll lose it again.'

'I fervently hope not. I'm almost sure I won't.'

He said, 'I can understand that you believe in God, but in Jesus . . . how can you? A man who lived two thousand years ago, somewhere in Palestine! The Jews don't believe in him. Millions of Muslims don't, neither do millions of followers of Buddhism and Hinduism. There are so many religions. Why this one? You must have been brought up with it.'

'No, not just brought up in it. Our entire civilization is pervaded with Christianity, isn't it? But that is not the reason. God has taken hold of me through Christ, not Mohammed. I can't help that. As to other religions: we all honour the same God, there's only one.'

'Is God good?'

'God is far above our good and evil. I can't tell you. However, God's Son, according to the New Testament, has held up to us men clearly what is good and evil. Through the New Testament I know what is good and evil, even though I don't quite understand some pronouncements.'

At this he said: 'Why does your God allow this ghastly mess, this war, all this slaughter?'

'Because we don't do what He tells us, ever. Read the New Testament and you'll see that we live our lives contrary to all commandments and prohibitions. We abandon God, and then someone else comes along.'

'The Devil, you mean?'

'Yes.'

'The Devil reigns here?'

'Yes, but only because God, the Almighty, allows it. God reigns above the Devil.'

'God allows innocent children to be murdered, by bombardments?'

'Yes.'

'Then I don't want your God. I loathe a God like that.'

'It is the same God Who created you and all your dear ones and to Whom you owe everything that is good and beautiful in your life. Do you loathe all that as well?'

'There isn't any God at all, it's all fabrication. In underdeveloped countries, in savage tribes you find all sorts of forms of worship with pagan rites, medicine men and magic. We consider that to be primitive, backward. A time will come when Christianity will also be considered primitive. God as man nailed to the cross, murdered, buried, risen, ascended into heaven - what nonsense really.'

I said: 'You should choose your words with care. What you call nonsense has been a source of the greatest religious strength for two thousand years for hundreds of millions of people, the foundation of our entire civilization, the source of inspiration for great geniuses throughout history from year one onward. Incidentally, our calendar starts with Christ's birth. You call all that nonsense? Christ performs miracles here and now, day in day out, for everyone who believes in Him. He is alive.'

'That's what you say, but I don't see it like that. I see no miracles for me.'

'No? Your life, life itself, love, friendship, nature - no miracles?'

'All of it has been explained scientifically.'

'Nonsense. None of this can be explained scientifically.'

He would not drop it: 'Do we have a free choice between good and evil? I thought you Christians were of the opinion that everything was predestined. If this war is predestined then everything that led up to it was also predestined, for instance Hitler's birth, as well as that of his parents. If you think it through then really everything is predestined in

135

the minutest detail, now as in the future. Where does that leave your free choice?'

'That question is even more difficult, I can't answer it. When I read the Bible properly, for instance the Revelation, I have to believe that everything is predestined, yes, in detail. Yet at the same time I believe in our free will and choice.'

'Therefore if you get the choice to pinch someone else's bread or not to pinch it, and you do pinch it, has that been predestined or did you consciously choose evil?'

'I think this: I had the free choice between pinching the bread and not pinching it, but it was predestined that I'd do the first.'

'Again, what nonsense! A sophism if ever there was one. No, not for me the Christian faith. But I still envy you your faith.'

'Why?'

'Because you don't have to feel afraid, or alone and abandoned, or unhappy; because you hope to be blessed in the hereafter. Your faith becomes stronger and really useful as conditions become ever more wretched.'

'You're right. But don't think that we Christians always believe firmly. Sometimes our faith is weak, or even missing altogether. Just like Christ Himself, in the garden of Gethsemane, and on the cross. We shout: "Lord, I believe, help Thou mine unbelief".'

He continued, 'That Devil of yours, he interests me. Are the SS devils?'

'No, they are possessed. They are possessed by Satan, by demons.'

'Is God also present among the SS?'

'Yes. The Creator is in everything created. Indeed, occasionally you can see that even SS men have the vestiges of conscience, a recollection of good. They too are creatures. Children of one Father. We pray for their deliverance from evil. We mustn't sanction hatred - it requires a tremendous effort not to hate your fellow human beings. We hate the demoniacal spirit that has taken hold of them because they abjured God.'

'Everything is predestined, you say. Therefore also that someone will abjure God, can't believe in God, has consciously chosen Satan's side? Is that predestined?'

'Yes - if I argue consistently. It was indeed predestined that, for instance, Hitler, who may have been a very good little boy, has consciously turned away from God and chosen Satan.'

'Well, mate, we'd have to ask him himself about that. Perhaps he thinks he's serving God, some greater Germanic God, perhaps providence. Perhaps he really thinks that his people are the Herrenvolk (master race) and that the Jewish people are vermin that have to be destroyed.'

'In that case, he's mad.'

'That's what you say. He doesn't think so.'

'Perhaps a small operation on the brain would have turned Hitler into a modest bookkeeper of a nice little business, with a loving wife and virtuous children.'

He stopped me. 'Have you noticed that you've contradicted yourself repeatedly?'

'Yes.'

'Your arguments, indeed your whole system just doesn't add up.'

'No. But sometimes I don't understand anything anymore.'

'Doesn't that confirm that your faith is a human invention?'

'No.'

He persisted, 'Have you ever thought how innumerable are the occasions during the course of centuries, when infamous deeds have been committed in the name of Christianity?'

'Certainly. Religious wars, crusades, the Inquisition . . .'

'Have you also considered how often the Church, the ecclesiastical authorities, have made common cause with the great of the earth, the rich and powerful, against the people?'

'Certainly. That's how it is. Meanwhile Jesus took up the cudgels for the publicans, sinners and whores. He washed the feet of His pupils. . . . You mustn't identify the Christian faith with the Christian churches. Perhaps even the very opposite. . . .'

'So we're agreed about that.'

'I'll go a bit further. Perhaps it's such a vale of tears here because the Christian faith, the preaching and guarding of it, is mostly in the wrong hands. That can be proved. Christ said: there is one shepherd, one flock, one Church. How many churches are there now?'

'I agree with you there.'

'In that case I'm going to shock you. Sometimes I understand absolutely nothing of Christianity, of the Bible, of Christ. God's Son Who gave His life on the cross in order to deliver us from our trespasses, by His blood - sometimes I really don't understand it at all.'

'Well, and? So?'

'So - I believe. I can't - and don't want - anything else. I have been seized. I get much comfort, peace of mind, sometimes great feelings of happiness, even here. Day upon day I get very great marks of favour. Not only me. Through faith the most fabulous works have been accomplished throughout the ages. I can only say: come and help my unbelief.'

SLOGANS

Many in prison and KZ sought certainty by inventing riddles in words or figures, notwithstanding repeated proofs that they didn't work, and indeed had no meaning at all. Crazy calculations were made: today is 12 February 1944, that adds up to $12+2+1+9+4+4=32; 3+2=5=$my lucky number, therefore it will be the 5th of the fifth month; that's when I shall be released, etc.

Crazy slogans were believed, rumours accepted, occult instructions were taken up eagerly, predictions made: a tangle of spiritual wanderings by people led astray by the fear of death.

Did you hear? All *Häftlinge* will be set free on Hitler's birthday. The Americans have landed (this was in April 1942, more than two years before the Normandy landings). We shall be home for Christmas! Have you heard? There will be a new, more gentle, commandant. Have you heard? Order from Berlin: no more death penalties. Heard the news? There will be an international exchange of prisoners. Have you heard? Churchill said that the invasion starts next week. Heard? The bread ration will be increased to 500 grams.

Rumours and fantastic slogans that brought a lump to the throat when one saw the bright, benevolent faces of the terrified people who uttered them. Then, inevitably, all these comforting thoughts left us in the lurch one by one. Slogans shot out to us like fiery flames of deliverance - possibly they were circulated on purpose by the SS or Gestapo in order to stimulate the collapse of morale that always followed when they turned out to be false. They died out, were extinguished, and all who had believed fell silent, small, crumpled up, as the colour of excitement on their deathly thin faces faded away. But there was still one certainty, as I knew, the only and eternal certainty! God.

This was why one was almost forced to seize God in the thick fog of existence where all worldly aids proved to be unsound, all worldly reassurances prevarications. There was nothing sure but God.

DER KREPIERT (HE KICKS THE BUCKET)

One night at half past one the lights are suddenly turned on in the warm, suffocating stable with its animal air. The two hundred and fifty men in this *Stube* wake up, ranting or quietly miserable. 'Get up! Stawatsch! You foul swine - you've got to be bathed, bathed.' Do not think. Look for your rags. As always your life is at stake. The delay caused by thinking might cost you your life. A few beds further on the cudgel cracks down. 'Up you get, you dirty bastards, to the disinfection room!' It has stopped snowing, a clear sky, there is a sharp frost. The millimetre of warmth between skin and rags has already gone. A glass dome. The feet, in wooden sandals, are stamping again and noses drip again, shoulders shake again and festering hands are wringing again. There is no moon. There are stars. I'm standing swaying like a child that cannot walk. I cannot walk, something sharp as a knife cuts into my right heel, in the centre of the heel-bone. My feet are like heavy clogs. And above them the gaps begin. Con Broers stands beside me. He smokes. He gives his cigarette to me. I smoke. Together we smoke. He takes hold of me under the arms. My stick-legs are moving. We stumble along the 'Lagerstreet' down to the crematorium. I drink the drips from my nose. The knife in my heel is down below, I am high up, far above the knife. The knife is not important. Far away, in a little village, an enslaved French village, the Germans sound the air raid alarm. All lamps go out, the searchlights and the spotlights. At 900 meters up in the mountains we are without light.

We arrive with our Block beside the crematorium. The *Lagerkapo*, in a heavy duffle coat, cap coquettishly askew, walks soundlessly around. From a distance we hear a voice:

'Undress, get on with it, you little ones, undress. Disinfection,' the jaws of the *Lagerkapo* snap. 'Come on, undress.'

It is said quietly, in a friendly voice, a whip under the arm. We undress. We gather the rags together. We are allowed to keep the sandals. Everything is thrown on a pile. We never get it back. My little book, my belt - I never see them again.

Two hundred and fifty of us are standing naked. Every second the knife pierces deeper. Nobody speaks. Nobody moans. Perhaps nobody thinks. We are still alive.

The heart is still alive. The heart, a red muscle pump the size of a fist, pumps. It hangs in my ribcage. My ribs around the red muscle rise and fall. I breathe, but without lungs. Whoo, whoo, the sound of the wind whispering through the slatted blinds of my ribcage. Softly the wind brushes the sides of the heart. That is all right. Otherwise I am a wasp, a connecting thread between ribcage and hips. My belly gapes. There are cavities, connected by threads. The mountain wind rustles softly. The snow glimmers bluish. There is no light anywhere.

I look up. I see the stars. I see celestial bodies. Not stars but little fiery globes. Not very far away, not even far away. Some are nearer than others. Fiery globes, and stars. Me, my eye, little planets, not so far away anymore. . . . I rise. They are all around me, and presently beneath me. I am on the way. I am rising among the celestial bodies. A globe, a black globe full of fire, is around me. It is not bad anymore. I am on my way, travelling. Be quiet, you're on the way. It is not really bad. This is your way. It is really a great moment, a great night, for God is now coming, it gets foggier, beyond the Milky Way He will come. . . .

Con bends over me. And there is someone else who gently prods my gaps with his foot. 'Der krepiert,' he says. I can see it is the *Lagerkapo*. He walks past.

'You take him under the other arm,' I hear Con say, 'he has slipped down. Hey, Floris, boyo, stay awake. Are you crazy, lying down here to sleep!'

They pick me up, those in front are already entering the bathroom. Light filters through the open door. I am hanging between two friends, my arms round their necks, stretched out. Another naked creature, arms outstretched, I now see hanging opposite. He looks at me.

We are going. The spotlights and the searchlights are on again. Yes, yes, we are going, we are coming but, be quiet, we are still here. . . .

[I found out what happened that night on 11 October 1976. After being disinfected, we were sent out still wet into the freezing night, but Con stayed with me and supported me. As a result of a bite from a dog he was suffering from an inflammation on his ankle which made walking almost impossible. Suddenly I sank limply down and slid out of his grasp. He then took me on his shoulders and carried me up all those steps, icy like glass, up to our Block, between the bodies of those already 'krepiert'. Con is of the opinion that in thus saving me he also saved his own life: the intense heat he developed during this climb probably saved him from freezing to death.]

REVIER (SICK BAY)

For the third time I was admitted to the *Revier* - after having been kicked away three times - on 21 January 1944 with a temperature of 40.4° and pneumonia affecting both lungs in turn. I had had pneumonia five times, but this one was extremely painful and made each breath abominable. I lay in a little room with one other prisoner and fought against death. Outside the snow on and between the barracks was one meter deep. I lost myself in inexpressible dreams.

In the middle of the night the light went on. A *Häftlingarzt* (a prisoner who happened to be a doctor and was used in that capacity; not all doctors among the prisoners were, of course, used as such) Fritz

Leo stood in front of me: a gnome, with fine curved lips, a communist, who on another occasion would snap at me: 'Your God won't help you, I will.' This time he said, 'You, can you eat?' He gave me a handful of tablets. 'You must eat these tablets at once, but really at once, understood?' For quite some time I was kept busy chewing and swallowing the thick chalky mass.

The next morning when the Polish *Sanitäter* came for *Temperatur und Stuhlgang* (to take my temperature and help me relieve myself), the temperature was down to 37.2°. Later I discovered that Con Broers had broken into the *Effektenkammer*, where our civilian effects were stored, endangering his own life to snatch some twenty sulphur tablets from his own luggage. These he had given to Leo, for me. That saved my life for the umpteenth time.

Later I was transferred to a bigger room with dozens of others. Occasionally we played intelligence games with the Dutch and Norwegians, such as composers or academics, or rivers or towns beginning with A, B, C, etc. At dusk I always got a visit from a mouse. I still felt so ill that I gave it some breadcrumbs without any qualms.

Once we received a visit from the SS-*Lagerarzt* personally. On the order 'Achtung', all those ill and almost-dead men jumped out of their beds and stood to attention. The 'doctor', gloved, decorated, walked past the beds, inspecting us. He was a handsome fellow with a sympathetic face - a smooth monster. He stopped at my bed.

'What country are you from?'

'Holland, Herr Lagerartzt.'

'Your profession?'

'Lawyer, Herr Lagerartzt.'

The doctor shook his head compassionately. Over his shoulder he said softly to the *Revierkapo* and his other followers: 'That man looks run-down!' He wished me 'Gute Besserung' and walked on. The SS doctor seemed to be pretending that strange, evil forces unknown to him were to blame for my lamentable condition.

The death of a Norwegian heavyweight boxer caused unprecedented consternation, even for us. The man was covered in ulcers. One evening he started roaring softly, got up and tore off all his paper bandages. They got him back into bed and he began to bleat like a sheep. He bleated and bleated. That night he got up again and again divested himself of all his bandages. He stood there, a giant skeleton full of deep red sores from which pus was dripping and flowing. A penetrating stench of old cheese permeated our whole room. The bleating became softer. Then it turned into roaring again, for hours on end. The roaring lasted until sunrise. He was then taken to the shed for corpses.

My afflictions did not stop at pneumonia. In mid-January my feet had been partially frozen. Fatally weakened, almost fainting from hunger, in driving snow I had dragged myself from Block to *Weberei* and back again. Now, suddenly, my bed was full of pus and blood. First the Czech *Sanitäter*, Dalibor (Dally) Broft, arrived and pressed out the boil. Next Leo came with 5cc of something which made me fall asleep. Operation. I awoke in appalling pain. The pain brought first a sob, then a growl, until finally I was roaring like an animal.

LEO

The *Häftlingartzt* in Natzweiler, Fritz Leo, was now and then slightly mad. He was gunning for me in a strange way. He knew I adhered to the Christian faith and never ceased mocking me. 'You God's clown. . . you Jesus-boy'. Meanwhile he saved my life several times.

This time I had a livid swelling about 10cm in diameter on my left hip. Leo promised to help me as soon as he had finished with someone else. He asked me to sit down in his little surgery facing the window, preventing me, over-sensitive *Jesuknabe*, from seeing anything. It was getting dark above the snow between the barracks where it lay one metre high; the window became a mirror and began to reflect the scene behind me. I saw how Leo and his helper removed the paper bandage from the right arm of my predecessor. On the back of that arm, from the armpit to beyond the elbow, I saw a deep gully, only a little blood but a lot of pus streaming out of it. A strong foul smell of cheese. Leo took a spoon and scraped a few times from top to bottom to clear the gully; the assistant caught the pus in a jar. The patient did not utter a sound. When his wound was not yellow anymore but blood-red, he was bandaged again with many paper swathes, whereupon he said thank you and disappeared.

'And now you,' Leo said kindly. 'Lie down, please.' I was assisted onto the primitive table. To my surprise and terror, the assistant tied me to the table, which had never happened at previous treatments. Leo stood over me, his sensuous lips smiling, and said: 'Your God isn't going to help you, but I will. Unfortunately we have to be thrifty with ether narcotics. It won't take long though.'

Immediately, my consciousness was cleaved by a dazzling flash of lightning, accompanied not by thunder but by a yell: mine, out of my throat. Leo had slashed my tumour open with a fierce slit, then with another one, he pulled the flesh on both sides apart and started wiping away the contents with swabs. Finally he wiped forcefully and deeply. The rank smell was again unbearable.

'Well, Bakels, you've got rid of this mess now, eh?'

He laughed, as did the Polish helper. I cried, yet laughed too. No stitches were applied. They put an enormous bandage on, circling my hips, and helped me to get up.

Back in bed a pain started that could only be tolerated as long as the umbilical cord between my soul and my Creator lasted. Did Fritz Leo not understand that my God had saved me for the umpteenth time, and through the medium of Fritz Leo?

My diary about this episode states:

Suddenly the knife in it, a couple of times. Agony, yelling. I have yelled and got hold of someone's coat. No more. I thought of you, and that I must be a man. I tried to move my spirit up to the ceiling; leaving the pain way below me. There's another drainage tube in the wound. Afterwards busy child-like chatter, as always from relief after a tremendous exertion. Funny chats while one's still shaking. Down to the *Revier* on a stretcher, under blankets covered with snow. Someone tucks me in, otherwise no affection or friendship. That was the worst part of it.

29 February: This morning, after some sandy soup, a dead body right opposite. Yesterday he ate enormous quantities, last night diarrhoea, this morning dead. One dies here before noticing it. Death here is deadly normal.

1 March: Was suddenly bandaged again, had a good look at myself. I'm now thin as a rail and dreadfully feeble, indeed dreadfully so, sagging on my constantly bent knees, faint and invariably icy cold. Awfully filthy, the feet especially. Muscles of arms and legs are like weak bags. My head is bald, my face, wide-eyed with big ears sticking out, looks like that of an old, grey owl. I'm smelling of pus and urine, sometimes also of shit. The skin on my legs is covered with desiccated cells, scaling off. On thighs and buttocks the skin hangs in folds. My lungs are not right, I'm coughing, my fingers fester, all ten of them. On my right foot two scars from Amersfoort in addition to the two scars from the ulceration of November. My left thigh covered with large scars, and also the four festering cuts on the hip and in the groin, with tubes sticking out. Just as well you can't see me like this, you would be fearful and cry. It is indeed enough to make one cry.

3 March: I'm learning to eat late. When I eat earlier I'm jealous of

the others who are still eating while I haven't got anything left. For that reason we play a game: who eats last eats best.

8 March: Last night J. was very quiet. Slower and odder than ever, eyes staring, cheeks pink, and moaning and crying. He didn't eat anything, asked for lemonade and visits from others. Gave him a *heisse Wickel* (hot compress). Someone spoke harshly to him; I pitied him though also being irritated. Many beautiful dreams later I wake up. Someone says to J: 'You may as well sit up to avoid being last served.' J. says yes, but doesn't do anything, his saucepan with porridge untouched next to him. He is being scolded and I say: 'Don't be silly, J., you've got to cooperate.' He's just lying there. Suddenly a Polish neighbour cries: 'Bakels, Kamerad kaputt!' And points at J. I look and see that J. is dead. At that moment someone enters with a *heisse Wickel* and says: 'It's his own fault, that one didn't want to live.' A German next to me says: 'He was so homesick for his parents.' A French doctor: 'C'était un tuberculeux.' I: 'Could I now eat his porridge?'

For this I have no words. Vulture. Hyena.

9 March: Schaeffer, a typographer from Sarrebourg, woke me up. He is sitting upright, panting and coughing. Foul smell of shit. Murmuring. It is pitch dark (air raid alarm), I put him down, tuck him in. 'Ne vous inquiétez pas, monsieur, on ne peut rien faire maintenant, attendez quelques heures, demain matin on pourra vous aider. Couchez vous.' He stammers: 'Oui, ça va, ça va, ça va.' I fall asleep, wake up, don't hear anything anymore. Damn it, he has actually died. Is carried away, stiff like a doll but his mouth bubbles.

11 March: I wake up in the middle of the night. A German sits upright on the edge of his bed above mine, panting, all his blankets are on the floor. I pick them up, put him back in bed, arrange the blankets, speak gently to him and stroke his hand and his head. It seems he later said - I was asleep again - 'Mein Herz!' (my heart) and slowly passed away.

13 March: The great day dawns, I've been discharged and must rejoin the chilly, even icy society. I've been granted four weeks *Schonung*. I've been here for seven, nearly eight weeks, spring approaches. I'll be seeing many loyal friends again. The French ask me to come and visit them sometimes, they all know I'm leaving, I was well-known here because to general silence I would read out in French the German Wehrmacht news (*das OKW gibt bekannt*).

There is no limit to love's faith, its hope and its endurance. Love never comes to an end.

This has been a long quotation. It will give the reader some impression - though no more than a sketchy one - of the German conception of a hospital: the *Krankenrevier* in Natzweiler.

WHERE NO MAN COMES

I have already mentioned that certain emotions proved too big for me and made me choke, almost suffocate. They could not be digested; calamity followed. What kind of process was this?

In 'ordinary' life too one is sometimes faced with something too powerful to absorb. It can happen suddenly or gradually. To be suddenly confronted with calamity, but also with great happiness, can, I believe, have a fatal effect on the human spirit in the sense that one succumbs to a heart attack or a cerebral haemorrhage. Sudden realisation of an undigested calamity can, it seems to me, result in mental illness, in madness. Now I believe that as far as people in a KZ are concerned, the satanism which dominated our lives, night and day, was in such unacceptable contrast to our memories of the beautiful and the good in our earlier lives, that they became indigestible. The channel became blocked instantly, you suffocated mentally, the regulatory mechanisms faltered. Someone said to me once: 'I've gone beyond my gearbox registers.' Someone accustomed to witnessing, even enduring, crimes, in a continuously and unfathomably contaminated filth, and who has thereby developed a way of life which may safeguard him from ruin, cannot switch back to normal at once. Remembering something normal, like the good and lovely life of the past, could hit one hard. In the same way that the first introduction to the KZ, the *Empfangszeremonie*, caused a perilous mental blow from which you could recover only slowly (or not at all: many succumbed in the first weeks), each association with the pre-KZ life also caused a mental blow which could only be absorbed with difficulty, if at all. I could get terribly upset, with my highly emotional character. God had to be called on with the prayer: 'Please help me bear beauty as You have helped me bear evil.'

What really happens when the spirit cannot bear something? One does not have to perish. One can lose consciousness. One can also cut oneself off when sensing the shock, step aside, put up a barrier. In such instances I have noticed in myself I became two persons, not one; I could see myself - a quickening of the pulse, a tremor throughout my body, goose-flesh, and eyes opened wide. I thought: can you bear this?

I replied: yes, I shall remain standing, God is behind me, I can lean against Him. Afterwards I felt as if I'd trespassed on forbidden territory. You have been forced to go beyond your mental limits. You have been at a place where no human beings can go, an undiscovered territory of suffering as well as ecstasy. A high tension held sway there which you could perhaps endure for one second; two seconds would have meant death. Sometimes I felt: You've been on the other side briefly. And, astonishingly, on the other side ecstasy and grief turned out to be melted together.

MORE ABOUT HUNGER

The kitchen in Natzweiler occasionally received a parcel of meat for mincing and adding to the soup of swedes. Once in a while we found a piece of such meat. It seemed to be horse meat. Or mutton. One day part of a human jaw turned up in the soup. That made it much clearer.

In the KZ and especially during the transports cannibalism has occurred. I have never witnessed this. SS dogs also had a preference for tearing the flesh from the buttocks and the backs of the thighs of their victims. I do not know for a fact but I believe they were fed on human hams. Most of them were Alsatians.

Germans always shout. SS men shout. *Kapos* shout. The German shouting - often yelling - is an essential expression of German might. We could soon distinguish the yelling of one from that of others. It was always a sign of danger, murder and torment. But sometimes it sounded like music to my ears: when it emanated from the throat of a *Kapo* who was in a position to hand out *Portionen*. The prospect of extra-food outweighed that of immediate danger.

In Natzweiler *Häftlinge* were appointed in each barrack to carry the daily 50 litre mess-tins full of soup from the kitchen to the barrack. The immensely heavy kettles had handles on each side. When the carriers, panting from the exertion, dropped the kettles on the floor the iron handles clanged loudly against the kettles. (I can still hear that sound). This always triggered a stream of saliva with me. Just like Pavlov's dog test.

OUR JEW

Amongst us there was one Jew. How did he get mixed in with our company? What German whim, what German sense of humour had caused one Jew to be in the NN-Lager Natzweiler? It was obvious that something would be done about it.

Something is going to be done about it. The gallows have been erected, a black coffin placed next to it. With much glee the Jew, our Jew, is invited to lie down in the coffin. He does just that. Now he gets three hours to get used to his surroundings, that is what they tell him. After that the lid is closed.

Three hours later, with the entire camp assembled for roll-call, they hang him. This time it goes smoothly. Our Jew breaks his neck immediately.

THE GYPSY WOMEN

One day a special fence was put up around one of the Blocks next to the *Revier*. The next day, we were utterly amazed to see several tens, perhaps hundreds of dark-eyed women with brightly coloured head-scarves thronging behind the fence. They were wild women, spoke an unfamiliar language and made jokes about us. Did they not understand where they were?

A few days later those barracks were deserted. I found out what happened from the *Häftling* vet who treated the dogs and other animals of the SS outside the camp. Somewhat below the *Lager* lay a farm, called Struthof. This had been vacated and turned into a gas chamber. All our female friends, our gypsy women, had been killed there. One of them had given birth just before she and the new-born baby were gassed.

FATHER AND SON

Sleeping lightly, a *Häftling* in the *Revier* is woken up by a strange noise: as if something is being cracked. Silently he sits up and looks over the edge of his bed. Below him he sees a small figure at work on something. He soon recognizes the figure: it is the little Polish boy who was admitted to the *Revier* shortly after his father. In the lower bed lies the father who has been busy dying all day. The cracking noise emanates from there; also soft groaning. The boy is probably helping his father. . . .

The next morning the father turns out to have died. The son seems rather cheerful. Later that day some prominent men come to visit him, fat *Kapos* with bread, soup, cigarettes. The following day too he receives visitors, and food. He recovers.

Later the boy starts blabbing. He has been very clever. He knew that the dead before being cremated are stripped of their gold teeth and crowns. He also knew that his father was well provided with these trinkets. Well, he thought, gold has proved to be useful barter. Let me be one up on them.

6 x 2 CENTIMETRES

Those who died in the *Revier* of Natzweiler between morning and evening roll-call were not reported dead before the next morning's roll-call; these deaths were kept secret for twelve or more hours. That way the dead also received a food portion. With a high death toll ten or more *Portionen* extra were sometimes available in one evening. They rarely benefited the sick who were still alive; they were 'organized'.

Officially the dead whose numbers had been reported were laid down naked outside the barrack, a hard stone, or perhaps asbestos - certainly fireproof - disc, 6 x 2 cm, was attached to their big toe, with space on it for scratching the number. The dead went into the oven with their discs; later these discs were recovered from the ashes; these provided proof of a person's cremation.

This introduces a complex subject: exchange of identity. In every KZ a *Politische Abteilung* was established which did not come under the jurisdiction of the *Lager* commandant but was under direct orders from Berlin: a sort of Gestapo branch. It kept and administered a card index of prisoners together with all accompanying files. *Häftlinge* worked there too. When a message arrived from Berlin that no. x had to be executed or transported elsewhere for execution or interrogation, when there was a danger of his blabbing - in short when certain prisoners were in immediate peril for their lives - numbers would secretly be exchanged with that of a *Häftling* who was already dead, in the card files and the dossiers, as fast as lightning. As a result the person summoned turned out to be officially already dead. In this way some Jews were made Aryans.

This perilous and life-saving task was carried out by several Dutchmen in the utmost secrecy in many camps, including Natzweiler. Sometimes some cooperation from *Blockältesten* was necessary. Almost no one knows the ins and outs of it, precisely how it worked.

THE WHEELBARROW

Sunday mornings in Natzweiler held a particular horror. We did not march off to far away details such as the *Steinbruch* but were kept busy in or near the *Lager*, for example shifting a pile of bricks to a place from where, on another Sunday, another group of *Häftlinge* dragged the bricks back to their original position. During this kind of Sunday work you could not afford to relax for one minute; the SS watched us avidly and at the first sign of any slacking all hell broke loose. One Sunday my group had to carry pieces of granite on wheelbarrows - *Schubkarren* -

along a slippery path up to a tip on a hill above the camp. There were a lot of SS and *Kapos* surrounding us who made sure that we covered the road up pushing our heavy wheelbarrows at the double. As usual I was conspicuous because of my height, my skeletal appearance, my big ears - even more pronounced when your head is bald - and the perennial drips on my nose. Nor did I ever succeed in disguising my unfamiliarity with this sort of heavy labour in contrast to my comrades whose profession was builder, docker or gardener. Working with spade, pick-axe and wheelbarrow showed up my profound clumsiness. At the bottom we had to load the *Schubkarren* to overloading, until not one piece of granite more could be fitted on to it. You looked round with Argus-eyes for where to load what and how. I chose small pieces, stupidly believing these to be lighter. I did not then appreciate that many small stones fit together neatly and result in a chock-full and leaden-heavy wheelbarrow. One of my friends, an Amsterdam docker, was much smarter, choosing the largest blocks and slaving away reasonably industriously. In this way he loaded his *Schubkarre* instantly, topped up with a large block, to the evident satisfaction of the slavedrivers. Even the krauts did not see through this clever device: because of the large amount of air between the irregular pieces of granite the wheelbarrow looked full and heavy but was in fact half empty and fairly light.

After a few hours - the well-trodden path had meanwhile become a slide - the end of my strength was nigh. I became more conspicuous, stumbling and panting on the way up with my infernal wheelbarrow. This did not escape my friend. When we had again arrived at the bottom, after the umpteenth horror-trip, and loaded our wheelbarrows, he hissed to me: 'Swap!' He grabbed my wheelbarrow and walked off. I took his, which not only looked lighter but was.

That Sunday morning came to an end without my having collapsed and I owed it to my docker-friend with his heart of gold and shrewd comprehension of situations like this one.

SHARING
Particularly when I had somehow obtained a cigarette, I felt the need to isolate myself in order to find my own aura again, which smoking always helped. Once I quietly sat puffing when a Dutch friend joined me. He did not ask for anything. But, of course, it was not done to sit smoking on my own and not share a few puffs (I have known ten men sharing one cigarette). Therefore we smoked in turns. The cigarette finished, two more fell into my lap from above. Surprised, we looked

up. Two well-fed Luxemburgers passed by, one turned round, smiling.

FRIENDSHIP

Any book one reads about wars, ordeals and disasters, invariably praises friendship. Without friendship you could not survive a kraut camp, not for more than a few weeks anyway. Friendship in the KZ was not restricted to encouraging words, help with food and clothes and getting a better job. It went far beyond this, sometimes to the limit. Frequently risks were taken in full knowledge of the danger to one's own life to save someone else, to grab him from the threshold of death. In ordinary life friendship between men has a genial quality, crude, perhaps sometimes superficial, but in the camps this could turn into something else. There you could not leave it at: 'Come on, boy, chin up.' During the daily fight to stay alive friendship could acquire a tenderness, which had feminine qualities, somehow protective.

In Natzweiler I suffered invariably from almost frozen hands and feet. At the end of one free Sunday afternoon, one of my friends brought me a pair of small pieces of black cloth with ribbons. 'Here you are, Floris, I've sewn these for you. Experience shows they're useful, more than the thickest mitten.' They turned out to be wrist-muffs, made specially for me one Sunday afternoon by a civil engineer. The next morning I put them on. You could not see them, my sleeves were long, gloves were *strengstens untersagt* (strictly prohibited). My hands remained warm.

Friendship in a KZ had an element of Eros when it became really serious. Some books proclaim that men who are locked up for a long time without seeing any women can become temporarily homosexual. Nothing of the sort occurred in our KZ, all sexual curiosity of any kind had disappeared as a result both of fear and starvation. Yet friends could still love each other. One evening when I was lying on my bed deeply depressed, Con Broers brought me a saucepan of macaroni. When he noticed my deep distress he climbed onto the bed next to mine. He said: 'You should imagine that it was three months ago that you felt like this. You must move ahead in spirit. Then look back at yourself as you are now, crying.' He turned on his side, my way, and started stroking my stubbly head. That really helped, and forty-nine years later I can still feel it.

Also in Natzweiler, just discharged from the *Revier* after another bout of pneumonia, but still very very weak after a murderous roll-call in a driving snowstorm, I came across a Roman Catholic priest, a most gentle man with a provincial accent. We talked about the palpable divine presence. He stopped in his tracks and said, 'You're a Protestant but I want to bless you.' We were standing by the side of a barrack in a snowdrift. He whispered a great deal of Latin. He then made a cross on my face and chest, saying, 'In nomine Patris, et Filii, et Spiritus Sancti. . . .' That too helped considerably.

The list of friends who pulled, dragged and hauled me through an endless series of mortal dangers is a long one, a very long one.

EFFEKTENKAMMER

Con Broers has 'organized' for two of us, me included, to join the team running the *Effektenkammer*. The *Effektenkammer* is the barrack for storing the private property of the *Häftlinge* - all our old clothes and shoes but also valuables like watches and rings - not only smartly packed in paper bags one per *Häftling* but also perfectly documented on cards in special ink - a model of a warehouse. The Germans are like that. Our *Effktenkammer* was directed by a handsome, heavily built Bible researcher, Ernst Hassel, with his purple triangle. It was a fabulous team in the barrack next to the crematorium. Anyone who worked in it was a 'prominent'.

Among the of private property were suitcases. These suitcases contained clothes. And Bibles, in many languages. And various provisions. And tobacco, cigars, cigarettes. There were socks, shoes, letters, love-letters, prayer-cards, photographs. Photographs of Luxemburger, French, Norwegian, Dutch, Russian, and Polish women.

Unlike anyone else we had plenty of opportunities to 'organize'. You could steal and make yourself rich, because all these goods could be exchanged for food. You could 'organize' sweaters, socks, shoes. You could smoke. . . . Initially we did not indulge in it. Not only because Ernst often searched us, but also because we felt it to be improper to steal from fellow-sufferers. But the temptation increased and became irresistible when the food situation deteriorated from bad to worse and then to impossible.

Our Ernst treated us well, a heavyweight, conscientious, occasionally losing his temper for no apparent reason, occasionally having mad fits. It was my job to inscribe the *Karteikarten* (filing cards) of each prisoner with name, first names and number, in Indian ink, known as *Tusche*. For weeks, indeed months, I sat in a clean wooden room writing for some ten hours a day, with a view of part of a forest, a watchtower with SS and machine gun, and a part of the crematorium. Innumerable times I wrote TADEUSZ- IWAN-LEW- ALEXEJ-HENRI-JANUSZ to surnames ending with -witsch and -enko. Like a good managing director Ernst came regularly to check. He was pleased with my work, except for the 1 and the 8 of *Häftling* numbers. At last he was driven to frenzy:

'You, Bakels, may be able to get away with this nonsense in your lawyer's office, but not here.'

From then on I therefore wrote a 1 with a German stroke and an 8 starting at the top and then curving to the left.

Like all Germans Ernst too had a passion for *Saubermachen* (cleaning). Every Saturday afternoon we had to stop work, fill buckets with water and get hold of brooms - Ernst in front. First *Fenster auf!* (open windows), whereupon Ernst, followed by us, started splashing water on the wooden floor. It soon turned into a water ballet, with us wading through the innundations, and Ernst shouting, 'Always Ruck Zuck (in a flash), you, give the floor a good scrubbing, what, Ruck Zuck!' As I was too weak for *richtig auskehren* (good scrubbing) he often came to me, snatched the broom from me and started scrubbing with bewildering fury, splashing about, refilling the buckets again and again.

One day an expensive object was found to have been 'organized'. A bigwig from the kitchen came to complain. Ernst confined us to barracks and asked the offender to step forward. No one stepped forward. This could have ended badly, with for instance a posting to a punitive team for all of us, but it blew over thanks to Ernst, who was himself an important bigwig. The next day all of us were still suspects - as Ernst Hassel clearly showed. It was an extraordinary experience for me, being a suspect. You do not know how to behave, look or talk. You are inclined to fidget when a suspect, but that would be extremely stupid. When therefore you behave especially normally, almost too casually, you are even more conspicuous. Normal behaviour is impossible when you are under suspicion.

MURDER BY SPECIAL ORDER

On 2 June 1944 at noon, before serving the soup, all those assigned to inside jobs are lined up. On one of the higher terraces the gallows have been set up, a scaffolding about 4 meters high with a box-shaped platform with a lid underneath, fitted with a pedal. When one kicks the pedal the lid of the case is thrust open. Anyone standing on the lid, a rope round his neck, would crash about one meter down and break his neck. That at least is the intention of hanging.

A young Polish freedom fighter has to be hanged by special order of Adolf Hitler. He is standing beside the gallows, the upper part of his body bare, in striped pyjama trousers, bare feet, hands tied behind his back. A group of kraut bigwigs are standing by his side, among them a military doctor with instruments, and the *Lager* commandant. The commandant steps forward and starts reading a decree from Berlin, containing the death sentence and the reasons for it. Some documents appear to be missing, a few SS men are sent away to investigate. Some ten minutes later they return empty-handed: the key of the filing cabinet cannot be found. The commandant informs us that we will hear the rest later.

The Pole asks whether he should mount the steps. Yes. This he does without uttering a sound. Two *Häftlinge*, whose normal job this is, put the rope round his neck and return to our lines. Suddenly an SS man approaches the platform and kicks the pedal. The boy disappears in the box up to his knees.

Apparently he touches the bottom with his toes because the rope is not stretched tightly. He tries to mount the box. The SS man rushes forward and kicks the entire coffin away. We can now see that the boy is indeed standing on his toes. His face turns first deep-red, then blue and his entire body starts shaking, his handcuffed arms, his legs. He makes hissing noises.

A murmuring passes through the ranks of the thousands like the rustling of the wind through leaves. After some five minutes an order is shouted. The two hangman's assistants run forward to the boy. One of them lifts him carefully, the other loops the top of the rope over the gallows. They then lower him - carefully. Again the boy therefore does not break his neck, but he is now hanging. His face turns dark blue, yes, black as a result of blood congestion; in front of our eyes he is being strangled endlessly. Slowly he turns round, 180° to the left, 180° to the right, and back again, and again, with monstrous convulsions and sounds that should not be allowed to issue from a human being. The bigwig krauts disappear one after the other. I watch it closely. I want to experience Satan.

What can we possibly do about it? There is a double row of guards. Outside the barbed wire under high tension SS are lying behind machine guns. Everything is prepared for any irregularities. The silence becomes absolute. The Pole starts to retch. Suddenly his arms and legs seem to have been struck by electric shocks.

After a quarter of an hour, the show still on, we are suddenly ordered to break ranks. We are marched off past the hangman for whom we have to walk rigidly to attention, *Mützen ab* (hats off). Most of us unmistakably do not take off our woolly caps in the direction of the hangman but of his victim, who will never know that he received a farewell salute from thousands of his fellow sufferers.

Back in the barracks we gulp our *Bohnensuppe mit Fleisch dazu* and fifteen minutes later we have to assemble again for work. The Polish boy is still gently turning round, legs and arms still straining. His face is now leaden. His tongue hangs out of his mouth. An SS man with his boots, deathheads, revolver and Alpen hat walks up and down, yawning.

It took three quarters of an hour for him to die.

DÉBARQUEMENT EN FRANCE

On 6 June 1944, early in the morning, as I was writing cards quietly in my wooden room, I heard someone rush into our barracks calling softly. I thought I heard 'débarquement . . .' and ran out of my little room. Yes, indeed. It was true. This time it was really true! 'Débarquement en France!' a French friend called, slapping everyone on the shoulder, fiery red with excitement. Allied landings in Normandy after massive aerial bombardments and artillery fire from the sea.

Americans and English were now in the same country as us! Liberation from the west had started! After the initial ecstatic joy I retreated to my little room. I felt a need to pray. To pray for inspiration and strength for the Allies. I also prayed for the Germans, for whom this was now the beginning of the end. I thought about the thousands of ships at sea, the tens of thousands of soldiers, sailing, landing, fighting, falling. God, what sacrifice, what lives lost. . . .

My intense feeling of happiness was accompanied by a bitter taste. June, the Channel, the beautiful coasts of France, those assaulting the Atlantic Wall, the soldiers who would fall without living to witness the realization of their goal, the Germans for whom the bell now tolled. . . .

At the evening roll-call of 6 June the change was clearly noticeable. The Germans were more vicious than ever. *Häftlinge* with some light again in their eyes, sometimes smiling, sometimes winking. They are coming!

PARCELS

One day in Natzweiler a rumour circulated: parcels had arrived for the Dutch. This could only be a fantasy. As far as the homefront was concerned, we NN-*Häftlinge* had, after all, disappeared without trace. But the rumour turned out to be true.

A few days later each Dutchman received a parcel - opened, pillaged, as usual. The sender was not the Dutch Red Cross. The sender was the Mennonite Society of Amsterdam. With warm greetings from the clergyman and a prominent lady, their names mentioned in full, astonishingly.

We were overjoyed, of course, and bewildered. In Holland the existence of Natzweiler was therefore known, as was the presence there of Dutchmen. How was that possible? And how could the Amsterdam Mennonites have had the guts to invite danger by quite clearly showing they knew something they were not supposed to know? The parcels from Holland, apart from their excellent contents, meant an enormous boost for morale. There were therefore at least two people in our country who knew about us.

[When trying, in 1976, to discover how the Amsterdam Mennonites could have achieved this I met the current vicar. Because of the time that had elapsed he could not recall everything. But he did remember that the thousands of ration cards and the thousands of kilograms of provisions had been financed by two well-known food manufacturers at Zaandam, just north of Amsterdam. One started with 10-20 parcels per week; in August 1944 one ended with 600-700. In addition to the two people mentioned on the parcels, another famous lady had been involved, whose subsequent fame and decorations derived from her daring efforts to save Jewish children, one of whom is the fortunate foster brother of the translator of this book. There is a statue of her in Amsterdam. She also joined me and some friends on a 4th of May many years ago in establishing the Anne Frank Foundation which was set up in a few hours to acquire the Anne Frank House and save it from destruction. Long ago I gave up my role as chairman and member of the Foundation's Committee.]

At about the same time as the news of the landings was circulating another miracle befell me, the result of the fearless vigour and care of my wife, so far away too and despite prohibitions and other hurdles. One evening Wim Roessingh appeared with a food parcel, addressed to him. However, the handwriting on the label was unknown to him, as was the sender. Did I perhaps know? With throbbing heart I admitted knowing everything about it. The handwriting was all too familiar, as was the person hiding behind the fictitious sender's name. The contents had been composed with such subtle significance that I could not contain myself at this first sign of my wife's love in the hell of Natzweiler.

PROMINENT

In the summer of 1944 Dave van Eeghen and I became very 'prominent' (the reader may have guessed by now that the term stems from the German *Prominenz* and refers to a *Häftling*-VIP, a very important person indeed in the eyes of ordinary *Häftlinge*, and also most useful to our captors). Hundreds of new *Häftlinge* started arriving, almost all of them French, with much luggage, sometimes suitcases full of food. 'Organizing' now increased sharply. There was no more shortage of food. My diary mentions that in August I weighed 79.5 kg (in Amersfoort 53 kg, when liberated 49 kg).

This had various consequences. On the one hand it was, of course, a reason for deep thankfulness, ending as it did our starvation. We had also become real grandees and were treated with respect. We even had a batman: a Russian *traktorist* or labourer in a tractor factory. He functioned as our attendant in exchange for food and particularly cigars. He did our washing. He brushed our shoes (of course we had also 'organized' shoes). He also made up our tables, for Dave and I had become such high persons that we no longer slept in the over-crowded sleeping ward on wooden beds but on tables in the *Waschraum*. We did not go to bed but to table, and our Russian took care of mattresses, pillows, blankets, sheets.

On the other hand, our position was, of course, painful and in some ways shameful, especially with regard to the hundreds of new arrivals who initially found themselves in an awkward situation. Some may enjoy being a rich gentleman among the poor, I did not. I felt embarrassed. Of course we gave away a lot, but still. We were waited on and our friendship was courted.

I often had qualms of conscience and asked myself continuously whether our Lord would be pleased with our behaviour. True, we were not exactly thieves, but we were petty dealers, businessmen whose practices did not always pass muster. The flesh proved to be weak.

Fortunately we could also do a lot of good in the *Effektenkammer*. We tried to reassure the hundreds of haggard, frightened French, mostly maquisards, and to teach them the ropes. Now and again it was very hot. The French sweated tremendously, our barrack exuded a constant penetrating smell of sweat which rose up from their clothes.

Sometimes we worked throughout the night. For several nights on end I had only three or four hours' sleep. That too provided an excuse for at least eating properly.

Our transport group delivered a prince and a bishop. Their names are not to be found in my diary. As for the bishop: he arrived looking like St Nicolas with crosier and mitre and I was kept busy for quite some time helping undress him. Under his ceremonial dress he turned out to be wearing plus-fours with woollen kneesocks and sturdy walking boots. It really is true: I have undressed a French bishop. Later I found out their names: François Xavier Charles Marie Anne Joseph, Prince de Bourbon Parme, Piacenza and Guastalla; and the Bishop of Nancy.

ANOMALIES

More than once I have testified - supported by examples - that the German is unpredictable in his behaviour; one moment like this, the next one like that. Perhaps it was due to the new *Lager* commandant, Hartjenstein, or to the progress of the war, or to something else. Whatever the reason, in the summer of 1944 changes occurred. Once a week, on Saturdays or Sundays, we could sit on one of the terraces in the sun and drink a glass of beer from the German authorities. I have been to see a film twice. In Dachau there was a brothel (not visited by Dutchmen). In Natzweiler the *Krankenrevier*, however poor, had an operating room at its disposal and an X- ray apparatus. And ambulances. A dentist boasted a small treatment room, albeit with a prehistoric drilling apparatus serviced by foot like a spinning wheel. Some beds in the *Revier* had sheets and pillowcases with blue and white squares: at their base a temperature chart, almost like a real hospital.

On the one hand the Nazis did everything possible to annihilate us whether quickly or slowly, on the other they kept a *Revier* going to patch us up. It was pure schizophrenia.

I have talked to Germans who honestly seemed to believe that we were in the KZ to be re-educated: that it was an *Erziehungslager* (education camp). Perhaps certain German authorities cherished some desire to show us how magnanimous they could be towards us criminals: reflecting the oft-repeated phrase about the 'magnanimity of the Führer'. 'Wir sind nicht so gefährlich' (we are not that dangerous), etc. Perhaps in or above the camp management there were people or bodies who differed in their opinion about the treatment of *Häftlinge*.

THE FOUR GIRLS

On 6 July 1944 in the afternoon *dicke Luft* (thick fog) suddenly descended on Natzweiler. The outside work parties returned early. Soup distribution took place early. Everywhere SS men were running around. All *Häftlinge* were consigned to barracks, nobody was allowed outside, or in front of windows. Clearly something was about to happen that should not be seen. A new disaster, a new horror. I was lying on my upper berth and looked, like many others, for some time to the terraces, the granite steps, the 'Lagerstreet': all deserted.

Then I noticed two heavily armed SS on the sloping 'Lagerstreet'. And behind them - four girls. Four summery girls with lovely long hair and gently swaying skirts, some with bare arms, all with bare legs. They looked around. They seemed like angels from heaven. And behind them two more SS men. I followed them with stinging eyes, one moment invisible behind a barrack, the next re-appearing far down below, finally disappearing in the direction of the bunker.

The next day we heard it all on the network of connections via privileged prisoners who had connections with even more important *Häftlinge* working in the bunker and the crematorium. We had seen four English or French girls. Four female secret agents. Four women, murdered by injections of phenol. Four murdered girls, already gone *durchs Kamin*. Incinerated.

[The case relating to the horrible murder of four female secret agents was heard in May/June 1946 by a British military court. Until recently only three of the four girls were known: Denise Borrell (FANY), Section Officer Diana Rowden (WAAF) and Vera Leigh (FANY). The fourth girl is now known to have been Sonia Olschansky. The only death sentence passed was for the *Standortartzt*, SS Unterstumführer Dr Werner A.J. Rohde, the doctor-murderer who administered the injections of phenol. Lager commandant Hartjenstein was given a life sentence. It is possible that all the suspects in this case also stood trial before or after elsewhere for other offences.]

THE RED CHIMNEY

Shortly before the evacuation of Natzweiler as a consequence of the approaching Allies (August 1944), the Maquis became more daring in their resistance activities down in the valley. Part of the local male population was arrested in reprisal and sent to our camp for execution. We saw them arrive, by their hundreds. They were not registered, not given numbers and camp clothing, not shaved or put in barracks. They went straight to the crematorium. There they were first hanged, next to the oven, and then burned.

When this turned out to take too much time - there were only four hooks, and the Americans were rapidly approaching - the SS skipped the hanging and threw French resisters without further ado live into the oven.

In those days the flames shot up high out of the high chimney of the crematorium. The entire camp stank of burnt flesh. In the dark the chimney was red hot to its full height. It began to list over.

THE CARD INDEX

Towards the end of August 1944 it became known that Natzweiler would be evacuated. The roaring of artillery could occasionally be clearly heard; in the evening after dark we could see a reddish flickering in the northwest. The Allies were advancing.

Nervousness in the camp increased by the hour. Transport invariably meant calamity. Most of the *Lagerhasen* had done their best to find themselves an endurable job. We had made friends. A routine had been established. Everyone would have to start all over again somewhere else. Especially awful was the thought that we would almost certainly move eastward, away from our liberators - but there too liberators were advancing. What plans did the Germans have? To murder us somewhere midway between the western and eastern fronts? Did they want all the hundreds of thousands of inhabitants from the many camps surging backwards and forwards according to the progress of the battles?

The reaction of the very old German *Lagerhasen* - some of them had been in a camp for eight, even ten years - was often baffling. I remember an old German gentleman who held the high office of manager of the *Schreibstube* card indexes. I think he was in his own eyes a sort of chieftain of the civil service, a functionary without whom the entire human society would dissolve into chaos. This man - on a personal level a decent chap - went into a complete muddle, and was inconsolable. It had become apparent to him that his card indexes ('meine fabelhafte Kartei') would not be evacuated but probably burnt. His life's work - burnt! He had lost all sense of reality. For three long years with typical German devotion to duty and *Gründlichkeit*, he had carried out his administration of the living and the dead, to the satisfaction of his superiors, undoubtedly in fine handwriting, on coloured cards. Burnt! I got the impression that he had rather expected to be honoured at his tenth anniversary with a gold watch.

DEPARTURE

We were transported on 2 September 1944, after fourteen months, to as always an unknown destination. In the unimaginable chaos preceding the evacuation I had 'organized' a superb pair of shoes. As usual we had to line up for hours on end to be counted, counted and counted again. We went on foot through the vast pine forests down the small road to Rothau. I remember a desperate need to relieve myself. It was, of course, impossible in our marching columns with SS all around us to *austreten* (step outside). Therefore, at last, I had to let the urine go. This was not only inevitable and filthy but also exceptionally difficult. Urinating while walking is almost impossible.

Down in the valley we were deeply moved by the sight of the houses, the flowers, the women and the men and especially the children, who clearly sympathized with us.

Of the journey eastward by goods train I remember nothing. My diary notes between 2 and 20 September are missing. After a fairly short journey we arrived in the mammoth KZ of Dachau near Munich.

NATZWEILER

Natzweiler (department Bas-Rhin) - French Natzwiller or Natzviller - is a hamlet some 65 km west-southwest of Strasburg in the Vosges near Rothau and Schirmeck. Above it lies the mountain La Roche Louise (1100 m). Before the war it was a much loved ski resort. Skiers would come down the Louise to the nearby Hotel Le Struthof, stop off for refreshment and then continue down into the valleys. In September 1940 the SS-Standartenführer Blumberg appeared on the scene. He considered the north slope of the Louise a suitable place for a KZ. In that he was right. It is a lonely area, about 900 m high, often swept by icy winds and generously provided with snow in winter. The construction of the KZ Natzweiler - in French, Le Struthof - created rivers of blood, as did the steep road up to it. The original camp population, several hundred *Grünen*, built their own hell.

Natzweiler, an exceptionally dangerous KZ, was laid out in terraces, one above the other. On both sides of each terrace was a large barrack (Block), between these the roll-call yard. There were almost as many roll-call yards as terraces. The terraces were connected by steep flights of shallow, irregular, granite steps. These too have cost many lives. On one side a steep road led down to the bunker and the crematorium; between these was a quarry, where the ashes of the cremated were dumped. The camp was surrounded by a double row of barbed wire and high voltage electric fences, a small path running between them for the guards, and several watchtowers with machine guns and search lights, which floodlit the camp at night except during an air raid alarm. It has been estimated that in all some 20,000 to 25,000 *Häftlinge* passed through Natzweiler; shortly before the evacuation there were 7,000. The number of dead has not been estimated. The *Lager* commandant - first Hüttig, then Kramer, then Hartjenstein - lived in a villa with a swimming pool near Das Tor. Nearby were the SS barracks. These accommodated 160 to 200 guards (i.e. one SS man for nearly 40 prisoners!). Some distance below the camp in a brick barn near Le Struthof, a small gas chamber had been erected. From the camp up to the Louise a road of about 1 km led to the *Steinbruch*, the largest work detail, where some 1,000 men worked. On the site around the *Steinbruch, Hallen* could be found where they worked in two shifts (*Nachtschicht*).

The government of the French Republic has declared Natzweiler a *Monument Historique*. Das Tor, the fences, the miradors, a kitchen block, a few of the other blocks, the bunker and the crematorium have been preserved. In one block an exhibition was set up; in 1976 neo-fascists set fire to it and it remained burnt out until recently when it was restored. There are conducted tours, one has to pay an entrance fee. As an *ancien déporté* you are allowed in free, and alone without a guide. There are often visitors. Just above the camp a monument in white marble has been erected, 45 m high, in the shape of a flame. The figure of a *Muselman* has been vaguely carved on the inside. The monument carries the text:

Honneur aux héroes et martyrs de la déportation
La France reconnaissante

It was unveiled on 25 June 1967 by President De Gaulle. Around it a flattened site has been laid out with small white crosses. Below, in the camp, at the place where the ashes from the crematorium were dumped, commemmorative plaques have been fitted. Including a Dutch one. The chimney is still there, still leaning slightly: ever since August 1944. . . . Today there is a flower bed. Large stones make up the words *ossa humiliata*. *Ossa humiliata* means literally 'humiliated bones'. The words derive from Psalm 51: 8: 'Fill me with joy and gladness; let the bones which Thou hast broken rejoice'. In other words: evil, sin, they have broken man, but the prospect of resurrection from evil is held out. In that sense *ossa humiliata* is not just a negative concept but eschatologically opens up a great perspective. I had wanted to call this book *Ossa Humiliata* but that did not seem quite right.

Where once other blocks stood there are now neatly flattened terraces, covered with gravel. On each terrace a sign: Allach-Gross Rosen-Neuengamme-Dachau-Mauthausen, etc. Well below the camp is the café-restaurant Le Struthof. On Sunday French families visit it for a glass of wine, squash for the children. A sign 'Chambre à Gaz' points to a messy brick barn. You can still enter the barn, free of charge. There are a few cells in the barn. There is also a gas chamber, 4 x 4 meters at most. The spy holes are still there. You can enter the gas chamber, I always do. The concrete walls, of bad quality and dirty, have been scratched, unevenly.

Sometimes it is not reason that passes the wit of man, but the imagination.

Above the camp a road has been constructed. Somewhere a sign:

'Champ de Feu'. On these roads car-rallies with racing cars are now being held. It is rather difficult to find the branch off to the *Steinbruch*. The foundations of the *Hallen* are still visible. Further along, on the large plateau under and above the granite rocks where the Great Murders occurred, not much more than a trace remains of the path, winding between high bushes that are now almost trees. It is usually muddy up there and very cold. No living soul ventures here. In two places there are small caves, which you can enter by bending down and jumping from stone to stone across the yellowish water, which drips down from above. There are birds, wild flowers and butterflies. At the spot where we tipped the *Loren*, letting the granite blocks thunder down the ravine - sometimes together with the bodies of comrades almost or completely beaten to death - thick bushes have grown up too, from the very top to the very bottom. You can see the thousands of granite pieces gleaming through the trees and bushes. Underneath them a lot of bones can no doubt be found as well.

Once when I was leaving the *Steinbruch*, there were people there after all. At the entrance, near the *Hallen*. Two people. In a small French car. A boy and a girl, petting passionately. They looked at me, slightly embarrassed, and smiled.

6. AUSSENKOMMANDO
OTTOBRUNN
10-20 September 1944

A MISTAKE

On 10 September 1944 I left Dachau with a batch of some 400 men, again bound for an unknown destination. The group was rather arbitrarily put together, i.e. consecutive Dachau-numbers. Mine was 99718, and the 400 numbers around mine formed part of our batch. They were French, Belgians, Norwegians, Poles and approximately thirty Dutchmen. The journey lasted a full twenty-four hours, and we passed through Munich, amongst other places. Rain seeped through the numerous bullet holes in the cattle-wagon. On the afternoon of the 11th the train stopped in a large pine forest. It turned out to be standing against the buffer that marked the end of the railway line, which was rarely used and almost covered by tall weeds. Apart from us and the SS no living thing could be seen. For one moment I thought: our number's up. But after half an hour's march through extensive forests we arrived at a settlement of summer cottages surrounded by beautiful gardens in full bloom. Our camp was in the middle of this village full of women and children - evacuees from Munich - Aussenkommando Ottobrunn. Later on it turned out to be a *Lager zweiter Stufe* where NN-men did not belong at all.

It was a benign little camp. The low barracks were well kept: in the centre of the camp was a pond, and there were well-tended flowerbeds everywhere. It was, however, overcrowded. We slept in paper bags. The SS hardly ever showed themselves. There were two roll-calls of only fifteen minutes a day. I did not see any beatings. After arrival we were addressed by the *Lagerälteste* in the presence of the *Lagerführer*, a quiet individual who occasionally associated with *Häftlinge*.

'You'll have a good time here, it isn't Natzweiler,' he told us. Our spirits rose optimistically. In view of the excellent news from the war we fooled ourselves that we would quietly await the end of the war in this pleasant camp. Reveille around 8am. It was cold, sometimes freezing, before the sun had climbed above the huge fir trees. After roll-call we just walked around. When the sun appeared it warmed up at once; we shed most of our clothes and lay down on the bank of the pond, sunbathing between the flowers. We never had to work. At noon there was lunch, which we did not take in the barracks but in a canteen. You could also be there at other times of the day; there were games of chess and a stage used occasionally for music-making. It was rather like a soldier's hostel. We could watch the housewives in the surrounding summer cottages, busying themselves while their children shouted. The days passed without incident. After roll-call at night bread was distributed. The food was, of course, not sufficient, but otherwise satisfactory. The *Krankenrevier* was very small, could only hold nine patients and was managed by a doctor from Holland.

Then rumours started that we had been brought to Ottobrunn by mistake and would shortly leave. Four clever boys at once obtained work in the camp, to avoid being moved. We left during the afternoon of 20 September. We were told the journey would be westward to construct fortifications.

None of us knew what awaited us: the Great Suffering.

7. AUSSENKOMMANDO DAUTMERGEN
21 September-20 November 1944

BEYOND ENDURANCE

After a nightmare journey of more than twenty-four hours our cattle-train carrying 350 men arrived on the evening of 21 September 1944 at Schömberg, somewhere in the Swabian Alps. On a small upland plain between Schömberg (the site of a KZ) and the hamlet of Dautmergen was the Aussenkommando Dautmergen which was under the jurisdiction of Natzweiler. Half an hour's march took us in darkness to the camp. In groups of ten we were kicked into tents that were already overcrowded with Poles who raged and cursed as we stumbled over them. There was no light. The next morning the camp turned out to be some 500 meters square, with a simple fence, watchtowers and searchlights. Several barracks were being built but were not yet in use; as were the *Krankenrevier* and the *Schonungsblock*. One lived in tents. But only a few days later we were moved to barracks and the tents were gradually cleared away. However, the *Revier* tent remained until early November.

Dautmergen was a place of unmitigated horror, managed by Polish criminals. Dominating everything, however, was the mud. The mud, sometimes covered with wet snow, was ½ meter deep so even the lucky devil who had shoes was not protected: the muck seeped into his shoes from above. There was a special *Wasserleitung* (water-works detail), but water pipes and drainage were unknown in Dautmergen. Every day a tank lorry appeared with water for the kitchen. No water was available for drinking and washing. Anyone who dared 'organize' water from the tank lorry got coshed. During the full two months of my stay at Dautmergen I did not wash, except for a few times with water from a brook far away in the field where we worked. I shaved only once, and never had my hair cropped. Disinfection did not exist, everyone was covered with lice. Initially there was no electricity either. Distributing bread took place by candlelight, which facilitated all kinds

165

of deception. The food: in the morning one slice of bread with something on it, in the afternoon at work a slice of bread without anything on it, in the evening 1 litre of soup or 3/4 litre of soup with *Pellkartoffeln* (potatoes in their skin). The soup contained a lot of unwashed vegetables, so all *Häftlinge* suffered from diarrhoea. There was no question of parcels. Only once did the Norwegians receive parcels - and how.

Before our arrival Dautmergen was exclusively populated by Poles, captured during the Warsaw uprising of August 1944. The Poles, the dregs of the population, were real scoundrels. They were in total control and the entire gang of *Lagerprominenz* was recruited from amongst them, except the *Kapos* who were German 'Grünen' (green triangles). The *Blockältesten* were not equal to their task, did not have privileges, stole wherever they could and flogged anyone not Polish with cudgels. The German-Polish *Lagerführer* was clearly a sadist.

The sleeping quarters in two large barracks consisted of three-tiered structures of boards (not even wooden beds) covered with straw. Blankets were very rare and continuously stolen or grabbed in the dark of night, as were clothes and shoes. We slept fully dressed with our muddy shoes or wooden sandals as pillows. There was only enough room to sleep on your side. Anyone who had to *austreten* (get out) and succeeded in the struggle to liberate himself from his cursing neighbours, faced an expedition of 200 meters through mud. The *Abort* was a small drafty shed with a beam for sitting on when the weakness of your knees proved to be greater than your abhorrence of the shit that dripped from the beam. Paper was not available. Anyone in desperate need who tried to relieve himself just outside was certain to be beaten unconscious by the night-guards.

Only the dying were accepted in the tent that served as the *Krankenrevier*. Medical treatment was completely absent. The loathsome 'doctor' from Warsaw collected cigarette stubs and rewarded his suppliers with the soup intended for his patients. The dead were put three together in one coffin, kicked in when necessary. The coffins were dispatched to an unknown destination.

We were woken at 4.30am by loud blows on a piece of iron that hung outside and when necessary flogged into line while we held on to each other, legs pulling out of the sucking mud, losing sandals and shoes, grabbing to find them again. Then vaguely a roll-call, when we would stand until 7am, sunrise. Next we regrouped in details and left the camp, of necessity arm-in-arm to avoid getting stuck.

Most details worked several kilometers away at building sheds and small factories for 'artificial oil extraction'. I belonged to Kommando

III. When there was no snow we walked, 125 men, escorted by Wehrmacht and *Schutzkommandos*, on paths through hilly terrain for half an hour to a place near Dotternhausen, where little buildings were being erected by the side of the road. Engineers awaited us, supervisors and labourers of 'Organisation Todt' - an appropriate name. (*Tod* is German for death, Todt the name of a Nazi engineer who became Minister of Works). We were arranged in small groups under a *Meister* (master) and worked from 7.30am to 12.30pm. The work consisted of hauling bricks, beams, cement bags and rails, and shoveling sand and operating concrete mixers. It was very heavy work, particularly carrying rails for which, because of my height (187 cm or 6'2") I was invariably picked; my workmates took advantage of this characteristic of which I had formerly been proud.

On the job at least we were rarely beaten. The men of the OT were led by superior OT officers who also commanded Russian and French prisoners-of-war from neighbouring camps. These POWs, much better off than we were, sometimes threw us potato skins, hard apples and animal-fodder beetroots. As *Häftlinge* we were under the command of an SS-*Arbeitsführer*. If one did not behave satisfactorily, one's number was written down ('Meldung') and one was punished with twenty-five lashes when returned to camp. The superior OT officers behaved like the SS, the lower ranks were on our side and sometimes gave us breadcrusts, which was prohibited. The Austrian labourer Glauninger repeatedly passed me crusts in a paper bag. As he did so he whispered, 'There, behind the rock.'

We wore only underwear and cotton pyjamas. So to protect us from the increasing cold we stuffed empty cement bags underneath our pyjamas. This was deemed 'sabotage' and severely punished. Some of us occasionally risked leaving the work party to steal animal-fodder beetroots from the nearby fields. That invited the firing squad. It resulted in several deaths. I believe that for some this was a sort of suicide. Passing locals, who sometimes threw food to us, were chased away with loud shouting.

Between 12.30pm and 1pm we were allowed to rest and given our one slice of bread, which we wolfed down in the open air. In bad weather we were driven into a drafty *Zementbude* (cement hut). One day I was careless enough to produce a bag of bread crusts from Glauninger while piercing Polish eyes were watching. Suddenly the bag was grabbed, the crusts flying all over the floor, and the Polish bandits dropped on all fours, got up, stared at me and chewed.

From 1pm to 5.30pm work was resumed, after which we stumbled back to the camp at dusk. An hour of roll-call in the mud followed, when *Meldungen* (reports) were implemented. The day concluded with the tumultuous, violent soup distribution.

When it started snowing we no longer took the short cut along the path, but went instead along the road through the wretched hole of Dautmergen, where now and then housewives and children appeared in doorways to mock us. Apple trees stood beside the road. The trick was to bend down at top speed and pick up fallen apples without being noticed. If spotted it meant the rifle-butt.

The camp was commanded by a young SS *Rottenführer* who spoke Polish and preferred to execute the *Meldungen* himself. He used a whip which he cracked loosely before hitting, his left arm stretched straight forward. He hit harder the more the victim cried. He collaborated in these exercises closely with the *Lagerälteste* and the *Lagerkapo*, both Polish *Häftlinge*. Apart from headgear and clothes there was no difference between these three.

[After the war I testified some six times against SS and SD criminals before German courts, as well as before the *Schwurgericht* (assize court) at Ulm against this particular SS *Rottenführer*. Other witnesses, from as far afield as the USA and Israel, testified that this defendant had also drowned *Häftlinge* by pushing their heads in the mud. The President of the *Schwurgericht* sent a message after my testimony asking me to see him, 'if I had the time'. This I had. He received me in his room without his court robe. The President told me he got the impression from my testimony that I did not believe the assertions from Germans that the German civilian population were not aware of the atrocities committed in the camps: 'Wir haben es nicht gewusst'. I concurred. I considered this to be a downright lie, I said. He was annoyed. He himself had not known either. Would I accept this from him? I said no. The President was even more annoyed. He told me that the German civilians had been far too busy with the war: military service, heavy bombing, evacuation, lack of food. He had himself had his hands full with troubles and distress. Could I not believe him? I said no. I pointed out to him the clear visibility of many camps, the chimneys, the *Kamin*, the stench, the cattle wagons so visible at stations, the long processions of *Häftlinge*, often wounded, along the public roads on the way from KZ to work and back, the information from released prisoners, etc. etc. Did the Germans know nothing of all these maltreatments, illnesses, murders and killings? Come off it.

I persisted. He persisted. Irritably we parted.]

Those who reported sick in the morning at the *Revier* were removed with a cudgel and put into a camp work party. Early in November that was changed, as a result of the numerous deaths. The *Revier* was then housed in a wooden shed. A huge barn was also fixed up for those with *Schonung*, impossible earlier on. The *Schonung* clientele did not have to work unless the kraut needed some prisoners for minor camp duties. In that case nearly all four hundred wrecks were flogged with deafening noise from their berths. The *Kapos* with cudgels jumped, often from three stories high straight through the boards. That way they collected some ten or twenty men.

The situation in this barrack is difficult to describe. Only a few buckets were available for four hundred men to relieve themselves, so the floor was flooded with shit and urine. In early November some thousand more Poles were added to our number, but this time they were Polish Jews, curiously enough all wrapped up in heavy, long overcoats. The Polish Jews were angels compared to the non-Jewish Poles. I was told that the normal remuneration in Poland for denouncing a Polish Jew was one kilogram of sugar. Some clothes too now started to arrive. These were handed out only to Poles. During these two months not only did I not wash but never, not for one minute, did I undress. Underwear and pyjamas became inseparably attached to my skin by a thick layer of grime and faeces.

Even the strongest among us reached the limit of their endurance. One after another we were admitted to the *Schonungsblock*. I myself was one of the last Dutchmen on 10 November.

Rumours now abounded about 'sick-transports'. Some had a holy fear of them. Justifiably - as we discovered later - we felt that transportation of the sick could only end in our ultimate ruin. On the other hand, Dautmergen was such a godforsaken camp that you could not imagine anywhere else could be worse. Dave van Eeghen belonged to this last group and decided to apply for a transfer. (On 16 April 1945 he died in Bergen-Belsen from exhaustion.) But soon there was no choice. I myself left on 20 November with the last transport of sick to Vaihingen-Enz, together with twenty-two other Dutchmen, among them fourteen friends.

My diary from Dautmergen consists of only a few scraps, as the scarcity of detail above shows. Not until I ended up in the *Schonungsblock* did it become possible to dabble with such things as paper and pencil. I quote a few passages as far as they can be made out.

I know I'm upset. Strange: I can't cope anymore with my feelings. I can't cope with myself. What is 'I'? Contrasts too great. The past a fairy story, the present a hell, the future a fog. Here we talk about the paradise of Natzweiler. Is a 'paradise of Dautmergen' conceivable? Or are we now the poorest of all? This ordeal is no child's game. Often prayed ardently and aloud. Mother, if she could see me, would close her eyes. *Los, weiter*, consuming hatred and yet not allowed. Struggle of faith very hard, too difficult to rise above bodily misery. Lord, I believe; help thou mine unbelief. I'm getting there. It doesn't matter when. I'll be joining you. Childlike confidence in God. He watches and cares, clearly. My heart is not well, heartache, broken heart, Tristan and Isolde.... They want me to be an animal, crush me. Will never succeed. God is with, in me. I'm fighting for civilization, millions alongside me. One day the flag will flutter. The plain of mud here is one huge fear. More than just a fear of frozen feet: you sink away! Mental mud. Everything slips away, is uncertain. Man can't put up with having to rely only on God. He wants certainty. But that never exists! Only seemed to. Too complicated. We've had the worst, God steered us along the edge of hell. He'll lift us up all the higher. This morning in pitch darkness I softly sang the Wilhelmus (Dutch national anthem). God have mercy on our small country. Second world war battles are now being fought there. What will be left? Whom will we find on return? The *Schonungsblock* has small windows at the height of my third storey berth. When you look outside you usually see driving snow across the muck pool. But in my misery, between prayers, unexpectedly I saw breaks in the clouds and a pink glow of sunset. I saw a heavenly vista of undulating countryside, and behind it mountains, and on one mountain a distant fairy-tale palace, pink, with towers, like a creation of my childhood imagination, from my earliest youth. I thought God comforted me with a vision of future eternal bliss. But someone told me it was a real castle, though far away. Others saw it too.

THE HEEL

The heel of my right foot, wrapped in a rag and squeezed into a wooden sandal, quickly starts to be unspeakably painful. The pain started three days ago, but now with every step the heel feels like a white hot fireball. It isn't possible to walk with such a heel, but I still walk because the Lord on the Cross, positioned in a roadside shrine near a farm on the road to work, told me to continue walking.

Somewhere at the top of a hill, ploughing through a snowdrift, the pain begins to talk louder than the Lord on the Cross. I hear the soft whimper of a dog, from inside me. Alongside me walks Van der Sande, the man who told me of his desire to own a car with a white steering wheel after the liberation. He is a pitiful bag of bones, his face resembling the snow around us. He has got to help me because I can only do five more steps, four more, three more, two more, one more.... From afar a whisper: 'Help me, support me, I can't go on anymore'. It is Van der Sande, who is about to fall. With my left hand I grip his boney upper arm just under the arm-pit and push him along.

My right heel now functions like the left heel. The pain has gone, a hot tingle remains, we proceed walking together. Reach the place of work. Work for ten hours. Walk back.

This was a direct intervention by God, whose existence is sometimes denied.

I SHALL GIVE YOU RELIEF

Some of us were barefoot. As was, for four long days, our 63 year old friend, Judge Bommezijn, whose shoes had been stolen. Several of us offered him our wooden sandals or any other footwear, but he didn't want to know. 'You are still young,' he said, 'you've still got a chance.' On the way to work we passed a beautiful old farm and next to it stood a gigantic beech tree. Underneath the beech there was a gilded crucifix, quite beautiful and large, under a small roof. When we went past the first time I lifted my headgear. The next day more joined in; later the Lord on the Cross was saluted by at least half our column.

Not until midway through our stay did I notice that half a meter outside the barbed wire fence of our camp there was another crucifix. Just imagine the Germans who constructed a KZ half a meter from Jesus Christ. Every morning I talked to Him and He to me. This is not a false assertion, it is the truth, so help me God Almighty.

AN IMPREGNABLE FORTRESS

During my time in the two prisons and six concentration camps it happened to me on several occasions that I knew with complete certainty that I had to defend, entirely alone and without any aid, a twenty-five centuries old civilization. In my deplorable condition that meant a tremendous effort. I was left no alternative but to make use of an artificial aid: a silent but fast retrospective. I thought of the Persians, the Assyrians, the Phoenicians. I thought about the Greek world of gods and ideas. I thought of the immense Roman Empire. I thought about Byzantium; the Middle Ages with their great monasteries. In my mind I recalled the Renaissance, the emperors, the kings, the revolutions, the empires. I thought especially of the sciences, the painters, architects, composers, writers, the discoverers, inventors, technicians, merchants, industrialists. I reflected on all the great values handed down and multiplied by thousands upon thousands of great spirits throughout the centuries - at high speed. In this way I built around me an impregnable fortress of western civilization which I now had to defend; here and now, I, a shivering skeleton, a slave shorn bare, a hungry beggar covered with boils and lice.

In the end I appealed to Christ Himself, who would stand behind me - no, alongside me - when I tried regardless to stand up for what is good, beautiful and sensible. That gave a feeling of fearful pride. Occasionally I thought about events of ostensibly limited, passing importance which later turned out to have determined the course of history. A handful of ships, a few thousand soldiers. A particular person at a particular time in a particular place. One human being researching in a back room, another busy with paint on canvas, another one with pen on paper, another trying out melodies on a grand piano. All once born anonymously, later co-creators of a civilization. I needed to defend them and their works. I could not possibly do this, but God demanded it, therefore it had to be done. You might perhaps drop dead in doing so, it was nevertheless required. Damn it, those values were truly worth a great sacrifice. And many had already offered their lives for them.

On 20 November 1944 a transport left the infernal camp Dautmergen, among them twenty-two Dutchmen. It could not be worse anywhere else. Murmurings suggested we would go to a *Erholungslager* (recovery camp). We dragged ourselves along the snowy country road to Schömberg. The SS had no reason to speed us up. I do not remember anything about the transport, the train journey to Vaihingen. We were probably more or less unconscious.

Dautmergen is a hamlet that cannot be found on most maps. It is situated in Württemberg, in the Swabian Alps, some 60 km (38 miles) north of Schaffhausen, Switzerland. We knew that the Swiss frontier was barely ten hours' walk away from us, but even thinking about escape rarely occurred. The fence of the KZ was impenetrable, the guards were tough. An unsuccessful escape attempt was punished by death by hanging, preceded by torture. Our bare heads and ragged clothing would have been spotted at once. We did not have any money or papers. We were in the country of the enemy. Finally, we were more dead than alive; I would probably not have survived a ten hour walk.

The castle mentioned earlier was not a vision. It was - and is - a mountain palace, the ancestral seat of the Hohenzollerns (German princes, electors and kings like Frederick the Great), near Hechingen, situated some 20 km (13 miles) from Dautmergen, 855 meters (2,800 ft) up.

172

8. AUSSENKOMMANDO VAIHINGEN-ENZ
21 November 1944-2 April 1945

AN ERHOLUNGSLAGER FOR JEWS

The transport of 250 sick *Häftlinge* took a day and a half to reach Vaihingen-Enz station near Stuttgart. In the evening of 21 November we descended some concrete steps and after a short march arrived at camp Vaihingen. It was situated in a very narrow valley, whose southern slopes were covered by a forest of pine trees. A small railway line ran through it, occasionally supporting a little train. The northern slope was given over to arable land. The long, narrow camp was, as usual, fenced in and had watchtowers with machine guns and search-lights.

The camp population consisted initially only of Jews from Radom and Cracow. The krauts had used Jewish guards there to maintain order. When they decided upon the infamous *Aussiedlungen* (resettlements) and the murder of the larger part of the Jews, they kept the guards alive and took them to a KZ. The youthful Jews in Vaihingen told us the most gruesome stories about the extermination of their families.

For reasons unknown Vaihingen had also been designated *Erholungslager* a little earlier. Who will ever understand the kraut! Both a Jewish labour camp and a recovery camp at the same time.

Truck-loads of sick prisoners from several camps were sent to Vaihingen. At least three-quarters of the camp population always consisted of sick people who never had to work and were spread over the four barracks of the *Revier*. There was only one barrack with workers, mainly kitchen staff and *Leichenträger* (corpse carriers).

Almost all the important camp functions were carried out by Polish Jews. The young, powerful-looking Jews were extremely embittered, but good for us Dutch, efficient and competent organizers (in the

173

original meaning of the word). The Polish Jews in Vaihingen-Enz were as intensely cordial as their non-Jewish compatriots in Dautmergen had been intensely bad.

On the day of our arrival the first Dutchman succumbed.

Initially Vaihingen was a sort of paradise after the hell of Dautmergen. The roll-calls did not last longer than a quarter of an hour, we did not have to work, beatings occurred rarely, we hardly ever saw the SS. In addition, we Dutch were favoured by the Jewish *Prominenz*. However, the plague of lice gradually became indescribable. On the other hand I could wash, after two months. There was a *Desinfektion*, but only of ourselves and our clothes, not the barracks. It did not therefore help at all.

In Vaihingen a great many *Häftlinge* succumbed, among them almost all the Dutchmen. In Dautmergen our constitutions had sustained terrible damage and almost all of us had exhausted our reserves. The quite insufficient medical treatment (few doctors, no medicines), the scourge of lice that resulted in a disastrous typhus epidemic and the poor nutrition meant the finishing blow for the *Muselmänner* from Dautmergen.

While all around me friends were dying, I was kept alive by three Jewish doctors and a Jewish dentist, later too by my best friend, Wim Roessingh. They had noticed that of our group of fourteen only Bas Backer and I stood much chance of surviving. They supplied us both regularly with extra soup and pap, extra bread and even cigarettes.

After my stay in the *Schonungsblock* I was admitted to the *Revier* from 2 December 1944 to 2 February 1945. The doctors did their best but could only help with food. They did not have instruments for even the most minor surgical treatments. I once saw how they relieved someone of his frozen, blackened toes with a dental extractor; the toes were left lying all over the place like peanuts.

In Vaihingen we suffered most from the lice and the unrelenting cold. In the barracks the stoves were hardly ever lit, there were no clothes, we lay naked under two horse blankets together with an army of lice.

At a certain moment it must have become clear even to the SS that the entire camp population would succumb if this went on. In mid-January four *Häftlinge* from Neckarelz appeared: Norwegian doctor Poulsson, Norwegian nurse Halversen, Belgian doctor Bogaerts and Wim Roessingh. They had been instructed to improve the medical provision but without the equipment required; therefore a typically German order. What they did was to introduce cleanliness.

The number of air raids began to increase significantly in February as did their intensity. At times the sky above us was not clear of bombers and fighters for even fifteen minutes at a time. The tension of the last months - perhaps even days, we thought - of the war had started.

In mid-February the typhus epidemic came upon us. The hurriedly introduced *Desinfektion*, this time of the barracks too, had little effect. The disease claimed victims by the hundreds.

I wanted desperately to stay out of the *Revier*, it had become a place to die. As long as possible I tended my dying friends. When most had already succumbed I too had again to be admitted on 28 February. For several days I fought with death. On 13 March I was discharged. Almost none of my compatriots had survived their illnesses. It became lonely.

The Americans were approaching. There were days now when the sky was not without warplanes for even a second. They flew in squadrons apparently criss-crossing through, under and above each other, dropped their bomb loads on Stuttgart and attacked with their machine guns. Once fighters attacked the SS barracks next to our camp. We were all in mortal fear. Our fear far outweighed the satisfaction of seeing the SS being punished. We felt that important events awaited us.

Immediately after Easter, on 2 April, 300 men received some clothing and apparently were made ready for transport. I was the only Dutchman; a few other Dutchmen, Wim Roessingh among them, stayed behind. Our convoy left that evening in goodswagons. On the way to the station we saw the pinkish fire from the mouths of American artillery. They arrived too late for us.

TAKE ME

Released from infernal Dautmergen I could at last continue with my diary. The first few pages were completely illegible: long, long recitals of words and notions and names without any coherence, serving as grapnels tied to ropes along which I could slowly pull myself up out of the darkness, like the invasion soldiers on the rocks of Normandy. However, after a few days my brain started functioning again, more or less. Thus on 26 November, a Sunday, I find the following:

May God give my words substance and power to tell the world shortly what is at stake: civilization. Justice, which praises and fosters and rewards the good, prevents and punishes and removes the bad, but only after investigation and having heard out the threatened party. Justice, which doesn't want to simplify everything, ignore all distinctions, but distinguishes between individuals and individual interests. Justice, which respects promises, considers agreements binding, enforces deprivation of freedom with restraint, yes, considers human freedom, spiritually and physically, one of the highest goods and doesn't praise or glorify slavery as if man exists for the benefit of the State! Justice, which distinguishes between power and justice, which doesn't assume that right is on the side of the strong but is inclined to protect the weak, to offer him power in his weakness: equal before the law.

Civilization is also charity, the helping hand, the uplifting gesture, the inclusion of what is one's own good. I now see so many charitable, nursing, serving figures: missionaries, Salvation Army, deacons, doctors, clergymen; thank God they exist.

In addition level-headed meekness, a very Christian virtue, as is tolerance: no quarrelling, no fighting, no obtuse striking of one's own breast full of blind and inflated pride, but the consideration of someone else's position, the imagination that can appreciate another's point of view, the weighing of the pros and cons of his arguments, possibly yielding to them, and the respect for his opinions, religious and social.

The humility and self-denial which values the neighbour more than oneself, looks upon serving others as an honour, passes on freely what has been received freely and gratefully professes: what have I got that I have not received?

Many, many more qualities are the jewels in the crown of a noble human being - oh, how fiercely burning the desire in me, little, hard-headed, dirty, poor man, to be as noble as you, my noble wife, my heart, my dear lovely Angel!

But I need to divest myself of even more. My cry for civilization is also a continuous cry for beauty and knowledge, often so curiously related, often so wonderfully united. There are thoughts, memories as well as ideas for the future, which can hardly be borne because the contrast with the present is too great: the feeling organism cannot cope with the intensity of the feelings. But, be quiet . . . the civilization, that invaluable, sparkling civilization of our Holland, which expresses itself in qualities of character, soul, spirit and reason, in religion, art and science - which is being learned, poured out and drunk in our holy, Dutch family which I see united around a table in a warm room under the light of lamps. Yesterday, today too, tomorrow. Imperishable: no German can destroy that. This is immortal. I want to create a monument in a novel for our Dutch family, sketch our civilization and narrate how even the most develish power in the world has not been able to destroy this glory.

But one day later on 27 November 1944:

My Darling, I'm writing in mortal sadness. In the middle of one of those anxious moods when I fear madness. So afraid, so terribly afraid. So lonely. So bereft of everything. So lacking in love. A gesture of love, a caress, a friendly word - I could scream. Just one flower, a rug, some lamplight, a spark in golden spectacles - I could cry. I am crying. I'm thinking of you, why do I cry when I'm thinking of my darling? It doesn't do any good. And that makes me cry more. Weak, endlessly weak. Very occasionally I'm thinking: please let me die, my Lord. Just take me to You. Here on earth I can't cope any more. It's not a real existence. Everything is hatred and death, everything falls to pieces, nothing remains. Do take me away, I'm a poor little creature who wants to die, so mortally cold, so mortally lonely. Only that flame of love; that still burns inside me that remains forever.

That night, end November with a moon when I woke up while turning over, I heard gnawing somewhere. Of course I immediately thought of mice and rats, but what would they find to gnaw in a KZ where even the last crumb of bread, fallen in the dust on the floor, was quickly snatched up? Furthermore, the gnawing was all too penetrating, even for the largest rat. I rose up a bit under my horse blanket, propped up by an elbow. In the moonlit bed below me on the other side of the central path in what seemed to be the direction of the gnawing, I suddenly saw something glitter. The bunk of that old Polish Jew - God, what teeth the man had, teeth glittering in the silvery light. But what a large head that man had. . . .

Then, at last fully awake, I could see it clearly. There were two heads in that bed. The head of the Polish Jew, and a colossal cow's head which he was busily gnawing clean.

28 November. One is optimistic, many bridgeheads on the right bank of the Rhine. Continuous air raid warnings. Disagreement USA-USSR? My God, how hungry I am.

30 November. Which way do I have to go with my thoughts? They aren't precise and go round in ever-decreasing circles and are now becoming nasty and lurid. They daren't enter the red shining grottos of the past anymore to relish those memories. After all, the memo-

ries are far too beautiful. The very fond moods - I can't cope with them anymore. The phantom of degeneration threatens. I'm poor, very poor, deadly poor of spirit.

2 December. The Jewish doctor: 'You'll be admitted to the Revier today.' It is like sailing into a harbour after stormy weather.

3 December. I surface from the most profound waking dream. I've been worshipping God. I've been visualising you, your face and figure: His work. I've visualized sweet peas, a large bouquet of sweet peas, violet, pink, red, white: His work. I saw a large warm hall with a Christmas tree, the candle flames reflecting in the large eyes of many children: His work. I saw a Dutch canal in January: mist, ice, seagulls, on Sunday morning, a father with a child wearing woolly gloves: His work. I saw a polder meadow in June, I heard black-tailed godwits, redshanks, the air was resonant, a playful calf with stupid head, large shining eyes, stick-legs and dribbling at the mouth: His work. I heard music, music from a large grand piano which soared up in a rising, lonely, passion - God, what outlet does this hot, sobbing, shaking passion have? - detaching itself from a gradually silent orchestra: God speaks. A varied range of beauty rich in treasures. Never before have I felt God's love so strongly, the love that permeates His entire creation. Love turned into physical shapes. I'm full of warmth. I'm over-full with happiness. I have You, God. I'm burning from Your power, I perish as a result of Your glory.

4 December. When it was dark, doctor Boyim woke me. He came to tell me what the Polish Jews had to go through. Gassed, burned, shot dead, raped, children smashed against trees and walls, wrenched apart, chlorophile gas in railwagons, stick in the gullet. All their family, wife, children, parents, friends: murdered. 'Ich möchte leben bleiben. Um Rache zu nehmen.' (I want to stay alive. To take revenge). On leaving he left me two thick slices of bread with butter and honey in blotting paper.

6 December. If only I had something. Man wants to have something. If only a crust of bread. I don't even have a vest. I have: three pencils, a toothbrush, three handkerchiefs, one belt. Nobody can be poorer than I. I have prayed. To the extent that grief and joy are deeper they come nearer to each other. Very deep grief can hardly be distinguished from very deep joy. Great joy stands next to eternal sorrow. I suspect why but am too tired to research it. I saw an old Jew, dressed only in spectacles, suspenders and wellies. Yesterday a madman ran yelling round the barrack. We ate potatoes, bread, sweet coffee, sour

milk and turnip soup. My little Polish neighbour prefers poached fish with raisins and sugar.

German legal procedures: one is arrested without warrant, waits weeks or months for a hearing, is tortured. Months later a court case: acquitted. That means: KZ. Many months later another court case, different court of injustice: death penalty. After another several months a third case, another court of injustice: acquittal. Different KZ. Oh, these bastards!

9 December. I would like to do something difficult. I'm desperate for a book. Last night the doctor brought me turnip soup, in the middle of the night a great deal more, my belly was like a barrel, 8½ litres (15 pints) in all.

10 December

Max And Hurry

An afternoon in December, four o'clock, the curtains are still open. Outside, snow covers the twilit town. In our drawing room a standard lamp is on. Max lies over there, at full stretch, snout on stretched legs, daintily like a stuffed fox. The fire in the grate reflects in his eyes. Why doesn't he slumber? Because now is a critical hour, for animals. ... Winter twilight in empty rooms - imagine, so much could happen, something will surely happen. To fall asleep would be reckless: it's far too quiet. Somewhere only the distant sound of a whistling kettle. It has started to snow again - now it will be even more silent. Something is threatening ... what mystery lurks in this room ... there it is! Indeed, and it emerges too: a phantom, a little phantom, an animal phantom appears from underneath the chest of drawers and walks with preposterous steps straight to Max. That should be Hurry, our kitten. She is unrecognizable. The silent twilight mood has become too much for her, a mad fit has got into her furry little head, and she purposely cultivates it - she flaunts with her own creepiness: ears in her neck, fangs bared, arched back, ridiculously thick tail held down, legs like sticks and eyes ... eyes like green lanterns. The phantom strides across the room, soundlessly and horribly, straight at Max. He would like to yelp, run away - it's impossible. Completely spellbound. His eyes become larger, once he suddenly sighs because fear made him forget to breathe. . . . It's coming nearer. It keeps striding obliquely. It's almost there, grotesque, awfully creepy - heavens!! That's it. Bolt upright, the forelegs of the furry creature stretched wide and high like a little bear, it jumps in the air - fluffy cross-caper - swipes the dog's nose lightning fast with one of its paws - he whines - and quickly crawls away, rapidly, embarrassed, under the sofa.

There's the key in the front door. 'Hello, darling,' she calls, she is already in the room. Outside it's dark, the curtains are drawn, the lamps turned on. There is no more mystery here anymore. Everything is normal and cosy. Max danced around her leaping up to her face and now sits full of expectation, tail wagging, for his first biscuit. And Hurry ... Hurry sits beside the fireplace like a sweet chocolate-box kitten, her right foreleg pulled up along her little belly, the easier to lick her chest. Well-brought-up drawing room animal ... but, Max, we know better, don't we. . . .

12 December. A 22-year-old Jew whose wife and family were exterminated: 'I did believe in God. Not any more, since He allows such things. I can't understand Him any more. I hope the war will last a long time. I don't want to be released. When I'm free I'll realize my loss, understand my tragedy. I'll then have to murder someone. And where can I go?'

13 December: We've had a *Kommission*. That means commotion for days in advance and orders with much shouting and confusion and usually no *Kommission* appears or only one simpleton who knows nothing. This time a *Kommission* did arrive, stuffed with food, wearing cheap uniforms, hands in pockets, big caps, cigarettes in mouths and then just looking, preferably shouting, even more preferably hitting. *Kultur*. What do they feel when they see our misery? Are they proud of it? Do they feel ashamed? No. They don't think anything. *Befehl*. A Nazi doesn't think. Once I tried to explain to them why we are weak and look foul. Something strange then appears on their face, speechless with amazement. It seems as if they try to think. Five minutes later: 'Sie faules Volk'. And now, this *Kommission*: 'Was über vierzig hat spielt keine Rolle. Ist sowieso bald tot.' (Those over forty degres of fever don't play any role anymore. They'll shortly be dead anyway).

We discussed Radio Orange (the Dutch service relayed by the BBC). What marvellous work it could have done! How I would have liked to be involved! But what a sad, insipid mess it usually was. Beware: the educated man doesn't dare abuse the service. He talks about loyalty, honour, Queen and Country. God and Orange. The simple man says: incitement to war, safely across the North Sea. Drive boys of seventeen, eighteen to their death. What misery they have caused, without any result. We've been cheated, with all these slogans, if only we'd stayed quietly at home. They should have taken the chestnuts out of the fire themselves. We prefer a quiet, peaceful life. Cosy. Lots of love for each other. Church, association, choir, bowling club. Radio, cigar, newspaper. The foundations of our State. These men don't want the hollow, shiny ostentation of ministers and generals. They want to see their families happy. That deserves quite a few sacrifices. 'As far as I'm concerned we shouldn't have fought 10-14 May 1940. Leave us alone in peace, what do we have now? Home and town bombed, son killed, son shot, poverty.'

These people are not defeatist, simply ultra-Dutch level-headed. Infatuated with Holland, infatuated with the Queen, full of criticism of the Dutch government in London. Infatuated with their family. The happy family is the foundation of the State. In this sense these defeatists are . . . more patriotic than the generals and ministers.

15 December. I'm deeply impressed by the stories of our Polish Jews. They want one thing: revenge. Are furious at everything and everyone: because no one takes up their plight. Are completely abandoned. Everyone at home has been gassed, burned, shot. They show their photographs. I see a lovely Jewish wife of rare beauty in white at the side of a handsome chap in tails. The woman has been murdered atrociously. The man sits next to me, crying, bald in a zebra suit. Who will later tell the world what happened? 'Es ist Keiner mehr da.' (Nobody is left).

More photographs, of Waynberg from Radom, happy families, beach chairs, canoes on the Vistula. Old men with skull-caps. Lovely dreamy Jewish girls. Wedding pictures. A synagogue. Now blown up, ploughed up, the gravestones used as paving slabs. An old lady in a hospital. Hospital emptied, patients machinegunned in open field, all of them.

The photographs show dear little children with large dark eyes. Their heads smashed against a tree, hurled out of a third-floor window. 'Eine neue Welt, ja, aber keine neue Frau, kind neues Kind.' (Yes, a new world, but not a new wife, not a new child).

More photographs. A lovely child, nine years old, Vita Gewatha, with plaits and a short dress, laughing and looking up at a slim dark woman, very beautiful. They are walking together in a park, blooming, mother and daughter. I see the daughter again, at thirteen, now a quite beautiful girl in a summer frock, with girlfriends, three

Jewesses in a train. A fence, a patio, french windows. His wife near a fountain, very delicate, lonely, aristocratic. All murdered by the kraut.

Most Jews want the complete annihilation of Germany. Pour petrol on it, then strike a match. There's a lot to be said for it, there's even more against it. But indeed, this scum should never be allowed to rise again.

THE DIAMONDS

In the hospital barracks the Jewish doctors from Poland did everything possible - which was almost nothing due to lack of medicine - to keep us alive, alas mostly without success. The chief *Häftlingartzt* was Doctor Boyim from Warsaw, who often came to have a talk with me. When I came to feel slightly more relaxed Doctor Boyim often gave me an extra piece of bread in the evening. Every time he walked in he must have felt my penetrating gaze on him: would he bring me something? No- yes-no-yes! Another Dutchman occasionally received something too, but I seemed to be the favourite. When I asked Boyim why he favoured me and the other one above the other Dutchmen who never got anything - a dangerous question, for imagine if he should change his policy! - he answered with a painful smile that we two were the only Dutchmen with a chance of survival. No bread would alter that.

My joy at this answer was mixed with feelings of shame and humiliation: in front of my comrades I was being nurtured.

One evening Boyim came for a chat on my upper bunk. He was clearly deeply distressed. His eyes were glitteringly wet. When asked what was the matter, he replied: 'I was a surgeon in Warswaw. I had a large practice. I was well known among the Jewish community of Warsaw. I was married to a beautiful lovely woman. We had a little daughter.'

The tears dripped down his cheeks in ever more rapid succession.

'They took our little daughter outside. They grabbed her legs. They then smashed her head to pieces against a wall. They carried my wife off, I haven't heard from her since.'

He sobbed loudly.

'And she was wearing her golden brooch with sixty four diamonds.'

When he had calmed down a little, I asked him how he could possibly talk in the same breath about the murder of wife and child and the loss of sixty-four diamonds. While holding his hand I told him: 'Boyim, we are friends, I'm very grateful to you, I like Jews a lot, you as well, and you must be suffering dreadfully, but how can you talk in one breath about this atrocity and a few damned diamonds?'

He seemed only slightly ashamed. 'Das erklär ich dir, Freund (I'll explain, my friend). As you know, throughout world history the Jews have been persecuted consistently and everywhere. Day and night we are subject to persecution, torture, maltreatment, arrest. We've always got to be mobile, ready to flee, or fight, but also ready to bribe. We're very fond of diamonds and brilliants because they give us a certain amount of power for they are easy to take everywhere and are highly valued everywhere, thereby making it possible to flee and rebuild an existence. With these sixty-four I had hoped to pay for an escape, bribe the krauts ... but my wife was wearing the brooch when they carried her off and therefore I didn't get a chance even to buy her out. . . .'

That is how I came to understand the interest of many Jews in precious stones.

1 January 1945: this will be the most important year of our lives apart from our birth and death.

2 January. Today I've been imprisoned for one thousand days. Just as well I didn't know in advance.

3 January. Letter to Jan van Brakel in the bunk below me: 'Dear Jan, I've got to make a confession to you, in writing because I dare not leave my bed for fear of the cold. Yesterday I did something irresponsible by asking you to lend me some bread. Today I already owe 250 grams (9 oz) to someone else. I had expected to wipe out this debt with today's margarine, worth, of course, 250 grams of bread, and to give you my bread ration. However, it seems that today we're not going to get any margarine. I tried to arrange the matter with him, but he wants the bread today because he hasn't got anything else. My request to you is whether you are prepared to - or could - wait until tomorrow. If not, I'll ask someone else with whom I'm on good terms to lend me his bread. Therefore, tell me completely honestly whether this suits you. My sincerest apologies for this incorrect way of doing business. Yesterday I felt terribly hungry and miserable. These days I'm going through a nasty mental crisis, you may perhaps feel it from the trembling of the bed. I feel guilty about you. You're just lying there and I don't do anything for you. Today I've been lying here for a month and I can hardly hear your voice. That's crazy. What are you doing? How are you? Miserable? It's after all my duty to help you. Tell me. We do need each other, friend. It's very difficult. For me too.'

Answer from Jan: 'Dear Floris, of course I can wait and everything is alright. I too suffer immensely but I'll manage. Pray for me, I for you.'

I discussed Albert Schweitzer with Bommezijn, who said he's no good. 'Because he's a German. Not one of them is any good.'

4 January. Bom again brought up Schweitzer and admitted he didn't mean it. Tomorrow my wedding anniversary, five years of marriage. Two years and nine months of these separated. Once more there are a few coals, there are some people in blankets standing round the stove. So am I. I fell asleep, sank on my knees, burned my 'tackle' on the stove. Doctor, when seeing blisters: 'Wenn Sie bei der Frau zurückkehren, ist nichts übrig.' (When you return to your wife, there'll be nothing left). There has been a *Kommission*, doctors Boyim and Wayntraub will leave for another Block, Norwegian doctors will replace them.

A THIEF

When you see someone else suffering and very slowly dying, it is natural that you should sympathize and try to support him; at any rate, you are moved. It is not normal but bad when you feel a strong desire for the dying man to die now: because he has a pan with cold porridge standing beside him and you badly want that porridge. You would even like to pinch it. The porridge is infinitely more important than the dying man.

Of course I too have stolen. On the bunk next to me, 40 cm (16") between us, Judge Bommezijn lay dying. A strong old man who had been dying for weeks. Laterly he ate hardly anything, he lacked the strength. I knew that under the rags that served him as a pillow at least three portions of bread lay untouched: a fortune. Being seriously ill myself this bread was on my mind throughout the day. The day before yesterday, the first time he did not eat his portion but hid it, and yesterday, when he put the second with the first, and today, when the third joined the other two, I prayed fervently: give me this bread! But he didn't give anything, talked a bit, dozed, sometimes told a story. And I tried to bring the subject round to my hunger and his bread. . . .

The third afternoon he was fast asleep. I thought: that bread is becoming as hard as stone, he will never eat that bread any more, I had to stay alive, others will pinch the bread, tonight the Russians will come and get it and be beaten to death; he has simply forgotten to give me the bread, he has forgotten what hunger is, he lets a fortune in bread swarm with lice, he is a rotter, what a bastard; I'm dying of hunger and he refuses to die.

That afternoon, while he slept, I saw a dingy thing move in the direction of his head. It was my dirty, licey paw, my stick-like arm which was taking a walk. I followed paw and arm with intense interest, they did not belong to me. Paw and arm bridged the space between the bunks, the paw arrived at the other end and dug softly underneath the rags. Then I was distracted by something terrible. I was looking into the open eyes of the Judge. But that night I nevertheless collected one portion.

11 January. Hard frost, frozen windows, no fire. Too cold to write. Just as well I've got so many lice, keep me moving. 'Der Laborant aus Natzweiler is da.' And there was Wim Roessingh. God, what joy! He and the new doctors are shocked by what they are seeing here. It is a lot worse than I realize. And we consider this a paradise compared to Dautmergen. He told me the Americans arrived in Natzweiler end November, the camp has not been burned down, my papers are therefore safe up in the rafters.

14 January. Cold as ice, I write in the dark of a blanket. We piss in a dish under the blankets. *Abort* (loo) too cold. Every minute struggle against death. Last night - how is it possible - at last a wet dream, it squirted right up to my mouth. The SS-*Stabsartzt* thinks that we masturbate to create sperm to use as phlegm in order to stay longer in the *Revier*. They are mad, completely crazy.

15 January. Yesterday all I could do was fight against the cold, rubbing my feet, rubbing and rubbing. I had to shit that evening. A horrible expedition. In twenty-four hours twenty-six men have died. Wim fights for us with the SS. Jesus himself is with me. It's improving. He speaks, and it becomes quiet. God gives me a lot. A lot. Thank You.

16 January. I pulled out one of my own molars. The Russians have reached East Prussia. Bom is very ill.

17 January. I have discovered that Mitigal helps against lice. I'm free of lice!

25 January. Last night Bom called me. 'Floris, I'm dying, pray for me, ask Doctor Poulson to finish me off.' God, oh God. It has snowed a lot. I read him Mark 10, 11 and 12. Poland has been reached. We were checked before being discharged from the *Revier*. Bom eats hardly anything, I'm now getting almost everything from him, give him margarine and jam in exchange. Boyim examines Bom and shakes his head at me: no. All of a sudden I've got a temperature

38.5° (101.3° F), I hallucinate, a rather nice feeling.

28 January. The fever has gone. There are many corpses, in our barrack ten a day. We are easily irritated, there are rows between the Dutchmen. And it snows, and snows.

Declaration of Love

You are opposite me, near the fire which makes everything into a secret. You're busy pouring tea. You're wearing a very lovely dress of grey/blue satin, short sleeves, fairly dark stockings, black shoes and against the pearly glow of your cleavage, adorned with a pink ribbon, an orange flame: nasturtium, Indian cress. A bit of gold here and there, I see the wide gold bracelet on your arm, sun-tanned, a left over from the summer. Your hands are as individual as faces. Your legs, pressed together, sideways. A cigarette in your mouth. Therefore one eye closed. Your mouth lightly painted. Blazing fire, singing water, chocolates in a small silver dish. And smoke rising from the blazing logs. On the sheepskin the sleeping dog. Now your sweet face is bent over pictures, every now and then you shout for fun, taking pleasure in the small, the charming. Your neck is very moving. And when something impresses you, you become silent like a child, a big female child, your large grey eyes, with spots of gold in the iris, notice everything: they're drinking it all in. Now you're laughing darkly and looking at me. What is it that radiates from under these long lashes that slowly turn up? It scorches. . . . It burns. . . .

30 January. Bom is about to die. Yesterday he became unconscious. Six of us busied ourselves with him for an hour. He is as heavy as lead because he is full of water; when turning him over his belly has to be dealt with separately. He doesn't eat, doesn't sleep, smells awful, is in a lot of pain. No animal expires as miserably as he does. There's nothing I can do except pray. He says: 'I feel weak. Tell my wife that I thank her for a pleasant marriage.' Nothing more. Deadly quiet. He seems almost cheerful. And I'm thinking: will he still get, will I get, his bread tonight? Lord, forgive me. Lord, be very near to him now.

It happened at 5pm. 'Everything will come right,' he said. With him and for him I prayed the Our Father, and 'into Thy hands I commend him'. They took him away. It's now ice cold, icy cold. He died, his hand in mine, his head in my arms.

31 January. Earlier Bom told me: 'If it's necessary for an early peace

that I die, please take my life quickly, Lord.' Now the Lord has taken his life . May He give an early peace. I've got his estate: belt, spoon, spectacles in case, soap, shaving soap, handkerchief and especially the cigarette-holder to which he had been so attached.

2 February. Time is up. Tomorrow I've got to leave here. Poulson wants it. Boyim doesn't. I feel reasonably well. Who knows what good it'll do. Apart from Wim Roessingh I'm the only 'healthy' Dutchman. I'll visit the other boys as often as possible. Perhaps shortly the end will come, or evacuation, or flight. I'll then be more or less fit to walk. I'll soon be the only Dutchman in Block 2 among strangers. I've lain here for two months. During that period we lost seven of the fourteen Dutchmen. I read aloud from *Prières d'un prisonnier*.

4 February. I've arrived in my new home. It is a relief. Nature is a revelation. I received a vest; a suit will follow. The Jews said I could come and eat with them every evening. I'm sleeping between a stove, which is sometimes lit, and a Norwegian, Christian Ottosen. There are also many Frenchmen who shout and never wash themselves. I slept wonderfully but have lice again. I visited a French priest, R.P. de la Perraudière, from Tours, a Jesuit. In his prayer book I read:

Que m'arrivera-t-il aujourd'hui, o mon Dieu, je l'ignore. Tout ce que je sais, c'est qu'il ne m'arrivera rien que Vous n'avez prévu de toute éternité. Cela me suffit, mon Dieu, pour être tranquille. J'adore Vos desseins éternels et impénétrables. Je m'y sousmets de tout mon coeur. Je veux tout, j'accepte tout, je Vous fais un sacrifice de tout, j'unis ce sacrifice à celui de Votre cher Fils, mon Sauveur, Vous demandant par Son sacré-coeur et ses mérites infinis, la patience dans maux et la parfaite sousmission qui Vous est due pour tout ce que Vous voulez ou permettez. Amen.

Back in the Block I had many contacts with Polish Jews, Frenchmen and Norwegians. Apart from Wim and myself all the Dutchmen were in the *Revier*; I visited them regularly. Many gave me extra food. The Jews said: 'Before 25 February we Jews will be with Bommezijn in heaven. You'll get home.' The USA and England would be grateful to Hitler: because he exterminated their Jewish competitors in Europe. Where do they get this madness from? The Russian State Police NKVD are supposed to be worse than the Gestapo but would not do anything to us because we had been in a KZ. From time to time we received strange white soups. 'On ne peut pas reculer jusqu'à Berlin et toujours servir de bonnes soupes,' said the French. The news was now followed even more closely.

I also made the acquaintance of a marquis, De Mailly, who called himself a bank employee. He told me that, having returned to Paris after two and a half years as a prisoner of war, he had come across a reason for divorce. From time to time we played chess on a homemade board. We also visited one another in our bunks. When once I returned an invitation to the marquis, he said, 'Oui, je te verrai sur ton lit à 16.00 heures après m'avoir dépouillé.' Thanks to the Mitigal I was usually free of lice.

Staying in an ordinary Block improved me a lot, after two months in the sub-human misery of the *Revier*. Thanks to the extra food, the new contacts, the approaching spring and the fabulous news I regained my fighting spirit; I achieved a weight of 62 kg (9 stone 11 lbs). It was of great importance that someone organized some shoes for me. Air raid sirens were continuous.

On 10 February I did a dirty trick. One of the Jews gave me a saucepan of soup to share with 'dem Konsul' (another Dutchman). On the way to the *Revier* where he lay I 'was tempted by the devil' and gobbled up all of it. I told the *Konsul* that I had stumbled and spilled the soup. To this day I feel ashamed: a nasty thief. Thank God the man survived the war. Wim told me: 'If you can't do a thing like that you haven't learned anything.'

We also got a Dutch Nazi: he threatened us. I wrote in my diary: 'The kraut is bad, a Dutch Nazi ten times worse.'

Another fellow-prisoner allowed himself to be ensnared by . . . the Wehrmacht and disappeared. Every day many inmates died. We often sat talking in the weak sun, our backs to a large fire: every day they burned the straw bags of the dead. Sometimes I got the impression that a few died through their own fault: they let go, lost all moral stamina, remained lying down, did not wash, did not move, did not organize, did not stretch their brains and ate dirt.

On 15 February in the middle of the night my roommates carried in a beam 5 metres (18 ft) long which was chopped into logs in fifteen minutes.

TYPHUS

End February in Vaihingen death came very near again. Gradually the camp had acquired several trillion clothes' lice which, as the reader knows, are responsible for the *Fleckfieber* or typhus. The lice were present everywhere, even on your crust of bread. Our grey horse blankets had become super lice-blankets: at close range the blankets swarmed with them. Anyone who felt very cold had less trouble from lice. Anyone who was ice-cold because he did not live anymore had no trouble at all: the lice departed.

The kraut was terrified of epidemics. He installed a barrack as a quarantine zone and did not ever show up there; the patients were tended by Jewish doctors and their assistants. For a short while I was able to keep myself outside that barrack; it was the gateway to the mass grave behind the hill above the camp, to which the *Leichenträger* made their daily journey. But my day had also come.

The typhus-quarantine barrack of Vaihingen was an endless nightmare; you had to be constantly reminded that it was not in fact a nightmare but reality. Hundreds of *Häftlinge* were at various stages of a miserable death, shouting, moaning, chattering, shitting and pissing from the top bunk down through the second and first to the floor. I was put at the top in a corner, and there my poor remainder of a lousy body began to boil with fever. There were a few thermometers: once I could vaguely discern that for me it climbed to 40.8° (105.5°F).

Worse than the fire in the body was the axe in the skull. Typhus causes the sort of headache that you cannot imagine, unless your imagination is so strong that you understand what it is like to have an axe imbedded in your forehead, where the hair line starts, a couple of centimetres deep. And in addition to the fire and the axe, everything glowed yellow.

Those who still had a grain of animal cleanliness left and did not want their constant diarrhoea running, from the top row of bunks right through the second and first rows to the slippery floor, went for relief outside. Close to the stable door of the barrack stood a rusty oil barrel, filled to the brim with shit, therefore some 200 litres (352 pints) and consequently impossible to lift up and clean. You had to relieve yourself there. Of course there was no paper. The soil around the barrel, already soft from persistent rain, was completely soaked with shit and urine.

One night was the worst of all. That evening a great many typhoid infected sufferers had died. They had been dragged to the long corridor in the centre of the barrack but no further because the *Leichenträger* were, of course, not allowed out in the dark. That night bladder pressure forced me to try to get out. I did not have the strength to climb down more or less normally, so I somehow fell from my bunk, rolling and clinging to anything hard. I had to grope my way between the bunks filled with dying men and found the door to the corridor. At the end of the corridor I saw a yellow, shining patch where the doors to the *Kübelton* were supposed to be. But then I got into great difficulties.

Continuing to grope and stagger, my hands and feet struck large, icy, slippery masses. The wooden floor was dangerously smooth as if it had been soaped. Now and then, when I tried to get a firm grip, there were dull smacks of arms and legs sliding down from a great height. A moment arrived when I stumbled and landed between the limbs with my yellow, fractured skull burning.

But still the shit barrel was finally reached, and in the icy cold another bit of life came out of me and splashed beside the barrel in the dung.

Back through the night on the bunk there was only room for fond dreams, the greatest melancholy, prayers to God and a longing for fruit and, especially . . . yoghurt. It was a new and devastating experience when I could not get the bread through my gullet.

Slowly the fever subsided and my skin became less sallow; the axe was wrenched from my skull. I started walking round with a urinal bowl and a pan to see what could be caught. The two urinals looked dark brown, when I no longer saw everything as yellow: this was because there was no way to clean them. With an iron constitution, a strong skeleton and sinews, the skin hanging like loose parchment, Our Lord had once again pulled me through.

From my diary, almost illegible for I was close to dying:

27 February. The weather is mild with a radiant sun, I'm sitting outside. While feverish I refuse to go into the *Revier*. Am almost suffocating. All seems really well. For someone who can eat that much can't be very ill. Still, I'm spinning on my legs and my eyes glaze over. A little white house, rain on the lawn, and violins, especially violins. Inside - french windows open - a young girl, seventeen, dark in a white dress, plays *Jardin sous la pluie*.

28 February. I must write, but find it almost impossible. Have quite a temperature now, excruciating headache, diarrhoea and rheumatism. Typhus? They say I'll be in the *Revier* tonight. So be it. But it's humiliating. Notwithstanding the grace of God it's horribly difficult. For almost three years now. Critically ill again. Your prayer will save me. Germany has already gone bust. Good. I can't carry on. Holland, truly a country worth dying for. Temperature over 40°.

1 March. Must write first; can't sleep otherwise. Yesterday 40.8°. A newly arrived Dutchman dragged me to *Revier* 4 ward 7. Suspected typhus. Tonight swerved along the pitch dark corridor to the open air

Abort, stark naked. When I come back to you - I believe that like a rock - God will have produced His umpteenth miracle and thwarted the cunning efforts of the kraut. Another Dutchman died, only five left. I see everything as glaring yellow.

2 March. Fever, billowing fever. A pile of thirty-two dead bodies. Tonight thirty-nine. Friends are helping me. I depend entirely upon God. Lord, I'd still like to live on for a little while with her. The warmth and light of Jesus envelop me. I firmly believe. Protect her, God.

3 March. Last night I was high up and far away. I think I'm allowed to live but tried to prepare for God. Didn't dare go to the very end. Got far, then drowned in tears. Angels. Black tubes and towers, golden inside. Flames, Jesus Himself next to them. I'm at the end of my tether. This morning 38.7° under the arm. A bit better, God wants me to succeed. I fight like a lion. I'll do anything. All the time I see you. Anything can happen. Perhaps the end is just behind the door. This evening: a shock, 40.3° rectal, yet feel better. Walked along the corridor full of corpses, zig-zag, all bright glaring yellow with silver stars. I'm close to God and to you and will get through all right. But extremely tough.

4 March. Sunday. My text: 'Draw near me, all of you . . .' I'm now dangerously ill. A delicate matter. I'm still confident of pulling it off. Monstrous neglect. They throw shoes with shit on your blanket. I'm already filthy. What have I got? No doctor. I'm not afraid. God looks after me, and observes me, and will bring me to you. I've wept loudly from longing for you. Summer in Holland with Anne-Marie. My lovely child, your husband fights in deadly earnest for his life. With God anything is possible. Lord, we desperately need You again, don't abandon Your little children. Amen.

5 March. I'm continuously in faraway firey flaming worlds. Shafts, ovens, skyscrapers, Swedish forests, Kager Lake, Pynacker. . . . Temperature ranges between 39° and 40°. The neglect here is awful. No washing at all. They call this a *Revier*. Oh, they are such bastards. Every day lots of corpses in the corridor. Well, I'm eating as much as possible even though it's difficult. Darling, please pray for me a lot, now. You surely feel that your husband is in danger. Angel. It is typhus, and soon I move to another ward. Will take another two days, according to the doctor. I'll wait like a good dog. It'll be alright in the end. Jesus Christ died for us. With temperature 40.8° taken to Ward 1. Suddenly feel lifted up above all people, close to Jesus. His angels

are defending me. You are among them. Marvellous to be ill that way. *Gloria in excelcis Deo*: that You have made her and consented to give her to me. Re-unite us. Amen.

6 March. It's Tuesday. I spent a most glorious night. My urine bottle was full. When the bottle is full I'm satisfied. It's full again. But: 'Do not be anxious about your life, what you shall eat or what you shall drink, nor about your body, what you shall put on.' I live close to God. Today 39.4°. They say: only a few more days; this is the crisis.

7 March. Have made it to another day. Temperature 38-39°. I dream and dream and dream. It's going well. You are with me every minute. The future beckons again. I am, of course, unsound of mind. God and you, they are the gigantic strength and the Almighty Angel. They keep me going. I can't do anything.

8 March. Too ill now for writing. Temperature 38°, now 37.6°, seems alright, crisis passed. But awful diarrhoea and filth in bed and vomiting as well. In addition: unfathomable depression. Together we were on the beach with balloons and sausages and beach chairs. Oh God, I love her so much! Protect her, Father, and re-unite us soon. This is such an awful horror. Amen.

9 March. For the first time 36.7° (normal). Don't know what it'll be tonight. No appetite at all and rather sad. I'm far away, very far away. But all will be well.

10 March. Saturday, all day temperature normal, what luxury. Didn't eat anything for forty-eight hours, stomach upset. Diarrhoea now could be fatal. I have the most wonderful dreams, many about you, just had a wild wet dream. Where does the energy come from? That's how much I love you. Oh dear, I'm tired.

11 March. Strange Sunday. No fever, no more diarrhoea. This morning my own church service: 'In the world you shall find oppression but be of good cheer: I have conquered the world.' Dear Father, You are all-knowing. We'll build on You, never again leave us (part of the Dutch National Anthem). Amen.

12 March. A tough day. Moved to Ward 3, two men in one bed of shit. I'm very melancholy, don't see any light at the end of the tunnel except above, there God sits in all His glory and witnesses what happens to me. Well, this is the last stretch of troubles. I'd like to get out of here.

13 March. Slept well, of all things. Tired, no appetite, but did eat:

macaroni with blood. Americans crossed the Rhine at Remagen! It's very, very difficult, but: (1) I'm alive; (2) God is with me; (3) the liberators are approaching from several directions.

16 March: This is it. Exactly two years ago they arrested you. I've left Block 4 and am back in Block 2. Such exertions! First, vomit due to the awful stench. Then soup, I'm famished and yet the *Lager* food disgusts me. Now, a triumphal procession to the bathing place through the spring. I wept profusely. Saved!

One Dutchman after another departed for ever. The hell of Dautmergen had sapped their strength. It was a refreshing spring day, 16 March, when I left the quarantine barrack with a few others and tottered naked outside in the sun on the way to the Baderaum, a shed with several showers. For the first time we saw the SS again, or at least krauts. They sat on a wooden bench, watching us getting under the showers. At their feet stood a large tub. When some twenty walking skeletons were assembled underneath the showers the taps were opened. Weak groaning followed immediately. The skeletons began to move with unusual liveliness: the water turned out to be virtually boiling. Instantly the shed was full of steam while we rushed back and forth like madmen. Some soon lay scalded and dying on the stone floor. One of them was put in a tub filled with boiling water by the Germans and drowned like a cat. It was a scene straight out of hell.

Back in the barrack I ardently prayed to God: 'Lord God, may I ask You to damn the Germans, the Krauts, the Monsters? Lord God, these are not human beings, are they? Oh God, are these not *Untermenschen*? Has this not been a mistake by you? Lord God, O God, all faith, all Christianity, all Bible texts, all and everything, may I not ask in Jesus' name that you annihilate this scum, abandoned by You. Do it quickly, now, and all of them.'

For some minutes I felt that indeed this could be asked of God. Afterwards I knew this to be a terrible error. I should have prayed for their deliverance from evil. Whereupon I did just that. And yet, doubts have remained - to be honest to this day.

[I realize that this book consists of one long condemnation of Germany and the German people. Now in 1993 I am trying to stand with both feet squarely in the present and even to think about the future as well - hardly surprising when one has five children, has worked at the heart of society, in, of all things, the information industry, and is trying as far as possible not to relive memories of 1940-1945. Well, I can fully appreciate that young readers in particular, while understanding my attitude, will nevertheless consider it far too harsh and, what is more, unChristian. Do they know a different German people to the one we have known? There are indeed differences. Are these profound or superficial?

In 1961 as Chairman of the Royal Dutch Publishers Association, I attended a formal dinner in Frankfurt of our German sister-association and sat next to my German colleague. I was rather taciturn but my neighbour clearly wanted to chat. He started talking about *das schöne Holland* where he had often been.

'Auch im Krieg?'

'Jawohl, auch im Krieg,' in 1940. Perhaps in May 1940? Indeed with the Luftwaffe. Taken part in the bombing of Rotterdam?

'Jawohl. Leider.'

Yes, reader, it's like that. I left to eat somewhere else.

Yet, I now feel a little guilty. After all, for the first seven years after 1933 concentration camps were full of Germans. There are also quite decent Germans of high moral standing, for instance young people who go to Israel to work for nothing in kibbutzim to atone in some way for the sins of their fathers.

One beautiful Sunday afternoon, a Dutchman had a flat tyre on a very busy Dutch motorway. He did have a spare wheel but no jack (unpardonably stupid). He therefore moved to the hard shoulder and put his arm up. Tens, even hundreds of cars loaded with daytrippers passed by without batting an eyelid. After about an hour a formidable Mercedes pulled up in front of him. The Dutchman got a shock when he noticed the number plate had a K for Köln (Cologne). In the Mercedes sat a trim man and a quite beautiful woman. Having heard the Dutchman's plight, the German got out, took off his jacket, dug out his jack and helped our Dutchman quickly and expertly to change his wheel. His hands had become dirty, his previously spotless shirt as well. Our Dutchman thanked him profusely. He also apologized for his hundreds of compatriots who had driven on - a painful apology. The German then said, 'Wir Deutschen haben hier in Holland ja etwas gutzumachen, mein Herr. Also, gute Fahrt.' (We Germans have something to make up for here in Holland, Sir. Well, have a good journey). And, covered in grease, he disappeared in his £40,000 Mercedes.

Since then something in me has changed. Perhaps I could summarize it like this: our legal system is based on the assumption of good faith as long as bad faith has not been proved. With regard to the Germans the reverse applies for me. 'None the less' quite an improvement.

That was written in 1977.

Sixteen years later, in 1993, my appreciation of the Germans has further improved, and measurably so, but some ambivalence remains, perhaps inevitably in my case.

The reader will also have noticed repeated discrepancies between my Christian faith on the one hand and my cursing of the Germans on the other. He may ask himself: does this author really mean what he writes or does the practice differ from the theory? He is right - and wrong. At times of comparative peace, as in the Utrecht prison, I could more easily rise above my fate than when in direct confrontation with those possessed by evil. In the quiet cell I could contemplate God's ordained neighbourly love and write about it in all honesty, and yet later in Natzweiler and in another KZ, I yearned passionately for our tyrants' destruction, even once praying aloud for their extermination. Understandable. But weak, yes. I am certainly not above reproach. Like everyone else I am a sinner; that becomes clear on many pages. I had moments of fear and of bravery; of hope and of despair; of belief and disbelief; of love and hate. Just like everybody else.]

Shortly after I returned from the showers, the air raid sirens started wailing in the SS-camp next to ours. This time there were no distant explosions behind high hills. This time fighter planes swooped screaming down just above us, again and again. They used machine guns, the barrack shook, debris fell, dust and chalk. God, we've had it, I thought, the result of my miserable prayer, the end of a wretched sinner.

I then became aware of something amazing. For days I had lived in this barrack on the top bunk, but I had never yet noticed it. A little wooden cross, 6cm (2½") high, crudely carved, hung on the wall above my bunk, clattering against the wall with the shocks and shaking of shells hitting the buildings and the anti-aircraft guns wreaking death and destruction outside. The crucifix, symbol of the Cross on which Jesus suffered and died for us, to deliver us from all evil and our sins. A minute piece of wood. A piece of wood with a radiating power over me at that moment of, initially, unChristian anger, then fear of death. The fighter planes had disappeared. In the distance there was uproar in the SS camp. None of us were hit.

SEED

One day Wim Roessingh, busy with his 'instruments', was approached by an unknown high-ranking SS officer of the guards. He entreated Wim to help him.

'Have had gonorrhea, nevertheless want to have children, could you see whether my sperm is still alive?'

Certainly, replied laboratory worker Wim, on condition that you provide some semen at body temperature. The officer disappeared without a word, returning a quarter of an hour later with a tiny dish wrapped in a handkerchief and shouted: 'Have wanked a bit off, put it on the radiator, now have a look and see whether there's still some life in it.'

Wim examined the SS-glue under his old-fashioned microscope. A little later the philanderer appeared again.

'Well, and?'

Wim jumped to attention and shouted: 'Herr Obersturmführer! Häftling number 313 reports obediently that there's life yet.'

The candidate for fatherhood stumped away beaming.

Wim told me this story while still in Vaihingen. It was one of the very few times during 1942-45 when I was doubled up with laughter.

THE WRONG HORSE

It was mid March and less cold. Dressed in a 'vest' and a blanket I started with small walks behind the barracks on my stick-like legs. Naturally, this KZ too was surrounded by an electrified fence. Outside the fence were a few scattered guards, armed with carbines.

One day one of them accosted me, which made me freeze with fright, then with surprise: the man called out, in our language: 'Dutch?'

At once I stood to attention, an automatic reaction.

'Jawohl, Herr . . .' I could not remember the SS ranks, and he was not SS.

'We are Volkssturm. Have you been in a long time?'

'Almost three years.'

'Are you hungry?'

'Yes.'

The man took something from underneath his military coat and threw it over the fence. It was a packet of bread.

'Thank you, thank you very much.'

He came closer, so did I.

'I've bet on the wrong horse. I'm not afraid, you know, not afraid of anything, but we're doomed. My name is Westbroek. Westbroek's my name. From The Hague. They'll carry us off to Siberia, I think. Well, bet on the wrong horse, you see.'

The man continued his lazy walk along the fence. For some minutes I considered whether I could eat the bread of a traitor to our country. I then sat down behind one of the barracks, out of sight of Mr Westbroek, and gobbled up the bread.

Among the French there was a Catholic priest who could barely stand on his own two feet and whose face already bore the traces of death. Strangely he carried a large wooden cross round his neck although this was strictly prohibited. He still carried it, and continued to do so.

Every day this man got up from the bunk where he was to die to visit his compatriots who were dying. He ministered to them even in his last hours. Whenever they wished it, he also ministered to non-compatriots and non-Catholics.

Once I too went to talk to him, when I was deeply saddened because almost all my friends had succumbed. He told me: 'Clearly the Lord has a soft spot for you. I can't imagine that He, having inflicted all this upon you, would suddenly have any other than good intentions.'

My depressions in Vaihingen came often and were dreadful. What caused them? I had already survived umpteen more or less fatal situations and illnesses. I had been surrounded continuously by good friends. I was deeply pious. And the victors, the rescuers were approaching fast from all directions, the end would surely be very near.

I think that this last reason was the main cause of the attacks of wretchedness. They were approaching, they were quite near, but they still had not arrived. The proximity of the end made me feel the present reality all the more.

There was too the sorrow about all these good, gallant fellows who had given up, and the secret thought that we, the last of the group, might have to offer our lives as well. Would that not be right? Like them, we should give up too.

In addition, the food situation had become desperate. Hunger almost suffocated me, notwithstanding so much help. We were also very irritable, despite the friendships we had formed and all our good intentions. We knew that we were at the dawn of great, critical, events and might even be embroiled in the fighting.

Meanwhile, even then, the German newspapers did not stop preaching the *Endsieg* (final victory) by the use of secret weapons. Should we have been more sensible? The Germans were, after all, fighters. Who knew whether they did not have some decisive invention up their sleeve? And, if there were no such weapon, what could be expected from the meeting between Americans, English, Canadians, and the Russians? Would that bring peace?

24 March. We talked about the behaviour of the Germans in Holland, particularly about the stealing and pillaging. How they cavorted in the most expensive, most elegant shops, with their idiotic

caps and boots, and bought dresses and suits, and bought and bought with newly printed paper money and endless textile and clothes coupons. 'Für die Frau in der Heimat' (For the wife at home). They emptied everything. And we talked about Rotterdam, about their entry into the city with tanks under yellow banners, and about the dirty way they waged war, about their arrogance, notwithstanding - or perhaps because of - their incompetence. About the many friends they murdered, quickly or slowly, and about the Gestapo's tortures, about the systematic destruction of our cities, of our beautiful countryside; about the wicked carrying off into slavery of so many men; about their loathsome propaganda aimed at the level of young children and the use they made of despicable Dutch traitors.

When reflecting on all this I have to say I'm glad I did something against this viperous brood, and when necessary I'll do it again. I can't help it. I accept the consequences. This rabble must first be cleared away, for otherwise we can't live.

26 March. Great news. Montgomery has started a new offensive, Americans are crossing the Rhine everywhere, we can really expect anything now. I'm going to give myself a real wash, I want to look entirely proper when the Americans arrive.

28 March. All of a sudden things turn very critical. We are to be transported. America has a bridgehead near Karlsruhe only 60 km (37 miles) away! Everyone is extremely nervous. Perhaps tonight American tanks will arrive in front of the gate? I'm dazed with hunger, lie on my berth all day, walking makes me dizzy. Will this be the end? How could the kraut move a thousand sick men? Fourteen hundred dead lie behind the hill already. I regularly visualize our reunion, hallucinating. Macaroni and bombed horses. Everyone very depressed. Again nothing happens. I'm praying desperately. I'm also very afraid.

30 March. Good Friday. Jesus Christ has died. One of the last Dutchmen has died, today, at 5 o'clock in the morning. In Dautmergen we wept together and comforted each other, particularly motivated by the idea that our wives feel and see everything and watch our behaviour. They shouldn't have any reason to be ashamed of us. I've got my friend's estate: amongst which a little notebook crammed with words. He had many excellent plans. 'If only I don't kick the bucket at the last minute.' I've got to pray to God for more understanding. I want to try and comprehend more. Only two of

fourteen Dutchmen are now left. I can't take it in. But I do know that my hatred of the krauts is mortal. No more about that on this special day. I want to be with you. Each new loss brings us closer together. I want to fight and I shall fight like a lion, every minute, every second. They want me dead as well, these scoundrels. But I want to live. I want to return to you. The end is now rapidly approaching. America captures one kraut city after another. The Americans will make mincemeat of the swine. But they'll want to drag us down with them. I shall resist.

Did those *Häftlinge* with a little energy left, capable of assisting in whatever form, really do everything to save those who could still be saved, and relieve the dying of their suffering during their last days and hours? I too asked myself that question. Quite often. Even to this day. The answer is yes and no. There are many examples of actions that showed great caring, self-sacrifice, even heroism for the benefit of fellow-men, whether friends or not. I have mentioned many. I myself owe my life several times over to such help. But some were more able to help than others, on account of character or position. If you were in a slightly better condition, for instance because you were lucky enough to be in a reasonable work detail and got a little more food, it was of course much easier to help someone else, with food but also morale. Anyone who was in a desperate condition could only help with great effort. On the other hand, I have experienced that he who gave his last powers to help fellow-men, totally unexpectedly would receive more in return than he gave. This book provides examples of this as well. We should have risked really everything, including our own lives, to save those who were even weaker. That too has been done. But it was also left undone. Sometimes, when at the threshold of death, I also felt insufficiently confident that God would replenish the strengths and means I had myself given away.

This is one of the reasons why KZ-survivors will always retain a sense of guilt.

1 April. Easter. At crack of dawn, sorrowful women, snow-white angels. 'Why do you seek the living among the dead? He is not here. He has risen. The God who was murdered - He is alive.'

2 April. Again there is talk of imminent evacuation. I hope not: wait for the Americans. But this camp is beginning to be boring, it is a dirty, gruesome death-camp. Dachau, while of course crammed to over-crowding, would be paradise. I feel very weak, occasionally diar-rhoea, breathe with difficulty and sometimes my heart gallops.

almost new woollen vest, wonderful though ugly. Are we really off? It seems nonsense. We'll see. I leave everything to God.

After the German offensive in the Ardennes (16 December 1944 - 26 January 1945) had been repulsed it was clear even to the most pessimistic in the KZ that the krauts were about to lose their war, and very soon in view of the rapid Russian advance in the east and the allied crossing of the Rhine in the west. The impending apocalyptic downfall of the Third Reich could not be doubted any more even by the most fanatic *Parteigenossen*. How did this prospect influence the German's conduct towards us *Häftlinge*? It is difficult to answer this question. On the one hand, the kraut became more murderous: if we perish you'll go down with us. There are many examples; I only mention the numerous murderous transports of *Häftlinge* on foot, in open railway carriages etc., criss-cross through the land of the Teutons. This tallies with the German character: that they should dramatize the final downfall as much as possible.

On the other hand, there are a host of examples of SS men etc. who started eating humble pie with the *Häftlinge*, who lightened the regime, took care to save their own skin. In many camps discipline slackened; but that had other causes as well: the SS guards were more and more replaced by *Volkssturm*, the resources dwindled, particularly food. Things clearly ran out of control, certainly towards the end in Dachau. Even when killing abated there were still plenty of deaths. What firearms, cudgels and gas could no longer achieve, typhus and hunger still did.

However, it is even more complex. Not all Germans were fanatical Nazis. As the war took a turn for the worse, so some slowly came to recognize that they had been deceived by their own leaders with all their absurd ideologies. They woke up from their dream of power as *Herrenvolk, Blut und Boden*, and *Lebensraum*, and began to understand that they had behaved like criminals.

Indeed, the eyes of some Germans were opened. There were some - only a few - who started chumming up with us, not particularly in order to be on good terms but because they began to understand how much they had been 'mistaken'.

The party leadership clearly belonged to the first category. As was revealed later, Reichsführer SS Heinrich Himmler had ordered the commandants of concentration camps to finish us off as the enemy approached: 'Kein Häftlinge darf lebendig in den Händen des Feindes fallen.' (No prisoner must be allowed to fall alive into the hands of the enemy). An order which several *Lagerkommandanten* sabotaged. Was this for fear of reprisals by the victors? Or from moral objection? I do not know. I suspect that, once taken prisoner themselves, they claimed the second but that really the first represents the truth. All in all, I believe that those who wanted us to share in their downfall were in the majority.

WORSE THAN ANIMALS

From Vaihingen to Dachau is 200 km (125 miles) as the crow flies: it took us three full days. Our train consisted of three goods-wagons, we were three hundred; easy to calculate. We received 750 grams (1lb 10oz) of bread; that proved to be all for three days. No drinks. Nothing. *Austreten* outside the train was allowed only once, otherwise we relieved ourselves in saucepans, or just as it came. Sitting was an art on its own. You slowly let yourself down and waited to find how, where and on whom you landed, whether they would tolerate you or punch you up again. Those who, having sat down, got up again lost their place and had to fight for another one again.

Sometimes someone died; that provided some relief because you could then sit on top of him. If someone dropped a piece of bread, a dozen men pounced on it, grabbed at it amid the faeces, some using their homemade knives. According to my notes - even in this racket I wrote something - we could look outside through bullet holes. I saw vineyards on mountainsides and blossoming fruit trees, magnificent castles, monasteries.

Our *Krankentransport* on 3, 4 and 5 April was the target for allied air attacks. Pure fear of death in the carriage; some shouted for their mothers. On 3 April at 4pm near Plochingen we were attacked by fighters. The guards fled across the railway embankments into a wood, we were standing, defenceless, locked up. On 4 April we travelled all of 30 km (19 miles) in twenty-four hours, endlessly shunting. At night I could see the Danube and Ulm cathedral, women with spades, columns of prisoners of war.

At one station we could make some contact with a group of American pilots, prisoners of war. There they were, Goebbels' 'phosphorus-throwing Anglo-American negroes'. Fine men, normal faces. They threw us cigarettes. They called to us.

'You'll be free within three, four weeks.'

This turned out to be correct. One entire night stoppage at Günzburg, the guards in the air raid bunker underneath the station.

At times when the air raid alarm sounded in the distance they hid the train in the forests. I made arrangements with some Belgians to save all my diary pieces of paper. By 5 April morale had vanished. Everywhere complaining, shitting, fighting with knives, lice. In this horror train I wrote: 'How can man survive this?'

9. KONZENTRATIONSLAGER DACHAU
5-29 April 1945

THE DEATH BATH

Our stay in Dachau started with *Desinfektion*, in the middle of the night. We undressed outside, in a heavy shower of rain. Our clothes had to be packed in a bundle, jacket with breast-number on top in order to be able to recognize the proprietor by his number after the disinfection of the clothes, apparently the whole bundle at the same time. That did not work of course: the bundles fell apart.

When we were petrified with cold after a few hours standing in the dark and rain, we were driven into the *Baderaum*. Those who could walk, walked. Those who could only limp, limped. Those who could just crawl, crawled. Those who could not move any more were dragged, as were those who were dead.

The *Baderaum* of Dachau was large, the showers were warm, soap and towels unknown. But the sight of our transport under the showers of Dachau, in early April 1945, one month before Germany's complete downfall, was so awful that the eyes hesitated to pass it on to the brain other than in a blurred way. A small number stood under the shower and tried to wash the shit off the skeleton; cakes of shit slowly floated into the drains. A larger number knelt, lay or sat in the warm water. Blood and pus and bandages floated off into the water.

Another group lay stretched out under the warm water of the shower in Dachau, mumbling, crying, twitching. Some of them let faeces and urine just run, it flowed whirling along to the drains. Beside those bathing. . . . Among those bathing, but also under the showers themselves, the *Waschraumkommando* was in action, in bathing trunks. Strong baldheaded men piled up the corpses higher and higher, one,

202

two, heave-ho! - another corpse smacked on top of the pile. They also picked up many who were lying down, those gasping for breath in their death agony: one, two - *Hoch Amerika!,* and threw what would be (would have been) human beings on top of the ever-growing mountain, and I could still see hands moving, and feet, and blood, pus, shit, urine was leaking from the pile; in that pile there was still rattling, coughing, groaning - but, one, two, heave-ho! And they dragged them away from under the farthest douche, by the feet, *los! los!* right through those standing, kneeling and sitting, and then: one, two, heave-ho! Until they started a new mountain.

After the death bath we were driven into the night again, wet and naked. This was followed by a trip across the roll-call yard to the quarantine barrack. Once there we had to try and push ourselves into the overcrowded sleeping hall.

I met many friends again who had remained in Dachau after Natzweiler. Notwithstanding quarantine they were able to make contact, through the windows between barracks. One of them appeared at a window. On noticing me his mouth fell open. 'Floris, you are dead!' he called.

'Not so,' I replied.

'Wait,' he said. A little later he returned with a large sausage. 'Because you're still alive.'

It was like that. We exchanged news. Who was still alive, who was dead? I made my sad report: twelve, fourteen, even twenty names. And they named their dead. Death was so common, at first you took fright, but you could not mourn all the time. Who was still alive? That was more important in those final days.

THE GERMAN - A PORTRAIT

One question has still got to be answered in this book and answered honestly: what did the prisoners really think of the Germans?

After all that has been written here, it can hardly be expected of those who suffered most to answer in any other way than along the following lines: We hated and still hate the Germans like vermin, and if there are good ones among them they will first have to prove it. We did not - nor do some now - make a distinction between Germans and Nazis. The Germans allowed the rise to power of the National Socialists. As long as the Nazis were successful, almost the entire German people supported them, with only a few exceptions. When things started to go badly there was some German opposition, but rather because the Führer failed as Commander-in-Chief to win victories than because they abhorred his bestial regime.

Still, I must of course try to give a more balanced opinion.

During our imprisonment we also came across 'good Germans'; this book contains examples. We encountered good Germans among those outside as well as inside the barbed wire. They were conspicuous because of their rarity. But, of course, those who guarded the KZs, like members of the SS and Gestapo, did not belong to the cream of the nation.

It is said that the Germans are *gründlich*, industrious, disciplined, precise and competent in everything (including industrious murder). That may be true today, we did not notice it. The Germans who dealt with us were not *gründlich*, though certainly industrious, not precise and almost always very incompetent, cumbersome, slow in action and comprehension: in short, stupid. We continued to be surprised by the stupidity of the Germans, even those in the police apparatus. Their organizational talent too was well below standard.

What also struck us was their strange combination of bloodthirstiness and sentimentality; this book gives examples of this as well.

The German is morbid, sinister, often preoccupied with death. His notion of *Oberster Kriegsherr* (the supreme warlord) has romantic parallels: field of honour, heroic death, *Heimat*, *Valhalla*. The German huntsman, in green, killing animals in forests, is like a miniature *Kriegsherr*. His sentimentality, of the coarse kind, is inseparably linked with it. Siegfried falls for the blonde, blue-eyed Kriemhilde, who can be seen as a *vollbusiges arisches Edelweib* (full-breasted Aryan noblewoman). This encourages the belief that the German often looks on human beings as animals. Everything in him seems to show something bestial. The SS advertised for *vollbusige Edelweiber zwecks Erzeugung arischer Kinder* (full-breasted Aryan noblewomen for the purpose of producing Aryan children). Himmler therefore set up coupling and breeding stations for human beings.

A human life had little value for the Germans (probably even less for the Russians). They did not spare either us, or themselves. As for the Jews, they were not considered to be human but *Untermenschen*, good only for destruction - a plague of rats.

Certainly, the German was disciplined and obedient, criminally so: *Kadaverdisziplin*. That came out at the Nuremberg trials. Anyone who received an order, whatever it might be, executed it. The idea of not executing it never occurred to them.

The Germans were coarse even unto death. They devised brutalities which only a sick mind could have thought of. Corporal punishment has existed since time immemorial; one has only got to think of the tough regime in the British (and Dutch) navy. But though these ratings were occasionally beaten on their backs, even until blood seeped out, or worse, it was typical of the Germans to cook up as an official corporal punishment *Fünfundzwanzig auf dem Arsch*. Beating grown-up men in public on government instruction on their bare bottoms is typically primitive and Germanic.

Also, the Germans seemed seriously convinced of their superiority as *Herrenvolk*. In a good mood they could be paternalistically good-natured to wretches like us, *dumme Holländer*.

One clear example.

In 1943, when I had been in prison for quite some time, my wife rented a rowing boat for a day on the Kager Lake. She rowed a bit, steered into some reeds, undressed and sunbathed. Soon enough she was startled by approaching footsteps in the march. A kraut, armed to the teeth, appeared on the bank and viewed the reeds and rowing boat.

'Gehört das Boot, Ihnen?'(Is that your boat?)

'Nein, es ist gemietet.' (No, it is rented).

The kraut then shouted: 'Kann da liegen bleiben.' (Can stay there). And marched away. That was all he was able to say to a beautiful naked woman, but he meant well.

The Germans were none the less asses when it came to administration and organization. As soon as they gave us prisoners a little more self-government, for whatever reason, everything improved. Their woolliness also showed in their slogans, written announcements and rules, including those from the highest authorities: gibberish, often pure nonsense. But industrious they were, in everything (also in Auschwitz). They could work like the devil, in both senses. They were strong, healthy, indefatigable.

Musical too. In the same way that the Dutch are traditionally steeped in the art of painting, the Germans are steeped in music. Sentimental music mainly, romantic. I think the German people are at the top in the world of composers, musicians, orchestras.

That was noticeable in the KZ too. The Germans wanted music there as well, even at executions, and the *Häftlinge* made music at their command.

A special idiosyncrasy of the Germans was their tendency (not unknown for that matter in Holland) to do something in a complicated way when it could be done in a simple one. To them, extreme complexity in regulations, coupled with verbosity and endless poring over documents, signified an educated and erudite approach.

In addition they displayed a curious desire to put an end to any agreeable situation. Even in a KZ it happened once in a while that one had eaten enough and, being out of immediate danger of death, could sit chatting pleasantly with friends. A situation like that could never last long with the Germans - it was as if they were ashamed of it, pressurised by the tough duties of service to the Führer and Fatherland. The awful cry would soon be heard: 'Fenster auf!' (windows open), which resulted in icy draughts, food gone, cigarettes extinguished, a general disintegration of the group and 'Ruck Zuck an die Arbeit, auf geht's'. (Work, get going!).

These paragraphs have turned out rather negatively, but I have to stand by them. In a positive spirit one might add that Christian neighbourly love demands that we take this strange, lost, yet talented people by the arm to show them a better way. One could acknowledge that a people of, at the time, ninety million souls must have included men and women of high character. With a few admirable exceptions, however, these men and women of high character kept as quiet as mice during the twelve years of the Thousand Year Reich. On the other hand it has to be admitted that among my own Dutch people there were many thousands who were just as wicked as the Germans - to our eternal shame - and some of them were even to be found within the barbed wire fences. However, I do not accept at all the suggestion sometimes made that if the Dutch nation had been in the same situation as the German nation between 1918 and 1933, we would probably have walked the same path, in other words, that any nation could behave like a collection of criminals. That is impossible.

Because of its history, its veneration for *das Militär*, its traditional educational methods, the unassailable prestige of the father figure, the paternalism, the over-compensation for its inferiority complex, the over-sensitiveness to hypnotic leadership, its death wish and its sentimentality, the German people were predisposed more than any other to march en masse and with hysterical joy behind their Führer, to their ruin.

In Holland the man would have been laughed out of court much earlier.

HOW DO YOU SURVIVE?

The reader will probably have noticed by now how much I have been protected and privileged, before my arrest but even more so after. Left, right and everywhere the fury of the Nazi-demons held sway. All around victims fell, usually after unimaginable suffering. During their interrogation they were tortured. They were locked up in bunkers. They were beaten to within an inch of death, or entirely to death. They were buried alive, burned alive, hanged, shot, gassed. They were starved to death, kicked to death, smashed up with cudgels, torn to pieces by dogs. They were guinea-pigs for experiments, for radiation, castration, sterilization. They joined Jewish work parties, punishment details, punishment camps.

And I? I had a lot ranged against me. Though not a Jew, nor a Russian or Pole, I was a *Rechtsanwalt* (lawyer), an intellectual, an arch enemy of all the rabble inside and outside the barbed wire. I was a Christian and therefore highly suspect to all communists and Nazis. My appearance did not help either: a nasty skeleton 1.87m (6'2") tall, with large ears sticking out and an eternally running nose. I was a wet, a dreamer, clumsy with tools. I was slow, always hurt somewhere. I was conspicuous everywhere. I truly had almost all the qualifications for a speedy end.

Many fellow-sufferers have continuously held their breath for me, surprised when they saw me surface somewhere time and again: from a murderous work detail, from the *Revier*, from another camp. How could this happen?

Only one answer is valid: because it pleased God to save me.

There are also a few subsidiary answers. I was absolutely convinced that one day I would be free; I considered this to be God's promise. I wanted at all cost to return to my wife. I held on to that. That was why I was rarely at the end of my tether, and then only fleetingly. I also felt I had a mission. I had been converted to Christianity, I therefore had to spread the word. I believed this to be God's intention and that therefore I would be kept alive.

I had inherited an iron constitution. I was really strong when an undergraduate. My entire being was healthy.

I had many, many friends. Elsewhere in this book I have described the priceless value of friendship. Friends kept your morale as well as your body intact. Not only did friends take care that I would be less conspicuous, they also protected me. Friends helped me get jobs and food. My diary records hundreds, perhaps thousands of such cases. Almost continually throughout those three years I was dreadfully hungry. I don't want to think about what such hunger would have been like if I had had to rely solely on official rations. Hundreds of pounds of extra food were given to me by friends.

And lastly, imagination. Unlike many others who went to pieces when thinking about home, I steeled myself against the reality, consciously or unconsciously, and while indulging in memories of the past also made plans for the future. I felt that the reality of the KZ would derange me, lead to madness (as it did on two occasions). Indeed, I used imagination as a weapon. I could also write down what I imagined, almost everywhere and always. Writing was a necessity of life comparable to eating. By writing everything down I forced myself not to digress but to concentrate on the subject. The memories that materialized in the written word kept up a flow of everyday thoughts - sometimes rather over-excited - and these mental images helped my mind to survive.

Because the mind is more vulnerable than the body, some men, although physically as strong as iron, lost heart. Their character was perhaps too refined to accept the villainy around them, and they gave up in a few months. On the other hand, small, slight men, physically not strong at all, often survived by force of character or faith or philosophy of life or shrewd adroitness or sheer obstinacy and acceptance of their lot.

You had to try not to let go. Many neglected themselves, often out of pure weakness. They did not care a damn any more. They became dirty outside and in. That was fatal. You had to stay civilised, behave politely, engage in proper conversation, discipline yourself.

In particular you had to keep on washing yourself, even with icy water without soap or towel, in a *Waschraum* full of wrangling *Häftlinge*. You had to try and get clean clothes, to keep your bunk clean, as animals keep their nest clean. You had to try on Sunday mornings to get a shave even though twenty others were ahead of you in the queue. You had to try and wash sceptic wounds and boils, grease them with margarine, and bandage them with a strip of your vest. You had to try to protect your health, however strange this may sound in the appalling circumstsances. In outside work details and roll-calls you could often chose places where you were less exposed.

In almost all the camps the beds were arranged in three tiers; you should always try to sleep at the top because that is where it was warmest, because men who had to *austreten* (go to the loo) did not climb past you - their feet in your face - and because no one could dirty you if they were incontinent. You should never exchange your bread or other food for cigarettes (as happened often).

Still, often cunning came in useful too, pure selfish cunning. Take the bread distribution: when the queue began to form you had to get a quick glimpse of the portions, in what order they lay and which were (or seemed to be) the largest pieces. You then had to take the place in the queue that would assure you the biggest piece when it was your turn. . . . The same for the soup distribution: you had to make sure it would be your turn when they ladled the last and therefore thickest soup from the mess-tin.

Also - and this was very important - you had to try and win over the powers that be to your side when you wanted to be admitted to the *Revier* or the *Schonungsblock*. That was a great art. If your appearance was too pitiful the guard could be sufficiently annoyed as to chase you away. If you took great care to look reasonably well he would certainly do that. It required a great talent for acting to make these dangerous criminals sympathetic to you. You had to be silent, very quiet, humble, ingratiating . . . but still pitiful. It is disgusting, but that's how it was.

With the SS it was different again. Extreme self-discipline was required in any contact with the SS. You had to put on an absolute stiff upper lip, *militärisch*, stand perfectly straight to attention, and speak good German loudly, with as Teutonic a bearing as possible. Otherwise the bastards only held you in contempt; they mocked you, beat you, chased you away. They did not want to see you. This too is disgusting, this too was how it was. Much could depend on it. For instance: obtaining a better job. You then had to put on your best behaviour to be accepted. You had to hit it off with a German! It was humiliating, but this time the end justified the means.

The reader should remember these guidelines. One day they might come in useful.

THE LAST DAYS

Towards the end of the war the krauts dragged their prisoners from the west to the east and those from the east to the west. They could not give them up. They did not want to set them free, apparently, nor did they want to murder all of them. In that way they expended manpower, railway capacity, money and food on herds of human wrecks who had no value to them, as experience had shown. Instead they should have been using every means available to step-up the war effort even if this led to the total annihilation they seemed to want. Because eastern Bavaria was among the areas that were last to be liberated, massive multiple transports arrived in Dachau. Gradually this resulted in an almost complete disruption of this, the oldest KZ in Germany. Discipline slackened, the food in the *Lager* was slowly exhausted.

We knew, of course, that the American armies were not far away any more. Bombers and fighters flew unhindered in several layers one above the other over us. On the other hand, we, *alte Lagerhasen*, knew that calamity threatened us. During the last days all 32,000 *Häftlinge* had to attend repeated roll-calls on the interminable parade ground. We were kept standing for an hour or several hours without the usual terror-discipline of the krauts, only to be sent packing unexpectedly. During these disorderly roll-calls we were prepared for anything, particularly for air attacks or artillery barrages. Would the krauts really allow us to be liberated by the Allies? On the other hand: would they be capable of *umlegen* 32,000 men? This state of mind characterized every minute of the last weeks: liberation could hardly be visualized, nor could massive slaughter. But perpetual imprisonment was impossible too, because Germany was collapsing. What would happen? Fog coupled with fear, coupled at times with ecstatic joy, sometimes with despair from impatience. I had many friends who were surprised that I was still alive, as described earlier, and they slipped a lot of food my way in order to further improve my condition. They were able to do this because they had been in Dachau much longer, had become *Prominenz* and therefore had at their disposal all sorts of extra food: in addition food parcels had arrived from all over, *mirabile dictu* - though of course again not for Dutchmen. Yet, my friends could 'organize' a lot.

From my diary:

19-4-1945: The water reaches my underbelly, I've also got fatter. Yesterday a beautiful sunset: 'They'll come from that direction', and I started crying. In that direction we'll go as well. After having been shaved bald again I had to wait an hour; naked into the night, naked under one thin wet blanket. Ruffians. Bastards. Always, always hungry. I'm querulous, because of the horrible cold. The sun isn't warm. Everything here is treacherous. They're fighting in Nuremberg. That's good. I feel rotten and I've lost my head.

20-4-1945: AH's birthday (Adolf Hitler). No roll-call today!! Serious amount of water build-up in my genitals and face. Tins of Ovomaltine are being distributed. I'm still convinced that the USA will arrive soon. Perhaps next week. After a nap in the sun two litres of carrot soup, one 'organized' by me: watch out carefully - left, right, behind - nothing? whoopee, in between others, keep going, scram - success! The struggle for - naked - life. Now great alarm. I'm lying on a table in the sun and listen to a Hungarian violinist playing Schubert's *Ave Maria*. I'm sure: shortly the Great Event will arrive: armistice, journey home, reunion. Spring 1945 will bring the happiest day of our lives.

22-4-1945. I'm extremely blessed. I met an Austrian priest who lent me his New Testament until tonight. I've got it here, it's lying in front of me on the bed. I devoured it, especially the Revelation of St John.

23-4-1945. Yesterday also jazz on an accordion. One Dutchman tap-danced. Last night everywhere theft from the parcels. Today monstrously cold. My oedema begins to disappear. Confusion. I'm still full of the Apocalypse. All of it points to this war. I'm frightfully cold and sitting against a stove, outside Jabo's, USA fighter bombers, are busy. The Jews are on the move. No news.

24-4-1945. Yesterday 1/8th of a loaf and so much song-seed soup that I nearly burst: ¼ of a 4-litre (1 gallon) bucket in one go. The Americans appear to be past Augsburg and close. Continuous alarm. We can expect anything each day. My brain simply can't cope. It got a hard knock. This time is so overwhelming, events are of such immense importance, the future is so dazzling, that I could yell as well as cry as well as roar with laughter. I take refuge in the New Testament. And in eating and sleeping.

I can't imagine anything any more. It's far too big, I choked at once. Smoking, I could smoke continuously and eat chocolate, sausage, cream, pancakes. I've read a pamphlet about Lourdes which impressed me very much. I thought about my own 'visions' on 9 April 1942 near Delft and on 25 December 1943 and in January 1944 in Natzweiler. Sometimes I reflect on how it would be if I became a Catholic. That religion is steeped in great charm. One has a lot more anchorage, they 'do more about it', and there is also their great power, their internationalism and especially their artistic mysteriousness. I drank tea and have been shaved. There is still alarm. All transports, all movements, have been cancelled. It's an extremely tense mess. Shortly we'll be eating dried vegetables. A kind Russian from Marioepol [now Zhdanov] will cook them for us. Suddenly soup is brought in. I talked to a 'comrade' who lives 600 km (380 miles) north of Vladivostok, 12,000 km (7,600 miles) from here. Tank squadrons are in the neighbourhood.

25-4-1945. The night promised at first to be quiet, but in the evening 166 men were added to our *Stube*. Four thousand men had walked here from Nuremberg in three weeks. Now they slept three men to one bunk without mattress and without blanket. However, I, suddenly 'prominent', am alone in one bed with two mattresses and four blankets. And alas, again lice. I'm thoroughly ashamed.

The work parties don't march out anymore. USA appear to be only a few tens of kilometres from here. Today or tomorrow? April 1945, will this finally be the month? When thinking about everything that could still happen I tremble like a reed, flush hot and cold, shake and sweat. If only they won't evacuate us, 32,000 men! Though where would we go, and how? I've got an idea that AH is fighting in the ruins of Berlin with his men, the city seems to have become one big fortress. He will die or commit suicide. What a terrible time for this man, who perhaps had ideals. The news is now quite tense, it's going to happen one of these days; that is the general opinion. Suddenly artillery firing, clearly audible.

26-4-1945. That's it. Evacuation of Dachau at 12 noon. The Americans are advancing. It is unbelievable. I think also impossible. They'll catch up with us; may God make sure that this time the krauts have left it too late.

Evening. We're still here. Dutchmen and citizens of other Red Cross countries would stay. I repeatedly prayed for it. Have had a truly festive meal: 4 litres (1 gallon) of brown-bean soup, quite thick (*très épaisse, pas de la flotte*); a Dutch friend had thrown half a pound of meat in it, coffee (!) with sugar, and a Laurens cigarette, unbelievable. I've learned to be grateful for everything. Where tonight? On the march on the road? Here in my own bed? When America? When Holland? When you?

27-4-1945. We're still here. There's still food. Everything is in complete disarray. A little while ago loud shouts of joy: Americans! Turned out to be nonsense, were *Volkssturm*. People here are all nerves. Important is that I'm still here. It seems that they have after all evacuated several thousand Jews. Last night I saw you quite clearly before my eyes, you're becoming much clearer. It's difficult to write, it rages and hisses and buzzes in my head. I've washed myself entirely and greased myself with Mitigal against the lice, my body is far from perfect, scars all over, but oedema almost gone. Shaved myself and had boils bandaged. Am now ready to receive the Americans. I don't want my hair cut anymore. The French again receive parcels. Why don't we? They will be leaving for Switzerland. It's really cynical that we don't get anything. Five hundred parcels were on the way, they were bombed, only forty are left. The big question is: do we go or stay? I believe it'll be the latter, I'm constantly praying for us to stay.

28-4-1945. Yesterday terrible confusion: thousands of *Zugänge* (admissons). After apocalyptic thunderstorms we moved to Block 19 in torrential rain, where a Dutch friend helped me get a bed. The French are eating without a stop, I have nothing, truly a torment, difficult to control yourself. Slept fully dressed: one never knows. This morning: biscuits with sweets, paté de fruits, soft cheese and white beans with cocoa, presents from a few Frenchmen. The USA have surrounded Munich and are supposed to be quite near. Today? Tomorrow? The birthday of Princess Juliana? [30 April, subsequently Queen Juliana, now retired and Princess again]. Keep calm, read your Bible, that's best, and forget the guzzling of the French all around you. God, pray help us in these interminable important days. The envy of people who don't receive parcels could lead to revolution. It is too bad.

29-4-1945. Sunday. Where do I start? The confusion is ridiculously great. *Keine Namen, keine Nummer, keine Listen* (No names, no numbers, no lists). Is the camp free? New governments, republic of Bavaria, what rumours. I don't believe anything any more. Only know that I can't get out yet. I'm not a 'prominent' any more but suddenly an ordinary man.

NB NB: from about 12 noon all watchtowers carry white flags. What the hell does this mean?

After the soup a strange sort of extreme despair came over me, just like that, impatience and loathing of all the filth and ruffians around me; hunger, a feeling of guilt too, and loneliness and nervousness and disappointment because tomorrow again we wouldn't be getting any parcels, and because I haven't got anything to smoke any more. God, what a weak, ungrateful, faithless devil I am! Anyhow all will be well in the end. That seems to be clear. I haven't got any words left. I'm brimming over. I've got a burning, fierce desire for the divine.

Later: white flags still fly from the machine guns on the watchtowers.

It's getting serious now. The Americans might be here tomorrow. Or tonight. Or right away.

10. LIBERATED
29 April-9 May 1945

'YEAH'

Sunday evening 29-4-1945, 18.00 hrs. The first Americans. Dead SS. Kick in the arse, disarmed, dead. Red flag. Other flags. Have just eaten bread with cheese and sugar. Cigar. Only American. Hitler dead? Are we rid of them or will they still shoot? Now big explosions. Tanks? Chocolate milk. For a full hour I cried. Saw women! After ten minutes a Harley Davidson thunders in at full speed with a painted sixty-year-old woman in the saddle, armed. Film, paper, pencil. War correspondent. Saw more women. Some prisoners fell dead against the electrified barbed wire fence. Will leave in a few days. Is Holland free? All those dead bodies. Dust storm, grey dust storm. I don't know. Heavy shocks.

This was an exerpt from my diary notes. The liberation of Dachau by a combat team of the Rainbow Division of the VIIth US Army under General Patterson took place at 17.31 hours.

The fact that American soldiers liberated us in Dachau has resulted in my everlasting devotion to the US of A. They could have been French, British or Russian soldiers. True. But they were American. Our, or at least my, slight anti-Americanism because of the absence of the second front in 1943 and early 1944, had disappeared. When in later years there has been exasperation or disappointment about American policies, this can be compared with exasperation at the wrong turns of a brother or another dear member of the family.

At last I had squeezed something out of the French again and was lying on the floor of the Block eating when I heard an unusual uproar outside. I hobbled along the narrow corridor between two Blocks to the fence, ditch, high tension and mirador and there saw a sort of robot from another world: helmet like a potty with tree branches, a belt with bullets around his waist, hand grenades in the belt, a large machine pistol, high brown boots. I called out: 'Are you American?' He turned to me: 'Yeah'. He then turned again to the watchtower with the white flag. A kraut stumbled down, hands high. The American tore some medal ribbons from the uniform, turned him round and ordered him to walk away. When the kraut walked off the American shot him dead.

We now saw more Americans in small open cars, some with caterpillar tracks. Several prisoners broke through the first fence and stopped at the ditch. A few went through the ditch and tried to break through the electrified second fence - and were electrocuted. I raced to the parade ground with thousands more. Soon the Harley Davidson with the painted blonde American war correspondent rushed in. I saw a *Häftling* - no longer a *Häftling* - climb the *Jourhaus*, the high entrance gate, with reckless disregard for his life, and attach a huge flaming red flag to the mast on its top. An hour after the liberation the bodies of Germans shot dead lay everywhere along the wall, particularly near the watchtowers. They were not alone. Poles and Russians were busy crawling over them. They stripped them especially of boots and watches. Later on you saw Poles and Russians with kraut boots and watches everywhere. As dusk set in, a storm rose which blew up a lot of dust. The Russians had already found the SS vegetable gardens, pulled up the tubers and potatoes and cooked them in huge saucepans in the *Lagerstrasse*.

A little later there was the deafening sound of shooting. We thought the Germans were firing on us from afar, but it turned out to be American soldiers who had found German Flakgrenades which they considered obsolete and therefore set off as a sort of fireworks display.

Nobody took any notice anymore of designated sleeping places. The quarantine barracks were also ignored. I joined friends, we cried, ate and listened to the American radio in Germany with delightful jazz music. Suddenly a few girls also turned up, God knows where they came from.

Not until March 1985 did a report about the liberation of Dachau reach me, written by (then) Lieutenant-Colonel Felix L. Sparks, CO of the 3rd Battalion, 157th Infantry Regiment, 45th Infantry Division, VIIth US Army. That report tallies with almost everything mentioned above. It was in fact Sparks and his men who had liberated us.

The next day we received food that was both too rich and too plentiful (pork). I ate everything too fast. Some died as a result. There was a religious ceremony on the parade ground, led by an American army chaplain. The sermon was about those who give their lives for friends (John 15:13).

I visited the *Pfarrerblock*, knelt down, prayed and made friends. I also made the acquaintance of two well- known Dutch poets and journalists who were busy preparing a newsbulletin for the Dutch contingent, *The Voice of the Low Countries*. I offered my services. These were accepted. I wrote a piece. It was published. On the parade ground five hundred Dutchmen assembled in honour of liberation, by chance on Princess Juliana's birthday. A handsome Dutch flag was hoisted, speeches made. We sang our national anthem (the Wilhelmus) as far as our tears allowed.

That evening many Russians entered our Block who had clearly made a tour of the surroundings. They roared up on large German motorbikes. They wore snow-white German shirts and smoked cigars. They cooked all sorts of food on fires in the middle of the barrack, they also had bottles of wine. In due course they started singing and dancing Tartar fashion, squatting down, legs flying. It was a mystery to us how they could produce such energy.

Friends had offered their services to the Americans as interpreters - *Dolmetscher*. The Americans banned us from leaving the camp for fear of infectious diseases; they threatened to shoot at us. In the surrounding area many SS were caught. Ex-prisoners beheaded a *Kapo* who had been in league with the SS with a kitchen knife from front to back and played soccer with the skull in the bathhouse.

An American three-star general visited the camp and was also shown the pile of 2,800 corpses near the crematorium. The corpses, surrounded by droning flies, had not been cremated for lack of fuel; there were rivulets of blood, urine, shit and pus. The general bared his head and said, 'We have occasionally been blamed for not knowing what we were fighting for. But now we sure know.' We got more food.

The next day, 1 May, I stood staring with open mouth and strange stirrings at a group of elegant, enchanting girls in blue uniforms. They looked terrified and walked carefully on their high heels through the rubbish, rags, and puddles. They belonged to a section of the *Ambulance Automobile Française* that had come to nurse our French comrades. There was a May Day celebration too. Lots of news came from the radio. The last resistance was being cleared up. AH had committed suicide in his Berlin bunker. Holland was still not free. It seemed to be terrible there, bombers dropped food parcels.

I was told that important SS officers were not killed but taken prisoner and interrogated. The *Lagerkommandant* must have sabotaged Himmler's order to murder us all.

A friend had been at the gate as interpreter. SS were brought in as prisoners and stood up against a wall, arms lifted. He told the nearest US soldier that during his interrogation he had had to stand like that for twenty hours. The American, chewing, asked, 'Shall I shoot them for you?' Incredulous, my friend chuckled and made some gesture that was interpreted as consent. The American ordered the SS to walk into the camp. They did. He shot them dead. My friend was severely shocked.

During the first few days after our liberation many of us were knocked off the rails, sometimes downright mad. I think that we were not the only ones. When the krauts surrendered all Europe was in confusion. My thoughts could not find anchorage anywhere. The old familiar had long since gone, broken down, washed away. Imprisonment was over and done with. The future lacked any form. You had Churchill, Truman and Stalin plus a number of allied ministers and generals, but we did not know anything about their ideas. Strictly speaking we were sure of only one thing: we wanted to go home.

When I complained to a friend that I did not know what I should think about anything anymore, he admitted to the same empty feeling but he did know one thing: he would follow the course that HM Queen Wilhelmina would take. That was his only certainty.

And yet, in those days I was slowly swept back to the trusted sense of national affection and pride, especially during and after the Dutch celebratory meeting at the parade ground on 30 April. I do not think anyone had dry eyes. All at once I had become a nationalistic, chauvinistic, proud Dutchman - and why not? God, Holland and Orange! We had fought for the humiliated, trampled fatherland, we had contributed to the victory with our lives in danger, the enemy had been defeated. And so on, and so on. The chest, the thin carcass expanded proudly.

I now wanted to forget completely many of my experiences, fears, judgements and observations. At least for a short while. This primitive reaction was surely understandable as well as pardonable. Under the Dutch tricolour I simply wanted to sing the Wilhelmus and pay tribute to our Queen. There wasn't really anything against it.

THE LAST NIGHT

While I tried to fill the days, the camp began to slowly empty. Diplomats arrived, so did military missions and Red Cross authorities. The Norwegians left, as did the Luxemburgers. No one came for the Germans, Poles and Russians. And as for the Dutch no one appeared for us either. Clearly Holland had completely forgotten its political prisoners.

On 8 May I 'organized' a brand new dark blue suit with wide red stripes down the trouser legs, probably a uniform of an SS band. I tore the stripes off and put on the suit. I 'organized' some biscuits. That evening a Dutch friend had disappeared, and he was not alone. I heard that he and several others had 'decamped'.

Somewhere in a corner of our barrack three Dutchmen were whispering. I felt that perhaps they had plans to follow this example and so I joined them. I was not mistaken. The three planned to leave Dachau the next morning, to get to the Rhine somehow and take a boat to Holland from there. Of course they had no possessions: no clothes, no money, no papers. Nothing. I asked them to take me with them.

They objected. They were three helpful boys from Rotterdam, not afraid of adventure, still fairly strong of constitution. What would they do with 'the lawyer', rather weak and unsteady on his legs? I would never pull it off. No, I was not allowed to join them.

During the remainder of that evening and part of the night I lay on my bunk fretting. What should I do? I could stand it no longer. Ten days had gone by since we were liberated, but we were still locked up. Our country had also been liberated. A piece of elastic stretched to its limits linked me to Holland, I was pulled by a strong power. I had to go.

11. JOURNEY HOME
9-28 MAY 1945

An Odyssey in the Spring
It is 9 May 1945 and at last spring weather.

I'm sitting outside in the early morning sun, looking at the Dutch flag against the bright sky. The sky that also stretches above Holland. ... Do I hear someone calling? 'Come! Do come along!' Sometimes an important decision can be taken in a second. We shall be going, the four of us after all. I put the biscuits in my new blue suit, gather my diary papers and walk in a trance out of the Block, along the lane, across the parade ground to the entrance/exit gate. Like others I had 'organized' a document allowing me outside the compound and even outside the fenced larger camp.

We quickly walk through the gate in a cloud of dust thrown up by lorries, waving our papers, call 'hello' to the heavily armed guards and turn along past the SS barracks, now totally ransacked. Silence. Flowers. Birds. Stench of burned things. At random we walk into a wood, look around us, walk on again.

The firing of an automatic weapon rends the silence. We get the shock of our lives. Behave naturally. In our path a soldier lazes in a deckchair, his back to us. Again rattling. I go to have a chat with him. 'I've just shot a bird,' he grins, chewing. A jeep full of officers storms up the path.

'Why did you shoot?'

'I've just shot a bird.'

He is severely dressed down because all sentries had been put on alert. He laughs, embarrassed. Quietly we make off.

Further along there is again shooting, now clearly in our direction. We notice a big hole in the barrier beside the road. We race across the road, dive through the hole, crawl underneath goodswagons, steal alongside some military barracks. In another wood we stop, gasping for breath. Already tired! And we are on our way to Holland, without papers, without money, weak, many hundreds of miles through a newly defeated country that teems with soldiers and rabble and mines and other dangers. 'Come. Do come after all.'

Walking fast now, straight on; we struggle through barbed wire, and are now in some bushes. I look at where the sun stands in the sky, estimate the time and thereby determine which direction is south. We continue to walk in a northwesterly direction, towards Holland. A road turns up. There are people, a couple petting, therefore harmless. I go up to them and simply ask the way to Holland. They understand at once, clearly this happens often. 'Sie gehen am besten erst zum Rhein, also Augsburg, Ulm, Stuttgart, Karlsruhe.' (You had better first go to the Rhine, therefore . . . .)

'Jawohl.'

This is followed by complicated directions of which I remember only 'Reichsautobahn nach Augsburg' (motorway to Augsburg). The girl gives us rather frightened looks, half hidden behind her slavish friend. We do look rather sinister. Move on.

Easier said than done. Our feet are aglow, our knees of rubber. One of us feels ill. We hear the autobahn at a distance because of the thundering traffic. We shall tell them who we are, the Americans will surely give us a lift.

No chance! For a long time we walk alongside the autobahn. Columns, columns, more columns. Lorries, Red Cross vans, breakdown lorries, small tanks. Nobody stops. One has engine trouble. 'Not allowed,' the black driver explains, chewing. Right, then we shall walk home. There is no lack of cigarettes. The hard shoulder is awash with hundreds of large stubs, mostly Lucky Strike, some still burning.

In the same way that water wells gradually up until it breaks through a dam I suddenly realize: you are a free man. You can do whatever you like. You are alive, and free!

I nibble at my biscuits, take a new large stub from the ground and look up and down the autobahn. To the right: interminable columns, weaponry never seen before, with a white star. Lorries crammed with prisoners of war, all ranks mixed, fatigue caps and enormous pancake caps, red collars. And above it all: fleets of aircraft and still more aircraft shake the heavens. To the left are rolling meadows and villages with little towers shaped like onions, far and wide. Bavaria. Nearby on a hill is a cloistral group of towers. Well, for today we have come far enough, it must be a monastery, let us knock on its doors.

Slowly we climb the hill, the roar of traffic gives way to the buzzing of insects. I salute a crucifix; it has become a habit. When we arrive at the top the bells start ringing. We sit down on a bench under a blossoming hedge, women and children with prayer books pass by and look surprised at the four tramps with their hollow jaws and stubble heads, smoking beside the church. I follow the faithful.

I now find myself in the German House of God full of friendly silvery holy men and candles and smells and singing children near a small organ. Monotonously we repeat the 'Vater-unser Der Du bist im Himmel . . .' (Our Father who art in heaven) and now I let myself go completely, kneel like the others, I let it wash over me while I pray wordlessly to the Father who never left me.

The church empties. Everyone looks at us. The priest approaches: 'From which Block?' He has himself just walked out of Dachau. He tells us that we are in Lauterbach, 16 km (10 miles) from Dachau. The priest takes us to a farm with many barns, where we are welcomed by a friendly family. We receive a lot of food, warm milk and a cigar. I tell them about Dachau, while stroking the head of a child. Everyone falls silent. And then we hear for the first time what all Germans to whom I talked after April 1945 have told me: 'Wir haben es nicht gewusst.' (We didn't know).

Ascension day, 10 May 1945. Right in front of my window an apple tree, glowing pink in the early dawn, is in full blossom. A vast dawn chorus of birds greets the rising sun. Is it really true?

However early you are, farmers are always earlier. I walk round the dim stables, and stroke the many horses under the hairy jaws. One has a foal, a brand new little horse on wooden legs with dark glittering eyes which takes my sleeve between its lips. When I return, one of my Dutch companions has been taken away by a Red Cross car. The other two are nowhere to be seen. I borrow our host's bicycle. This establishes that I'm still able to cycle. I am like a newborn, experience everything for the first time. I cycle to the edge of a wood and lie down stark naked in the sun, cabbage and lemon butterflies fluttering around me.

On 11 May the entire family is present to wave us goodbye. Ten Hail Marys are said as a farewell. Soon we, now three, are on our way through a medieval wood. In the hamlet of Sulzemoos a woman serves us with a huge pancake; the priest had given us her name and address. We then hit the autobahn again.

Half of Europe seems to be travelling along Germany's roads. I hear many languages. Some walk, others cycle, ride on farm carts and cars. Entire families are on the move, often barefoot, all their belongings on carts: folk in search of their ruins.

We reach the village of Ober-Elzhausen towards evening. The baker gives us a large loaf for free. The local priest asks: 'Haben Sie Geld?' (Do you have any money?) 'Nein'. Each of us receives ten bank notes of RM 5. [Reichsmark, the German currency at that time] He takes us to a farmhouse with barns as large as churches; this is the mayor's house. We are invited to join them at table. Ten of us eat from a sort of washbasin. Surreptitiously the best pieces are pushed our way. Well, they do have to make up for a lot, these Germans. The farmer-mayor tells us to be present at 9 o'clock the next morning. That is when the milk van passes on its way to Friedberg near Augsburg. The farmer-mayor does not have any beds for us. There are many more guests, but they do not show themselves. These days many have reasons for not coming out. Along the way I saw many who, clearly in borrowed or stolen clothes, preferred a long journey on foot above prisoner-of-war camps. Ah, well, it does not interest me now.

I drink two litres (3.5 pints) of warm milk straight from the cow and look for a nice place in the straw in one of the giant barns. Everywhere I hear the rustling of people hidden in the straw.

On 12 May my diary records: 'No despot in the world has ever had such a magnificent bedchamber as I did this night.' Awake, the fiery morning sun beams through the wide-open gates and turns all the straw into vivid pink-gold. We wash in a little river, are crammed with bread and eggs and catch the milk van, already loaded with goods and people.

There we are now, sitting precariously in the back. With any sudden acceleration, sharp bends and low branches we have to take extra care. I roll cigarettes and crack eggs. There is little conversation with my two travelling companions, their interests differ too much from mine. I do not believe they are in much of a hurry. Other travelling companions tell us that trains for foreigners are running from Augsburg. We shall see.

We get off at Friedberg in a good mood, eat and drink without ration cards and for almost no payment in a cafe and walk to Augsburg. It is the first thoroughly devastated city we come across. Almost everything is in ruins. A citizen tells us the station is on the Adolf Hitler Platz. As he mentions the name of the square he winks at me but otherwise remains completely serious. I laugh at him, we walk to the demolished station and learn that there are no trains. I sit down to read a newspaper for a change, *Die Mitteilungen*, distributed by American soldiers to eager hands. It contains an illustrated article about Dachau. Later this paper would be of great use to me.

Now we start walking again. At a large cross-roads, military police regulate the traffic. Columns of tanks as large as houses shake the earth. Steel contraptions on caterpillar tracks come thundering past. One tank carries a big soviet flag at the front! All vehicles carry mascots, toy animals and dolls. A formidable break-down lorry, towing an articulated lorry, is driven by an attractive black girl in a fiery blue jersey, tightly stretched over her ample bosom, cigarette between purple lips.

What a contrast between the Wehrmacht and this victorious army! The Germans still squeezed in their cheap uniforms, bent under their hoorah caps, stamping along on their coarse studded boots, all the time *schneidig* (dashing) and *militärisch*. But these farmers from Texas, office staff from New York and metalworkers from Detroit behave as if it were all a game. They do not wear jackets, their shirtsleeves are rolled up, they wear sunglasses and colourful scarves, smoke, chatter like crickets and let their legs dangle from their vehicles. It is easy to see that they do not care a damn for the military life and would like to return to their wives and children in the States. I read that in half an hour it is curfew and we are not allowed on the street anymore. I also read: 'Ausländer ohne Heim melden sich an die Arraskaserne.' (Foreigners without a home should report at the Arras barracks). I dislike barracks but we shall have to sleep somewhere.

The barracks complex is a town in itself. We try to report but no one knows where. The squares between huge buildings are littered with mountains of furniture, paper, rubbish and broken weapons. It teems with people. At last we come across a group of Dutchmen. They tell us that there will be transport to Ulm in a few days. Then there will be a medical check-up before travelling on to France and Belgium where we would be put in camps because the Dutch frontiers are closed for fear of epidemics. In addition we learn that this Arras barracks is guarded and that we cannot leave unless a special permit is obtained, valid for three hours. This does not please me at all. Those epidemics in Holland! To be once again imprisoned! Transport, check-ups, camps! And my two travelling companions, who chum up with the Dutch, appear to be in much less of a hurry than I to return to our ravaged country. The Dutch show us suitcases full of goods, small items of furniture, electrical appliances, bottles of wine, watches. We consult together. They advise me to stay quietly in the camp and wait. A journey on my own, without papers, almost no money and in my condition they consider dangerous, even impossible. The country is full of rabble. I also have a nasty festering toe.

All of 13 May I wait. A resolute plucky girl cuts open my toe and cleans the rubbish out. I tell my mates that I shall continue the next morning. They disapprove. I provide myself with a permit for three hours. Quietly I fall asleep. Tomorrow, no power on earth will stop me.

On 14 May I am on my way to Ulm, thank God. Alone. I remember the bombing of Rotterdam, this day five years previously. I do not make much progress, with my toe. I have now been on the way for five days and am still only just beyond Augsburg. This will not do. I need a bicycle. I search for a bicycle.

On a side road I meet a checkpoint. 'Your papers, please.'

'I haven't got any papers.'

'We are obliged to send you back.'

'Don't do that. I come from Dachau. I want to see my wife after three years.'

They salute and let me go on. But more luck is in store. In Zusmarshausen another checkpoint: five soldiers are sitting in front of a house, jazz music pours out of the open windows and a bicycle leans against the wall. I greet them, explain who I am and where I'm going, and ask for the bicycle. The tyre has a puncture, they say. I ask whether I can take the bicycle never the less, as it is.

'Sure.'

But then two men mess around in their jeep and an hour later all punctures have been mended. I jump on my bicycle, and in my excitement forget to say thank you, so turn back, shake black hands, they keep on waving when I pedal away.

I pedal like one possessed. This way I'll get there. With great difficulty I heave myself up the lonely hills, while whizzing down the other side all the faster. In this way I arrive at Glottweng that evening. It is not even on my 'organized' map. There is a *Wirtschaft* (inn). I ask an old woman for accommodation and show her my *Mitteilungen*. The result is a basin full of warm water on the doorstep in the evening sun, soap and clean towels, fried eggs and fried potatoes and an excellent sofabed.

On 15 May I want to settle the account. No way. I get RM 10 as a present and the old woman makes sure that my tyre, which has gone flat again during the night, is repaired expertly, quickly and free of charge. I ask her why she treats me so well. She answers that she hopes God will repay her by providing similar hospitality for her son, a soldier on his way home. In her inn she has had SS and Wehrmacht billetted on her. When the Americans arrived a brief battle erupted between three parties: the Americans started shooting at the Wehrmacht. These came out, their hands up. The SS shot at both the Americans and the Wehrmacht. I bid her a cordial farewell after she has warned me of an impenetrable checkpoint on the Danube bridge just before Ulm.

I'm quickly getting nearer the town. The silhouette of the gigantic cathedral looms closer by the minute. It is the only tower still standing.

I cycle close to the checkpoint, step down and wait to see which way the cat is jumping. A mass of people are tightly packed together, only two soldiers are checking. When they are busy talking I take my bicycle and walk as cool as a cucumber behind the soldiers onto the bridge, cross it and enter the monstrous ruins. Only the cathedral is still standing.

I'm cycling again. Indignant pedestrians point out posters stating that this is a military road and *strengstens verboten* for civilian traffic. The stupid Germans do not notice that the posters are faded and the text only in German, not in English. It is obsolete nonsense of their own Wehrmacht which is not my business. I throw this back at the protesters. They are deeply frightened.

Towards evening I arrive at Luizhausen. There is a large *Gasthaus* run by a very beautiful girl who provides me with what is most needed. Apart from her there is an older lady dressed in black, clearly on her way back to find her ruined home. Because she fixes me with a friendly look I go and sit next to her. She has walked 150 km (90 miles) with heavy luggage and has to go to Mannheim. I show her the Dachau article. She reads it and nods. She walks away. After half an hour she is back with a loaf, a bottle of wine, eight eggs and the information that a lorry leaves for Karlsruhe the next morning at 6. She has booked a seat for both of us and paid for both of us and tells me that I am tired and must lie down.

On 16 May at 5.30am I'm ready. I bring my bicycle outside, return inside for something to eat and am outside again in ten minutes: bicycle gone, stolen! I have learned to give up earthly goods and climb with my protector, Frau Lisa Sturm, onto the lorry, which runs on wood gas, is full of bags of logs for the fire that sets the engine running and overcrowded with people. We pass the ruins called Stuttgart. All passengers want to go to Heidelberg. We collect money, the driver agrees. Along the way everywhere there are tanks shot up, damaged farms, even dead animals. And one endless camp for prisoners of war, the hills and valleys to the horizon are covered with former German soldiers. I cannot help laughing; Frau S. understands that as well.

I now learn that I cannot possibly sail down the Rhine. It is blocked by 4,000 ships, all blown up, and 250 bridges, also blown up.

We arrive in Bruchsal. The driver tells us he will after all only go as far as Karlsruhe, not Heidelberg. He has got the money anyway. I tell him that this is a dirty trick typical of a German. We pick up our luggage and walk towards Heidelberg. All in all we are some 150 km (90 miles) nearer home.

Shortly afterwards we arrive in Ubstadt where Frau S. appears to have acquaintances. They take us in, hospitably, and a scrumptious dinner is served. I quickly go to bed.

On 17 May I am awakened by a princely breakfast in bed which keeps me happy for over an hour. I am very grateful - which I do not really have to be, I consider, because everything I am given has been stolen for five years from all over Europe. On the way I have not seen one thin German; I myself am now barely 50 kg (7st 12 lbs). The women have sewn a little red, white and blue flag for me. We leave late. I show my flag when allied vehicles pass by, not when it is German. It is nevertheless a German car that takes us at last to Mingolsheim.

And there we are now, sitting by the side of the road. It is too hot for walking. Frau S.'s luggage is also far too heavy. I myself have no luggage. Towards evening Frau S. goes to a large pink house across the road to make enquiries. We are welcome. Well-to-do, middle-class people, a woman with an 18-year-old daughter. German girls are often very beautiful. Certainly this Irmgard Leicht is beautiful. After a wonderful dinner - when I seem to have lost my table manners - the young daughter sits down at the piano. She plays Chopin, Beethoven, Schumann.

I go to pieces. Initially vaguely but increasingly stronger the music reminds me of everything that once made my life so beautiful: nice people, my beloved one, books, music, flowers and rivers, all the delightful things that made up our civilization. The other women have long since gone to bed, but this Irmgard, a daughter of my evil enemy, plays beautifully, very beautifully. Until well past midnight. She shows me upstairs to a fine guest room. I draw the curtains, open the door to a balcony. Above and around the balcony the spring night is silent. Again she enters, now behind me, with cigarettes and matches. 'Stehen Sie morgen früh auf, ich spiele fur Sie in der Kirche. Gute nacht.' (Get up early tomorrow and I'll play for you in the church. Good night).

That early morning of 18 May in Mingolsheim is unforgettable. Shortly after seven we climb a spiral staircase in a big church. Upstairs I sit down next to her. Never before have I been so close to a church organ, very complex. For some time she fiddles with switches, pedals and registers, several little lights start glowing. In the huge pipes far above us droning starts. Good gracious! It is the famous Toccata and Fugue by J.S. Bach. Mighty flows of sound thunder down into the church, the entire church shakes, chords once started complement each other, all the world is filled with music, I am overcome. . . . She has noticed something. She stops, waits awhile, then switches to Reger. But

I request Bach again and now I can bear it. I am sweating but can still watch her chubby arms and legs producing those immense sounds. It is heavy work, she swallows frequently, hisses 'verflucht' (damn it), she is very beautiful. . . .

Outside I am dizzy. I tell Frau S. that I am in a hurry and will search for another bicycle. I walk to the Town Hall. It is in the French zone of occupation, much stricter than the American zone. I ask for the French commanding officer and am allowed in. He has surrounded himself with a staff of at least twenty German beauties. I explain my situation and tell him what I want. He takes me by the arm to the window overlooking the square.

'Voyez-vous les bicyclettes?'

'Oui, mon commandant.'

'Elles sont toutes à vous.'

He pushes bread and bottles of wine into my arms.

'Bon voyage, Monsieur.'

Assisted by a cycle-repairer I compose one showpiece out of some six wrecks of bicycles. I ride it to my hostesses. At the last moment the three of them, kneeling, bandage a dirty boil that has suddenly appeared on my right calf. They give me a large package of food. I plant my flag on my bicycle and say goodbye. At the very last minute Frau S. gives me her address in Mannheim where her sister should also be, if still alive.

Heidelberg turns out to be completely untouched. It is a relief. I wanted to cycle on to Mannheim as fast as possible but it took a couple of hours. I do not feel all that well. Mannheim is one big nightmare, a lunar landscape pock-marked with craters as far as you can see. Some walls, however, still carry painted slogans:

'Der Endsieg ist unser.'(Victory is ours in the end).

'Mit dem Führer zum Sieg.' (Victory with the Führer).

'Wir kapitulieren nie.' (We will never capitulate).

'Räder rollen fur den Sieg.' (Wheels roll for victory).

I ask a roving character the way to Hafenstrasse. He looks at me with pity, points to a road between collapsed masses of stone. You can see what destruction one bomb can cause. Apartment blocks are now towers of rubble. Deserted. I have to be at no. 4. On a half-destroyed towerblock I discover a 4. I climb over the rubble, enter a gate into a wilderness. Incredibly a man sits there in a cane chair reading a book. I ask him about Fräulein X. He shouts upstairs and, surprise again, a face appears on the tower battlement. Face and appurtenances come down, I pass on greetings from Frau S. and ask for shelter. The bicycle is locked into a cellar where the man lives between mountains of saved furniture; I am to pass the night there as well. The Fräulein takes me upstairs: a den in the heaven of the sixth floor, the four floors above it have disappeared. You can see the sky through holes three metres across; the lavatory has landed in the living room. Yet there is electricity, there is water and everywhere left, right and underneath families are still living. After dinner I step onto the balcony and view the rubble- mountain that was once the Rhine harbour Mannheim-Ludwigshafen. I hurry down into the cellar.

Early morning on 19 May Frau S. also arrives. She is happy to find a sister again and something of a home; I am happy to see her again. She is German, true, but she has taken care of me like a mother.

The next couple of days were less traumatic though still harrowing. On 21 May the good old bicycle takes me to Oberlahnstein, a deserted ruin, in torrential rain. Suddenly a large piece of rubble tumbles down close to me. My Dutch flag! I quickly cycle on. French soldiers appear again.

'Vos papiers!'

They look fierce.

'Je n'ai pas de papiers.'

I am taken to an office full of officers, all of them stern, all of them surly. I explain who I am, where I come from, where I am going. The result is bewildering. They all laugh, shout, pat me (too hard) on the shoulder and in an instant my arms and coat are filled with bread, cigarettes and bottles of wine. What is even better: the next morning at four a train leaves Neiderlahnstein across the Rhine for Holland via Koblenz and Bonn.

Some soldiers help me along. In gratitude I offer them my bicycle. That makes them immensely happy, surprisingly. With great difficulty I enter a barracks. Inside are thousands of Dutchmen, all well fed and rather conspicuously, at least strangely, dressed in stolen clothes. I had had no time to steal anything, nor the inclination, anything I have was a present. At last I find something that could be called an office. I tell my story and inform them that I would like to join the transport tomorrow.

No way.

Why not?

I do not belong to their group, and the train is full.

Full? How many men per wagon? Thirty. Full. Can't be done. Sorry.

I remember the transportations when one hundred and ten men were pressed together in one wagon. I look at the fattened looters. To my surprise I suddenly lose my temper completely. I tell the fellows what I think of them. Immediately they put me on 'the list'. I receive a double food ration. And a bed.

On 22 May the long train with thousands of Dutchmen on the way home leaves Koblenz. The goods' wagons are decorated with flowers and flags on the outside. I cannot believe that we shall be in Holland that evening, as predicted. I am lying on a pile of bags full of loot, feverish, occasionally not quite conscious.

'Look, there!' a man next to me shouts many hours later, standing at the open sliding doors, 'that little house there, that white one, that is the first Dutch house, man!' I forget what I feel and move to stand next to him.

And then, at 9.15pm, I notice different signs, different railway barriers, different signposts - we are in our country alright!

When the people in the villages of Limburg, our southern-most province, run out of their homes and shout to the decorated train, yes, then it becomes too much for all of us. People cry, they shout, they embrace, they lean out of the carriages in the red of the evening sky - we are back in Holland!

The journey to Maastricht is triumphant, the sun has set behind the spring hills. For everyone the question is: where do we go from here? On Maastricht station a voice from a loudspeaker lets us know that the train will continue north to Sittard. Then ends: any political prisoners and/or prisoners of war should immediately get out and report to the Red Cross post.

For the first time in three weeks I do what an authority tells me to do: it is a Dutch authority. Apart from me two more get out. Very slowly I walk to the Red Cross post. There is a man in a white coat, there are nurses. I start telling them, they stare at me, they take me along in a car to the repatriation bureau. They give me a medical check up. They suggest taking me to a hospital. I am supposed to be ill. I tell them my story about wife and suffering and three years in hell. They say that Holland north of the rivers is closed and, again, that I am ill and have a temperature. Exhausted, I yield. We drive to a huge building that turns out to be a hospital for those being repatriated, in reality it is a Jesuit monastery. I receive papers as a Displaced Person. I also receive a pile of snow-white slices of bread. A bath is filled. A pretty sister with chubby bare legs helps me get in, washes me. She sits down beside the bath on a stool and feeds me the slices of bread. I now quote from my diary to the end:

23 May 1945. Holland is closed because of typhus. I can no more come to you than you can come to me. We shall see. Count on me.

This morning at half past three four doctors came to examine and bandage me. My temperature is 38.3° (101°F). They will send Uncle and Aunt Bax who live here. I had to cry again for all the friendliness and care. If I feel it is taking too long I'll leave nevertheless. Uncle and Aunt did appear. They brought photographs. Everyone still alive, there are more grandchildren than before. Doctor Erik Twiss follows and has another look at everything. He says I am a biological miracle. I also have a curious fatty ball on my coccyx. He says: stay here for a fortnight and ask your wife to come. 'You'll then have recovered your strength, fatty ball gone, better food here than in the west.' Large dinner. Again tired to death. Uncle was here, I asked for a typist. My diary has to be typed as soon as possible in view of the sad visits I have to make. Lord God, please let me see her soon, waiting is becoming unbearable.

I contacted all the relatives of my dead friends whose addresses I had, from Maastricht by letter. Some came to visit me there, defying the transport problems of the time.

[Later on a very special experience came my way when the President of the High Court in The Hague asked me to report verbally on the death of Judge Bommezijn. Upon arrival I found myself facing at least fifty people: judges, prosecuting counsels, clerks, lawyers. I made my report. The President thanked me, saying something like: 'We knew that our colleague Bommezijn and his wife were engaged in resistance activities, among them helping pilots escape. I often pointed out to him the dangers involved including to his own life. He disregarded my objections and continued. Consequently he has therefore sadly paid with his life.' The reader will understand what I thought about this. I left quickly. Mrs Bommezijn survived Ravensbrück KZ. She died a few years ago.]

24 May 1945. A lot of white bread with corned beef, eggs, oatmeal porridge, real coffee and Pall Mall cigarettes; smoking is allowed in this hospital. Why am I so confused? Everything gets mixed up. Oh, what tearing passion a man can have.

Walking to another building for X-rays proved quite an expedition. All well. Weight: already 55kg (8st 9lbs)! On arrival only 49kg (7st 9lbs). Therefore no TB. For the first time I walked along a Dutch shopping street, feel a bit firmer, everyone looks at me, I have very short hair. The doctor brought pyjamas and books, I've been shaved, parting in hair possible, just, I'm becoming fully human again. Doctor has just arrived with a doctor's wife - not his - who is prepared to type my diary. She seems to be perfect for the job: doctor's wives are used to a lot, she is not too young, and will perhaps do it for free as well. Feverish. That will remain as long as I have to wait. Tomorrow I can send another letter by courier. I am so very tired.

25 May 1945. Gradually this diary becomes of less importance as I can now simply send off what I write. Yesterday 39° (102.2°F). They can't find anything. I believe it to be the tension. I ate ten slices of bread with meat, jam, chocolate; a lot of porridge, a lot of coffee, again this morning. Today 38.4° and a puncture in my fatty ball which is not a fatball at all because it contains blood. A weird thing. I read Job, Isaiah and *Yank* and wrote home again, doctor enclosing a statement. Tonight I ate three plates piled high with salad, mash, fried potatoes, eggs, soup, porridge. Now tea with biscuits and chocolates. I'd better write less about food from now on! A priest has taken the letters. The doctor's wife can read everything and happily types on. Lord, reward all my benefactors for their kindness.

26 May 1945. It's possible you'll arrive today. Read newspapers, completely dumbfounded and overwhelmed. Princess Juliana distributes toys to children of three to twelve on Walcheren island. Prime Minister Gerbrandy says that the food situation in Holland has greatly disappointed him. The Canadians parade in The Hague - a nice spectacle for those who could still walk and stand up. A lot of very anti-German articles. I started to waver. I would say: 'Yes, what a sordid rotten people, really.' But then I remember the nice people I met on my journey home. Some were certainly cowardly but most were good, genuinely good people. I ate fearfully much, sweated terribly, today 38.5°. I wrote, studied the map again, took up one book after another, put them all down again, smoked, tried to do something. It failed, I can't bring myself to do anything. All thoughts are nipped in the bud. All activities bore me halfway through. Lord, send her now quickly, quickly, quickly. Asparagus, sausage, macaroni, rotten fever.

I am now very worried. How do I know how bad you all are? Perhaps your need for being nursed is greater than mine. Suddenly I'm in despair! Lord God, will You help us, please?

27 May 1945. Sunday. You didn't turn up yesterday. I had a temperature of 39.9° (104°F), doctor thinks I may have typhus in my belly and pneumonia at the same time and put me on a diet. Diet means hunger. I'm mortally afraid of it. I also feared secret rotten illnesses, there was shouting and singing on the ward. For the first time in days I was really unhappy. Couldn't sleep. Nurse Jansen, a lovely girl with very short skirts, sat down on my bed for a chat in the middle of the night, gave me a sleeping tablet. It's true: these days

are almost the most difficult of all. Woke up this morning soaking wet, got only dry bread and an egg and tried to read. Priests came to give communion. The doctor's wife might come today. What will it be like to see all those shameful intimate notes typed? The little nurse has prayed that you will be with me soon. Perhaps you'll come today. . . .

It's now Sunday evening. A high fever. I'm sweating like a pig. Again diet, dry bread and an egg, the most delicious food passes me by, rotten luck. At this rate I'll quickly relapse. This afternoon the doctor's wife arrived. It made me blush to see my 'confessions' so businesslike and neatly typed out. They contain very secret things. Uncle and Aunt also came. They say you'll soon be here. My brother is said to have a bride, maiden name Kasteel (castle). Doctor examined me again, and again found nothing, talked again about stomach-typhus and pneumonia. Quite possible. The swelling appears to be harmless: a lymphoma. Thank God.

[I did have pneumonia and typhus of the belly in addition to a vast lymphoma on my coccyx. I was admirably looked after in the repatriation hospital, or Jesuit monastery, by doctors Castermans and Twiss. Doctor Castermans went in person to my wife who then lived in Leyden to tell her that I was alive and in a hospital. Leading Maastricht families took care that we lacked nothing; they also came for visits. As did HRH Princess Juliana who wanted to talk particularly with the two political prisoners then in our hospital. For a quarter of an hour she sat on my bed as she did not want my wife to give up her chair. We had known the Princess during her undergraduate years at Leyden University where she played chamber music, like my sister Mia, in trios and quartets. I stayed three months in this hospital. On arrival I weighed 49 kg (7 stone 9 lbs), upon my release 94 kg (14 stone 11 lbs), a pig without muscles. My last sceptic sore from imprisonment led to the amputation of a piece of my finger in October 1946.]

28 May 1945. It is 6am. The sun shines golden. But within me a fiercer fire shines. Last night, just past ten, you came. I shan't try to write anything about that. It would be far beyond my powers. Just this: I will give thanks to the Lord with my whole heart. (Psalm 9). Of course I couldn't sleep. I, I, I. Stop that. At last: you, you, you!

This diary, in effect one single letter to you, has now come to its end. I don't have to write to you anymore. I can talk to you, look at you. I'm allowed to be with you, the rest of our lives.

Lord God: Hallelujah! Amen.

Epilogue to the English edition

I have recorded my life between 1945 and today in a diary which now fills seventeen volumes. The habit has stuck. I shall condense it here into a few pages.

The first piece of information, which may bewilder some readers, concerns my first wife, elevated in this book progressively to the status of an angel. She and I were divorced at the end of 1948 after an extremly grave and soul-searching struggle. I remarried in 1949, and she in turn in 1952. Her marriage remained childless, and her husband died in 1975. We remained on the friendliest of terms. She was recently in a hospice where my second wife and I took care of her. She died in 1991.

My second wife and I were blessed with a daughter and four sons between 1949 and 1964. They are all married and we have ten grandchildren. Our daughter is married to the son of Wim Roessingh, who has often been mentioned in these pages. He and I share three sweet grandchildren. If only the Gestapo and SS knew! My family now numbers 22 persons, all united in love and mutual support. The Lord be praised!

As for my career, it is difficult to determine whether it would have been more spectacular if I had been spared the road to Calvary described in this book. I did not return to the legal profession but opted for that of publishing, mainly with Elsevier, where I reached a satisfactory position as one of its directors. As a publisher of educational and academic books I have been priviledged to meet and encourage several hundred professors. This has given me great pleasure.

I am now (May 1993) almost 78 years old and occasionally startled when aware of my age. To me 78 is ancient. Mentally I sometimes feel 178 years old, sometimes six or eight, mostly between 25 and 30. Certainly age inflicts infirmities - small ones in my case, including exhaustion sooner than expected.

I do not think that I suffer much from the so-called post-KZ-syndrome, well known in Holland. I shall not burden the reader with a detailed definition. Just this: the syndrome is a particular combination of physical and psychological complaints, the result of a shortage of reserves. Too high a toll has been demanded of our nervous system and our mental stability. This book was written during a period when I could not do any normal work, and was indeed declared medically unfit. Writing helped me return to normality. Still, do not others suffer equally heavily and for a prolonged period, such as veterans of this horrible war?

As for politics, I do not belong to any party and am more interested in foreign than in domestic policies. But I am very proud of my country which achieves a lot despite its small size.

Of course I have great difficulty in accepting the *Wiedervereinigung* (unification) of the two Germanys. The United States can do little wrong, if only because American soldiers liberated us in Dachau. I always wave to cars bearing a US military registration plate. I do that as well to cars with British numberplates. As for the USSR, I am deeply grateful that the Russians, with whom we suffered so much in the concentration camps and who contributed so much to the allied victory, have been relieved without bloodshed of communism, a close relative of Nazism and fascism.

As a full-blooded gentile I have great sympathy and admiration for Israel, which I have visited twice and where my wife and I were baptized in 1981 close to the Dead Sea. I look upon Jerusalem as the capital of the world.

As a direct result of my stay in concentration camps I have a strong aversion to everything that is dirty, messy and faulty. I love cleaning and repairing things. To repair something defective is marvellous.

Like everyone else incarcerated in a concentration camp, I hold the complex concept of freedom very dear. Even a minor infringement of my personal freedom irritates me immensely. When circumstances allow I therefore disregard the speed limit. I am also suspicious of all public authorities, including government, any government.

My Christian faith, although occasionally overwhelmed by the worries of the day, has not suffered but has held out. Faith, hope and charity continue to give me wonderful strength, especially in adversity, when disappointed or at grave events like my father's death in 1956 and that of my mother in 1964. I remain sceptical about Christian churches, ecclesiastical institutions and organizations, theology and theologizing. I see hardly any progress towards the *Una Sancta*, the one and only

Christian church, proclaimed now as then by Christ. Therefore I do not belong to any reglious community and rarely go to church, unless it is to lecture. I fear the catastrophes which threaten to come our way; many are already on the way. However, basically I can only be an optimist in anticipation of God's promised Kingdom.

I regularly return to Natzweiler, about once every two or three years, sometimes with my wife, and sometimes also with one or other of our children, but, to be honest, preferably alone. The nearer I get to the camp the worse the weather invariably turns and the more nervous I feel. On reaching the top and parking the car I go into a slight trance. I wrap myself up well, with coat and scarf, and report to the ticket-collector as an *ancien déporté*. That allows me to enter free and roam around without a guide. The camp is usually deserted, fortunately; sometimes I see a little group with a guide wandering around somewhere below.

I take in the sky, the mountains and valleys and forests of the Vosges, the Gate, the camp. I listen carefully, take a deep breath - in, out - concentrate with all my senses: eyes, ears, nose. I saturate myself with the camp. In my mind I recall the faces and voices of my friends, dead and alive. I try to step out of my current self and be once more as I was in 1943-1944. I make an attempt to relive the KZ in all its extra-terrestrial, divine and infernal aspects.

And I succeed in reliving that phenomenon in the same way that lightning strikes - a discharge of high tension, which curiously enough you survive. I am back in the KZ, but never longer than a few seconds. Away from the earth. Away from the present. Out of myself. I return. This psychic experience cannot be described. It is like taking an unbelievable medicine, beneficial and mortal at the same time. You are 'outside yourself'. It is neither good nor bad, it is a mystery. This is accompanied by physical symptoms. I shiver from top to bottom, three or four times. I stand there shivering. I am sweating profusely. My pulse rate increases rapidly; I feel my eyes dilating. I am completely taken up by it. I am completely in the power of some force. It is neither pleasant nor unpleasant, raised above earthly qualities, above being human, while yet remaining a human being. It is not allowed, nor prohibited. It is the tidal wave into a river bed long ago dried up - a previous existence, a future existence. However much I try, it cannot be explained. But it is very real.

Nobody can visualize what awaits him after death. Sometimes I think it may be a bit like this.